COMMODITY

Commodity Derivatives: A Guide for Future Practitioners describes the origins and uses of these important markets. Commodities are often used as inputs in the production of other products, and commodity prices are notoriously volatile. Derivatives include forwards, futures, options, and swaps; all are types of contracts that allow buyers and sellers to establish the price at one time and exchange the commodity at another.

These contracts can be used to establish a price now for a purchase or sale that will occur later, or establish a price later for a purchase or sale now. This book provides detailed examples for using derivatives to manage prices by hedging, using futures, options, and swaps. It also presents strategies for using derivatives to speculate on price levels, relationships, volatility, and the passage of time. Finally, because the relationship between a commodity price and a derivative price is not constant, this book examines the impact of basis behavior on hedging results, and shows how the basis can be bought and sold like a commodity.

The material in this book is based on the author's 30-year career in commodity derivatives, and is essential reading for students planning careers as commodity merchandisers, traders, and related industry positions. Not only does it provide them with the necessary theoretical background, it also covers the practical applications that employers expect new hires to understand. Examples are coordinated across chapters using consistent prices and formats, and industry terminology is used so students can become familiar with standard terms and concepts. This book is organized into 18 chapters, corresponding to approximately one chapter per week for courses on the semester system.

Paul E. Peterson is a Clinical Professor of Finance at the University of Illinois at Urbana-Champaign. His primary focus is futures and options markets, particularly in relation to commodity prices and risk management. Other interests include marketing practices and pricing issues.

COMMODITY DERIVATIVES

A Guide for Future Practitioners

Paul E. Peterson

Routledge
Taylor & Francis Group

NEW YORK AND LONDON

First published 2018
by Routledge
711 Third Avenue, New York, NY 10017

and by Routledge
2 Park Square, Milton Park, Abingdon, Oxon, OX14 4RN

Routledge is an imprint of the Taylor & Francis Group, an informa business

Library of Congress Cataloging-in-Publication Data
A catalog record for this title has been requested

ISBN: 978-0-7656-4516-6 (hbk)
ISBN: 978-0-7656-4537-1 (pbk)
ISBN: 978-1-315-71843-9 (ebk)

Typeset in Bembo
by Apex CoVantage, LLC

To Peg
I couldn't have done it without you

CONTENTS

List of Figures   x

List of Tables   xiii

Preface   xvii

1 Introduction   1

What is a Commodity?   1

What is a Derivative?   3

2 Trading Futures and Options   7

Pit Trading   7

Electronic Trading   15

3 Understanding and Interpreting Futures Prices   20

How Futures Prices Are Quoted   20

Measures of Trading Activity   24

Interpreting Price Differences: Time, Space, and Form   28

4 Margins, Clearing, Delivery, and Final Settlement   37

Margins in Futures Trading   37

Margin Account Example   41

Final Settlement via Delivery   43

Final Settlement via Cash Settlement   45

5 Market Regulation   46

Futures as Contracts   46

Contract Specifications   47

Regulation by Exchanges   53

Regulation by the Federal Government   54

Self-Regulation by the Industry   57

Applications in Other Sectors and Countries   58

Appendix 5.1   59

6 Hedging with Futures   67

The Role of Correlation   67

Hedging Against a Price Increase   68

viii   *Contents*

Hedging Against a Price Decrease   72

More on the Role of Correlation: An Example from the Corn Market   77

Price Changes vs. Prices Levels: The Importance of Returns   80

7 Hedging and the Basis   82

Hedging and Basis Changes   82

Long Hedging and Basis Behavior   84

Short Hedging and Basis Behavior   90

8 Hedging Enhancements   97

Types of Hedges   97

Rolling a Hedge   99

Cross-Hedging   105

9 Profit Margin Hedging and Inverse Hedging   111

Profit Margin Hedging   111

Inverse Hedging   119

10 Hedging and Basis Trading   125

Redefining the Basis and the Cash Price   125

Commercial Hedging   129

11 Basis Trading and Rolling a Hedge   135

Rolling a Hedge to Capture a Favorable Basis   135

Spread Impact on Hedging Results   143

12 Speculating with Futures   147

Speculation vs. Investment   147

Speculative Styles   148

Commitments of Traders   152

Speculative Participation in Commodity Futures   157

13 Introduction to Options on Futures   159

How Options Work   159

Options on Futures   160

Options on Actuals   169

14 Option Pricing   170

The Black Model   170

Put-Call Parity   175

Option Sensitivity and the Greeks   176

Summary   183

15 Profit Tables and Profit Diagrams   184

Futures and Cash Positions: Linear Profits   184

Options Positions: Nonlinear Profits   189

Discussion   205

16 Hedging with Options   206

Option-Based Hedging Strategies   206

Delta-Neutral Hedging   217

Synthetic Futures and Options   222

17 Speculating with Options 230

Intrinsic Value Strategies 230

Time Value Strategies 231

Volatility Strategies 231

Spread Strategies 236

18 Commodity Swaps 251

Swaps and Forwards 251

Swap Features and Applications 251

The Market for Commodity Swaps 255

Index 257

FIGURES

2.1	Cross-Section of Trading Pit	8
2.2	CBOT Agricultural Trading Floor circa 1980s	9
2.3	Trader with Trading Jacket and Badge	9
2.4	Trading Ticket with Order Details	10
2.5	Hand Signals	13
2.6	Trading Card for Recording Trade Information	14
2.7	Hypothetical Order Book Showing Prices and Quantities	18
3.1	Corn Futures Prices from November 11, 2016	21
3.2	Forward Curve for Corn Futures as of November 11, 2016	30
3.3	Forward Curve for Sugar #11 Futures as of November 11, 2016	31
3.4	Forward Curve for Live Cattle Futures as of November 11, 2016	32
3.5	Corn Futures Contract Summary Specifications as of November 11, 2016	35
4.1	Direct Exchange of Cash Flows Between Buyer and Seller	39
4.2	Exchange of Cash Flows Between Buyer and Seller with Clearing House as Intermediary	39
4.3	Exchange of Cash Flows Between Buyer and Seller with Clearing House and Both Clearing Firms as Intermediaries	40
5.1	Disaggregated Commitments of Traders Report for Corn Futures as of December 27, 2016	51
6.1	Cash Corn Prices, East Central Illinois	78
6.2	Corn Futures Prices, December 2012 Contract	78
6.3	Cash Corn Prices, East Central Illinois, Corn Futures Prices, December 2012 Contract, and Cash Minus Futures	79
6.4	Long Cash Corn, East Central Illinois and Short Corn Futures, December 2012 Contract	79
8.1	Grain Sorghum Cash Prices ($/cwt), Texas Triangle Region and Corn Futures Prices ($/bu), Nearby Contract, January 2001–December 2016	106
11.1	Basis Values for Multiple Futures Contracts	136
13.1	Relationship of Strike Price to Futures Price for In-The-Money and Out-Of-The-Money Options	162

13.2	Time Value and Time to Expiration: $3.50 Call Option, $3.60 Futures Prices, 30% Volatility	165
14.1	Premium Over a Range of Futures Prices: Slope = Delta, $3.50 Call Option, 30% Volatility, 185 Days to Expiration	178
14.2	Time Value Over a Range of Times to Expiration: Slope = Theta, $3.50 Call Option, $3.60 Futures Price, 30% Volatility	180
14.3	Theta Over a Range of Futures Prices: $3.50 Call Option, 30% Volatility, 185 Days to Expiration	180
14.4	Premium Over a Range of Interest Rates: Slope = Rho, $3.50 Call Option, 30% Volatility, 185 Days to Expiration	181
14.5	Premium Over a Range of Volatilities: Slope = Vega, $3.50 Call Option, $3.60 Futures Price, 185 Days to Expiration	182
14.6	Vega Over a Range of Futures Prices: $3.50 Call Option, 30% Volatility, 185 Days to Expiration	182
15.1	Profit on Long Futures Position Established at $3.50	185
15.2	Profit on Short Futures Position Established at $3.50	186
15.3	Profit on Long Cash Position Established at $3.50	188
15.4	Profit on Long Cash Position Established at $3.50 Hedged with Short Futures Position Established at $3.50	189
15.5	Profit on Long $3.50 Call, $0.35 Premium	190
15.6	Profit on Short $3.50 Call, $0.35 Premium	192
15.7	Profit on Long $3.50 Put, $0.25 Premium	194
15.8	Profit on Short $3.50 Put, $0.25 Premium	196
15.9	Long Cash Position at $3.50 Hedged with Long $3.50 Put, $0.25 Premium	198
15.10	Long Cash Position at $3.50 Hedged with Short $3.50 Call, $0.35 Premium	200
15.11	Short Cash Position Established at $3.50 Hedged with Long Futures Position Established at $.350	201
15.12	Short Cash Position at $3.50 Hedged with Long $3.50 Call, $0.35 Premium	203
15.13	Short Cash Position at $3.50 Hedged with Short $3.50 Put, $0.25 Premium	204
16.1	Long Cash Position at $3.50 Hedged with Long $3.50 Put, $0.25 Premium and Short $4.00 Call, $0.1575 Premium	210
16.1A	Long Cash Position at $3.50 Hedged with Long $3.50 Put, $0.25 Premium and Short $4.00 Call, $0.1575 Premium (Rescaled)	210
16.2	Long Cash Position at $3.50 Hedged with Long $3.50 Put, $0.25 Premium and 2 Short $4.00 Calls, Each $0.1575 Premium	213
16.3	Short Cash Position at $3.50 Hedged with Long $3.50 Call, $0.35 Premium and Short $3.00 Put, $0.0750 Premium	215
16.4	Profit Diagrams at Various Times Before Expiration: Long $3.50 Call, $0.35 Premium	219

16.5   Synthetic Long $3.50 Call, $0.25 Premium Using Long $3.50 Futures
        and Long $3.50 Put, $0.25 Premium   222

16.6   Synthetic Short $3.50 Put, $0.35 Premium Using Long $3.50 Futures
        and Short $3.50 Call, $0.35 Premium   223

16.7   Synthetic Long $3.50 Put, $0.35 Premium Using Short $3.50 Futures
        and Long $3.50 Call, $0.35 Premium   224

16.8   Synthetic Short $3.50 Call, $0.25 Premium Using Short $3.50 Futures
        and Short $3.50 Put, $0.25 Premium   225

16.9   Synthetic Long $3.60 Futures Using Long $3.50 Call, $0.35 Premium
        and Short $3.50 Put, $0.25 Premium   227

16.10   Synthetic Short $3.60 Futures Using Short $3.50 Call, $0.35 Premium and
        Long $3.50 Put, $0.25 Premium   228

17.1   Long Straddle Using Long $3.50 Call, $0.35 Premium and Long $3.50
        Put, $0.25 Premium   232

17.1A   Long Straddle Using Long $3.50 Call, $0.35 Premium and Long $3.50 Put,
        $0.25 Premium (Rescaled)   233

17.2   Long Strangle Using Long $3.60 Call, $0.30 Premium and Long $3.40 Put,
        $0.20 Premium   234

17.3   Short Straddle Using Long $3.50 Call, $0.35 Premium and Long $3.50 Put,
        $0.25 Premium   235

17.4   Short Strangle Using Long $3.60 Call, $0.30 Premium and Long $3.40 Put,
        $0.20 Premium   235

17.5   Conversion Using Actual Long Futures at $3.58 and Synthetic
        Short Futures at $3.60   239

17.6   Synthetic Long $3.59 Futures Using Long $3.20 Call, $0.5175
        Premium and Short $3.20 Put, $0.1275 Premium   239

17.7   Reversal Using Actual Short Futures at $3.60 and Synthetic Long
        Futures at $3.59   241

17.8   Box Spread Using Long $3.20 Call, $0.5175 Premium and Short $3.20
        Put, $0.1275 Premium Plus Short $3.50 Call, $0.35 Premium and
        Long $3.50 Put, $0.25 Premium   241

17.8A   Box Spread Using Synthetic Long Futures at $3.59 Plus Synthetic
        Short Futures at $3.60   242

17.9   Bull Call Spread Using Long $3.50 Call, $0.35 Premium and
        Short $3.60 Call, $0.30 Premium   244

17.10   Bear Call Spread Using Short $3.50 Call, $0.35 Premium and
        Long $3.60 Call, $0.30 Premium   246

17.11   Bull Put Spread Using Long $3.40 Put, $0.20 Premium and
        Short $3.50 Put, $0.25 Premium   248

17.12   Bear Put Spread Using Short $3.40 Put, $0.20 Premium and
        Long $3.50 Put, $0.25 Premium   249

TABLES

2.1	Hypothetical Order Book	16
3.1	Month Codes and Corresponding Calendar Months	23
6.1	Results for Long Hedge: Rising Prices	69
6.2	Results for Long Hedge: Falling Prices	70
6.3	Results for Long Hedge: Stable Prices	71
6.4	Results for Short Hedge: Falling Prices	73
6.5	Results for Short Hedge: Rising Prices	75
6.6	Results for Short Hedge: Stable Prices	76
6.7	Results for Short Hedge: Falling Prices, and Futures Prices $100 Higher than Cash Prices	80
7.1	Results for Long Hedge: Rising Prices, Basis Zero and Unchanged	83
7.1A	Results for Long Hedge: Rising Prices, Basis Positive and Strengthens	84
7.1B	Results for Long Hedge: Rising Prices, Basis Positive and Weakens	84
7.1C	Results for Long Hedge: Rising Prices, Basis Negative and Strengthens	85
7.1D	Results for Long Hedge: Rising Prices, Basis Negative and Weakens	86
7.2	Results for Long Hedge: Falling Prices, Basis Zero and Unchanged	87
7.2A	Results for Long Hedge: Falling Prices, Basis Positive and Strengthens	87
7.2B	Results for Long Hedge: Falling Prices, Basis Positive and Weakens	88
7.2C	Results for Long Hedge: Falling Prices, Basis Negative and Strengthens	88
7.2D	Results for Long Hedge: Falling Prices, Basis Negative and Weakens	89
7.3	Summary of Long Hedge Results with Basis Impact on Buyer	89
7.4	Results for Short Hedge: Falling Prices, Basis Zero and Unchanged	90
7.4A	Results for Short Hedge: Falling Prices, Basis Positive and Strengthens	91
7.4B	Results for Short Hedge: Falling Prices, Basis Positive and Weakens	91
7.4C	Results for Short Hedge: Falling Prices, Basis Negative and Strengthens	92
7.4D	Results for Short Hedge: Falling Prices, Basis Negative and Weakens	93
7.5	Results for Short Hedge: Rising Prices, Basis Zero and Unchanged	94
7.5A	Results for Short Hedge: Rising Prices, Basis Positive and Strengthens	94
7.5B	Results for Short Hedge: Rising Prices, Basis Positive and Weakens	95

7.5C	Results for Short Hedge: Rising Prices, Basis Negative and Strengthens	95
7.5D	Results for Short Hedge: Rising Prices, Basis Negative and Weakens	96
7.6	Summary of Short Hedge Results with Basis Impact on Seller	96
8.1	Results for Long Hedge: Rising Prices, Basis Zero and Unchanged	98
8.2	Results for Short Hedge: Falling Prices, Basis Zero and Unchanged	99
8.3	Results for Long Hedge: Rising Prices, Basis Positive and Weakens	100
8.4	Abbreviations for Calendar Months and Contract Months	101
8.5	Results for Long Hedge: Rising Prices, Basis Positive and Weakens, Rolled Forward	102
8.6	Results for Short Hedge: Falling Prices, Basis Negative and Strengthens	103
8.7	Results for Short Hedge: Falling Prices, Basis Negative and Strengthens, Rolled Back	104
8.8	Results for Linear Regression of Change in Grain Sorghum Cash Prices on Change in Corn Futures Prices, Daily, January 2001–December 2006	107
9.1	Results for Long Hedge on Soybeans, Crush Margin Example	113
9.2	Results for Short Hedge on Soybean Oil, Crush Margin Example	113
9.3	Results for Short Hedge on Soybean Meal, Crush Margin Example	113
9.4	Results for Long Hedge on Feeder Cattle, Feeding Margin Example	116
9.5	Results for Long Hedge on Corn, Feeding Margin Example	116
9.6	Results for Short Hedge on Live Cattle, Feeding Margin Example	116
9.7	Incorrect Approach to Calculation of Results for Long Hedge on Grain Sorghum Using Corn Futures, Feeding Margin Example	119
9.8	Results for Short Forward Contract Offset with Long Futures and Price Increases	121
9.9	Results for Short Forward Contract Offset with Long Futures and Price Decreases	122
9.10	Results for Long Forward Contract Offset with Short Futures and Price Decreases	123
9.11	Results for Long Forward Contract Offset with Short Futures and Price Increases	124
10.1	Results for Long Hedge: Rising Prices, Basis Positive and Weakens, Basis Trading Format, Generic Dates	126
10.2	Results for Short Hedge: Falling Prices, Basis Negative and Strengthens, Basis Trading Format, Generic Dates	127
10.3	Results for Short Hedge: Falling Prices, Basis Negative and Strengthens, Detailed Dates	131
10.4	Results for Short Hedge: Falling Prices, Basis Negative and Strengthens, Basis Trading Format, Detailed Dates	131
10.5	Results for Short Hedge: Rising Prices, Basis Negative and Strengthens, Detailed Dates	132
10.6	Results for Short Hedge: Rising Prices, Basis Negative and Strengthens, Basis Trading Format, Detailed Dates	132

10.7	Results for Long Hedge: Rising Prices, Basis Positive and Weakens, Detailed Dates	133
10.8	Results for Long Hedge: Rising Prices, Basis Positive and Weakens, Basis Trading Format, Detailed Dates	133
10.9	Results for Long Hedge: Falling Prices, Basis Positive and Weakens, Detailed Dates	134
10.10	Results for Long Hedge: Falling Prices, Basis Positive and Weakens, Basis Trading Format, Detailed Dates	134
11.1	Results for Long Hedge: Rising Prices, Basis Positive and Weakens, Rolled Forward	137
11.1A	Results for Long Hedge: Rising Prices, Basis Positive and Weakens, Rolled Forward Using Spread-Adjusted Futures Prices and Basis Values	138
11.2	Results for Short Hedge: Falling Prices, Basis Negative and Strengthens, Rolled Back	140
11.2A	Results for Short Hedge: Falling Prices, Basis Negative and Strengthens, Rolled Back Using Spread-Adjusted Futures Prices and Basis Values	142
11.3	Excerpt of Results for Long Hedge: Rising Prices, Basis Positive and Weakens, Rolled Forward	144
11.3A	Excerpt of Results for Long Hedge: Rising Prices, Basis Positive and Weakens, Rolled Forward Using Spread-Adjusted Futures Prices and Basis Values	144
11.4	Excerpt of Results for Long Hedge: Falling Prices, Basis Negative and Strengthens, Rolled Back	145
11.4A	Excerpt of Results for Long Hedge: Falling Prices, Basis Negative and Strengthens, Rolled Back Using Spread-Adjusted Futures Prices and Basis Values	145
12.1	Calculation of Total Reportable Long and Short Open Interest from Disaggregated Commitments of Traders Report, Corn Futures, December 27, 2016	156
15.1	Profit on Long Futures Position Established at $3.50	184
15.2	Profit on Short Futures Position Established at $3.50	186
15.3	Profit on Long Cash Position Established at $3.50	187
15.4	Profit on Long Cash Position Established at $3.50 Hedged with Short Futures Position Established at $3.50	188
15.5	Profit on Long $3.50 Call, $0.35 Premium	190
15.6	Profit on Short $3.50 Call, $0.35 Premium	192
15.7	Profit on Long $3.50 Put, $0.25 Premium	194
15.8	Profit on Short $3.50 Put, $0.25 Premium	195
15.9	Profit on Long Cash Position Established at $3.50, Hedged with Long $3.50 Put, $0.25 Premium	197
15.10	Profit on Long Cash Position Established at $3.50, Hedged with Short $3.50 Call, $0.25 Premium	199

15.11 Profit on Short Cash Position Established at $3.50, Hedged with
       Long Futures Position Established at $3.50   201
15.12 Profit on Short Cash Position Established at $3.50, Hedged with
       Long $3.50 Call, $0.35 Premium   202
15.13 Profit on Short Cash Position Established at $3.50, Hedged with
       Short $3.50 Put, $0.25 Premium   204
16.1   Profit on Long Cash Position Established at $3.50, Hedged with Long
       $3.50 Put, $0.25 Premium and Short $4.00 Call, $0.1575 Premium   209
16.2   Profit on Long Cash Position Established at $3.50, Hedged with Long
       $3.50 Put, $0.25 Premium and 2 Short $4.00 Calls, Each $0.1575 Premium 212
16.3   Profit on Short Cash Position Established at $3.50, Hedged with
       Long $3.50 Call, $0.35 Premium and Short $3.00 Put, $0.0750 Premium   214
16.4   Profit on Long $3.50 Call, $0.35 Premium Combined with Short $3.50
       Put, $0.25 Premium   226
16.5   Profit on Short $3.50 Call, $0.35 Premium Combined with Long $3.50
       Put, $0.25 Premium   228
17.1   Profit on Actual Long Futures at $3.58 Combined with Synthetic Short
       Futures at $3.60   237
17.2   Profit on Long $3.20 Call, $0.5175 Premium Combined with Short $3.20
       Put, $0.1275 Premium   238
17.3   Profit on Actual Short Futures at $3.60 Combined with Synthetic Long
       Futures at $3.59   240
17.4   Profit on Bull Call Spread Using Long $3.50 Call, $0.35 Premium and
       Short $3.60 Call, $0.30 Premium   243
17.5   Profit on Bull Call Spread Using Long $3.50 Call, $0.35 Premium and
       Short $3.60 Call, $0.30 Premium   245
17.6   Profit on Bull Put Spread Using Long $3.40 Put, $0.20 Premium and
       Short $3.50 Put, $0.25 Premium   247
17.7   Profit on Bull Put Spread Using Long $3.40 Put, $0.20 Premium and
       Short $3.50 Put, $0.25 Premium   249

PREFACE

This book is a compilation of information and experiences collected during a career in commodity futures, options, and swaps that has spanned four decades. During this time I have worked as a market analyst, marketing manager, research director, and futures/options/swaps contract designer, all of which provided a broad exposure to the many facets of this dynamic industry.

When I became a professor in 2012, I found a lack of suitable materials for students planning careers as practitioners. Conversations with corporate recruiters confirmed my findings, and led me to develop classroom materials that provide the necessary theoretical background, but also cover the practical applications that employers expect new hires to understand. These materials have been used by more than a thousand college students to date, whose feedback has helped to refine the information presented in this book.

Derivatives can be a complex and highly mathematical topic, sometimes unnecessarily so. Every effort has been made to limit the math used in this book to basic algebra, and to provide alternate explanations – verbal, graphical, and/or numerical – whenever possible. The reader is assumed to have a working knowledge of economics and some familiarity with markets and prices, but nothing beyond what a typical undergraduate business or agricultural major should know.

The writing style is conversational and informal, with citations used only when the information is source-specific. It relies heavily on industry terminology, so new terms and common words with specific meanings are shown in italics and defined at the first usage. Gender-neutral pronouns "they" and "their" are used in keeping with the current style. Examples are coordinated across chapters using consistent prices and formats. This book is organized into 18 chapters, corresponding to approximately one chapter per week for a course on the semester system.

Three people deserve special mention for their invaluable assistance in this effort. My wife Peggy Peterson reviewed the early drafts and served as a sounding board at many important points in this project. My colleague Paul Stoddard reviewed the later drafts and offered valuable input from both the student and instructor points of view. My friend Rodney Connor reviewed the basis trading chapters from the vantage point of a grain merchandiser and provided many useful suggestions. Any errors are entirely my responsibility, and should not detract from the important contributions of these three individuals.

I have enjoyed writing this book, and I hope you find it interesting, useful, and rewarding.

Paul E. Peterson

Urbana, Illinois

August 2017

1 Introduction

The title of this book is *Commodity Derivatives: A Guide for Future Practitioners*. But what is a commodity, and what are derivatives?

What is a Commodity?

Undifferentiated vs. Branded Products

Commodities are *undifferentiated* products including tangible physical items such as wheat, gold, or crude oil. By "undifferentiated" we mean that every bushel of wheat, or bar of gold, or barrel of crude oil, is just like every other every bushel of wheat, or bar of gold, or barrel of crude oil with the same quality specifications. In contrast, most consumer goods are *branded*, which implies the presence of additional qualities – real or imagined – that set a product apart from similar but competing products, and typically allows them to command a higher price. For example, coffee is a commodity, but Starbucks coffee definitely is not. Most commodities are inputs used in the production of various other products, while most consumer goods are final or near-final products sold to end users.

By being undifferentiated, the same commodity from different sources can be *commingled* or combined. For example, wheat from multiple individuals can be combined in the same storage bin. If any of the individual owners want to remove "their" wheat at some later date, it is not necessary for them to receive the exact same kernels they put into storage. Instead, any wheat with the same quality, and therefore the same value, will be acceptable. Stated differently, commodities are *fungible*, so every unit of a commodity having a particular set of qualities is *perfectly substitutable* with every other unit of the same commodity. Because the underlying commodities are fungible, many of the exchange-traded derivatives based on those commodities – particularly futures and options on futures – also are fungible, so they can be bought and sold easily. Each exchange-traded contract is completely interchangeable, so it is not necessary for buyers and sellers to find their original trading partners to liquidate positions from previous transactions.

Perfect Competition Model

Commodities differ from most other products because price and quantity are determined by the market as a whole, through the forces of supply and demand. Consequently, commodity markets resemble the *perfect competition model*, which requires large numbers of buyers and sellers with no individual large enough to influence the market, homogeneous products, low barriers to entry and exit, and all decisions driven by profit maximization. This is in contrast to the branded products described above – for example, Starbucks coffee – in which the seller sets the price and then uses various marketing tools to create additional qualities to justify that price. If a commodity seller attempted to do this and demanded a higher price based on claims of some type of intangible benefit, potential buyers would simply buy the commodity at a lower price from someone else. Similarly, if a commodity buyer attempted to do this and offered a lower price, potential sellers would simply sell the commodity at a higher price to someone else.

One consequence of the perfect competition model is zero long-run economic profits. This does not imply that producers and consumers in commodity markets do not earn profits. Instead, it means that over the long run, they earn returns to capital, labor, management, and other inputs, but no consistent, above-market returns over an extended period of time. From basic economics, recall that the cost curve defines the supply curve, so a low-cost producer of a commodity has a definite advantage over its competitors. In fact, cost control is the only tool that commodity producers have to obtain higher profits. From history, we also know that commodity prices are characterized by boom-and-bust cycles and volatile prices which can be disruptive to buyers and sellers alike. Reducing this inherent price volatility is precisely the reason why commodity derivatives were developed.

Inelastic Supply and Demand

Another characteristic of commodities is *inelastic supply* and/or *inelastic demand*, where small changes in the quantity supplied and/or quantity demanded can produce large changes in the price. Most commodities are economic necessities in the production of other products, and have few close substitutes that can be used when shortages arise. When a commodity shortage occurs as the result of crop failures, labor strikes, transportation disruptions, or various other events, the market allocates the limited supplies of the commodity by increasing the price. Conversely, when a commodity surplus occurs, the market encourages increased consumption by decreasing the price. Commodity markets are particularly susceptible to supply shocks that can cause prices to spike higher or lower. Demand shocks also can occur in commodity markets, but tend to be less common. Most demand changes occur gradually over a period of years, but sudden shifts in government policies such as taxes or import/export restrictions are the most common examples of demand shocks that can affect commodity prices.

What is a Derivative?

Price Stability and Certainty

Derivatives include forward contracts, futures contracts, options, and swaps. They are called "derivatives" because their values are derived from the price of the *underlying* commodity – wheat or gold or crude oil, from our examples at the beginning of this chapter.

In a typical transaction for a physical commodity – and for most of the things we buy and sell in everyday life – a buyer and a seller agree to exchange a product today for a price established today. In most situations, and particularly for frequent transactions involving relatively small quantities of a product and relatively small amounts of money – for example, filling up your car with gasoline once a week – this simultaneous exchange of goods for money at the current market price is acceptable, because the price risk is manageable.

However, when transactions become large and/or infrequent – for example, a farmer who harvests and sells a crop once a year and needs the selling price to cover their costs, or an airline that needs to price its fuel needs so it knows how much to charge its customers for tickets, the risk of an unfavorable price can be devastating to the individual or firm. In these situations it becomes important to establish the commodity price before the goods and money are exchanged. The importance of stable, predictable prices typically increases as businesses become larger, and planning and budgeting activities become more formalized.

Separating the Pricing and Exchange Functions

Forward Contracts

Markets for physical commodities are designed for the simultaneous exchange of goods for money at the current market price. In contrast, establishing the price in advance of the actual transaction is beyond the capabilities of a regular market, because it requires the exchange of goods for money to occur at one time and the price to be established at another. However, the separation of the exchange of goods from the pricing of those goods can be accomplished with a derivative.

The simplest and most common type of derivative is a *forward contract,* commonly referred to simply as a *forward.* A forward contract is a legally binding agreement between buyer and seller to exchange a product later, or "forward" in time, for a price established now. A forward contract eliminates uncertainty about the price at the later date; it does not eliminate *buyer's remorse* or *seller's remorse* when the price at the time of the exchange turns out to be better (i.e., lower for buyers or higher for sellers) than the agreed-upon price. Forward contracts may be created for any product, not just commodities, and may include any terms to which the buyer and seller agree. Consequently, the market for forward contracts is both large and non-homogeneous, reflecting the high degree of customization and flexibility that is possible with forwards.

One version of a forward contract known as a *price-later contract* reverses the timing of the two components described above. As the name suggests, it is an agreement between buyer and seller to exchange a product now for a price established later. A price-later contract removes uncertainty about the availability of the commodity for the buyer, and allows the seller to select the market price at some later date as the price for the commodity they deliver today.

Futures Contracts

A *futures contract* is a more formalized version of a forward contract. Like forwards, futures are legally binding agreements between buyer and seller. Unlike forwards, which are completely customizable, futures are standardized in terms of the underlying commodity being traded, the quality and quantity of the underlying commodity, and the time, location, and other details for final settlement of the contract. Because all terms and conditions for a futures contract except the price are established beforehand, the price is the only feature to be negotiated between the buyer and seller.

    This high degree of standardization, with price as the only variable, makes futures contracts fungible. Consequently, someone who initially buys or sells a futures contract and later wishes to liquidate it does not need to find their trading partner from the initial transaction and then try to negotiate an exit at some price. Instead, the initial buyer or seller can make an offsetting trade with anyone who is willing to sell or buy at that particular point in time. Standardization also allows futures contracts to be traded on an *exchange*, which is a centralized marketplace that brings together buyers and sellers. This concentration of buyer and sellers enhances *liquidity*, or the ability to buy or sell quickly and easily with little or no impact on the price.

    The world's first futures contract was created in the 1700s at the Dojima Rice Market in Osaka, Japan (this market closed in the 1930s). The first commodity futures markets in the United States were created in the mid-1800s for corn, wheat, and oats, making them the oldest continuously-traded futures markets still in existence. Other crop and crop-based futures contracts, including those on oilseeds and the so-called soft or tropical commodities, were added over the subsequent decades. Among other physical commodities, livestock futures and precious metals futures were introduced in the 1960s, and energy futures first appeared in the 1970s.

    Today, corn is the largest of the three original US futures commodities in terms of physical production, value of physical production, and volume of futures trading. Given its long history and importance in the development of futures markets on other commodities, all numerical examples in this book will use corn-level prices, and the examples will be coordinated to allow easy comparison across chapters. However, the principles presented in this book apply equally to all commodities, so the reader can easily convert these examples into any other commodity by simply re-scaling the prices.

Options

From the descriptions above, both forwards and futures require the buyer to provide the agreed-upon funds and the seller to provide the agreed-upon goods at the termination of the contract. In contrast, an *option* replaces the buyer's obligation with the right to buy a specific commodity or futures contract at a specific price – known as a *call* – or the right to sell a specific commodity or futures contract at a specific price – known as a *put*. An option may be on a physical commodity, known as an *option on actual*, or on a futures contract, known as an *option on futures*. Our focus in this book will be on options on futures, which in the US were introduced in the 1980s.

If the price specified in the option is favorable to the option buyer – relative to the market price at some date or over some period of time – the buyer may exercise the option. Upon exercise the option buyer receives a futures contract at the specified price, and the option seller is assigned the opposite position in the same futures contract. If the specified price is unfavorable, the option buyer can simply abandon the option without any penalty. In return for this right to exercise or abandon, the option buyer pays the option seller a *premium* at the outset of the option. Similar to futures contracts, options on futures are traded on an exchange. All terms and conditions of the option are standardized except the premium, which is negotiated between the buyer and seller in the same manner as futures prices.

Swaps

Swaps are similar to forward contracts in many respects, beginning with the fact that swaps are traded off-exchange, so they may be created for any product and may include any terms to which the buyer and seller agree. Also like forward contracts, the market for swaps is both large and non-homogeneous, reflecting a high degree of customization and flexibility. The first swap was created in the 1980s.

As the name suggests, a swap requires the buyer and seller to exchange or "swap" cash flows from two forward contracts on the same commodity. While a forward contract has a single payment, a swap typically has multiple payments, so a swap can be described as a series of forward contracts with different maturities.

Organization of this Book

This book is organized into three parts. The first part focuses on futures, the second part on options on futures, and the third part on swaps. Each part will describe how the particular derivative and its market infrastructure operates, how it can be used for risk management purposes, and how it can be used for speculative or investment purposes. There is no section on forwards, largely due to the close similarities between forwards and futures and the duplication that would result from a discussion of both types of derivatives.

Forwards, Futures, and Price Discovery

As noted earlier, forward contracts may be created for any product and for any terms to which the buyer and seller agree. This means forwards are very flexible, but the unique nature of each transaction means that the price for one forward contract may not be a reliable indicator of the price for other forward contracts, or for the underlying commodity itself.

Each term and condition of a forward contract must be negotiated by the buyer and seller, so reaching an agreement can be a time-consuming process. Because there is no centralized market or other authority to monitor trading activity, enforcement of those terms and conditions is the responsibility of the buyer and seller, and resolving disputes can be time consuming and costly. Each party faces the risk of *default*, or non-performance by the *counterparty*, or other party in the agreement. On the agreed-upon day for exchanging goods for money to fulfill the contract, the buyer may not be able to provide the funds, and/or the seller may not be able to provide the specified quality or quantity of the commodity at the specified location within the specified time frame. Finally, there is no mechanism to disseminate the price, quantity, and other details of the transaction. Although some buyers and sellers might prefer to keep these details confidential, information about previous transactions can be useful to other market participants when negotiating new transactions and can make the market more efficient, even when the terms and conditions of previous transactions are substantially different from those being negotiated.

In contrast, futures are highly standardized, so futures can be traded rapidly and in large volumes because only the price must be negotiated, and the prices of all transactions are publicly available on a real-time basis. The exchange enforces terms and conditions of the contracts, provides facilities for rapidly resolving disputes, and provides financial guarantees against default, all of which facilitate additional trading activity.

An important side benefit of futures trading is *price discovery*, in which the forces of supply and demand find the equilibrium price for the futures contract at a particular point in time. This is in contrast to *price determination*, in which the price is dictated by an individual or entity, such as a monopoly or cartel, and likely does not represent the equilibrium price. Notice that the price for a futures contract on a particular commodity is not necessarily the same as the price for the commodity itself; recall from above that futures are derivatives, so the futures price is derived from the commodity price. Nevertheless, the price discovery process for futures is often more efficient than the price discovery process for the underlying commodity, because the futures price is more actively traded. It is increasingly common for the futures market to play a role in establishing the price of the underlying commodity. Thus, it is important to understand how futures markets operate, even for individuals who never use futures directly.

In the following chapters we will explore how each of these derivatives is traded, how prices can be interpreted, how the markets are regulated, how commodity derivatives can be used to manage price risk, and how commodity derivatives can be used for investment purposes.

2 Trading Futures and Options

Nearly all futures and options trading today is conducted on computer-based electronic trading systems. However, many of the practices and procedures of electronic trading were borrowed from pit-based open outcry trading, which in the US began in the mid-1800s. Pit trading is also the source of much of the trading terminology still used today, so it is important to understand pit trading as a way to understand electronic trading.

Pit Trading

The Trading Pit

Until recently, all futures and options trading took place in *pits* or *rings* located on the *trading floor* of an exchange. Usually just one commodity was traded in a particular pit, so a trading floor generally had multiple pits. Each pit had a set of steps, usually arranged in an octagon and resembling an inverted cone with the lowest point at the center of the pit and highest point near the outer edge. Much like slices of a pie, the set of steps for each side of the octagon corresponded to a particular *contract month* when delivery or final settlement occurs and the contract *expires*. A cross-section of a trading pit is shown in Figure 2.1.

One "slice" was designated as the *front month* and was the area where trading in the soonest-to-expire contract month occurred. Going clockwise, each successive contract month was assigned its own slice and was designated as the second month, third month, and so forth. This caused traders of the same contract month to be located in the same area of the pit, in close proximity to one another. Upon expiration of the front month, all contract months rotated counter-clockwise by one slice, so what previously had been the second month was now in the front month position, what previously had been the third month was now in the second month position, and so forth. At this time a new contract month would be added to the roster of eligible contracts, and this latest-to-expire contract month would be referred to as the *back month*.

The top steps along the outer edge of the pit provided the highest visibility and traditionally were reserved for traders known as *brokers* or *order-fillers* who executed orders to buy or sell on behalf of customers. Other traders known as *locals* or *floor speculators*, who bought

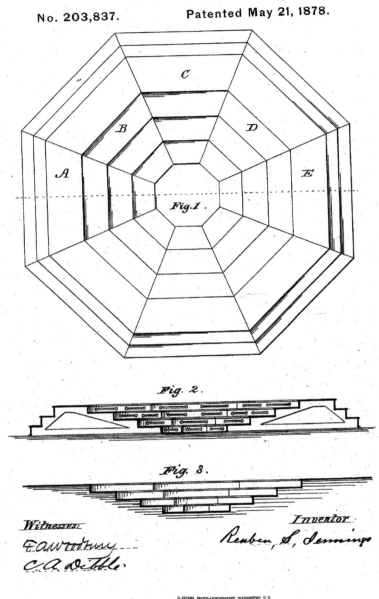

R. S. JENNINGS.
Trading-Pit

No. 203,837.   Patented May 21, 1878.

Figure 2.1 Cross-Section of Trading Pit
US Patent and Trademark Office

or sold in hopes of making profit and who provided liquidity to the market, populated the other areas of the pit. All traders in the pit wore trading jackets with many large pockets to hold order tickets, trading cards, and other paperwork. Locals had brightly-colored and patterned jackets so they could be seen easily by brokers; brokers generally wore solid-colored jackets. All traders also wore a badge with a unique 2- to 5-letter acronym that served as their personal ID and a 3-digit code for the *clearing firm* that financially guaranteed their trades.

Figure 2.2 CBOT Agricultural Trading Floor circa 1980s
Courtesy of CME Group

Figure 2.3 Trader with Trading Jacket and Badge
Image courtesy of Trading Pit History https://tradingpithistory.com

Order Types and Order Execution

Each trading session would *open* and *close* at fixed times for each particular commodity, signaled by a bell or buzzer. These times often were staggered so that individual traders could cover more than one commodity. Customer orders were phoned to a brokerage firm's *desk* located at the edge of the trading floor, often by the customer's brokerage firm representative. A desk clerk answered the phone and wrote the information – buy or sell, commodity, contract month, number of contracts, price, and other instructions – on a *trading ticket*, also called an *order ticket*. Information for buy orders was entered on the left side of the ticket, and information for sell orders was entered on the right side of the ticket. Each ticket was in triplicate with the original on top, a broker copy in the middle, and a desk copy on the bottom. A sample trading ticket is shown in Figure 2.4.

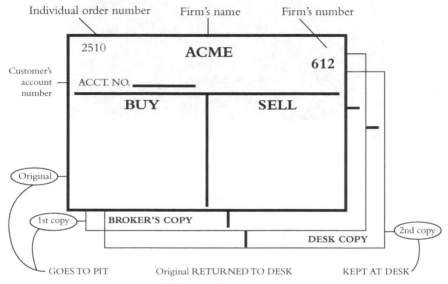

Figure 2.4 Trading Ticket with Order Details
Image courtesy of AMP Futures

One of these instructions was the *order type* that instructed the broker how the order should be *filled*, or executed. The most common order types and their abbreviations are:

- Market (MKT), which should be filled immediately at the best-available current price. This is the default order type if no other information is provided.
- Limit (LIM), which should be filled at or *better than* the price specified by the customer. "Better than" means below the specified price for an order to buy, and above the specified price for an order to sell.
- Stop (STOP), also known as a *stop loss*, which becomes a market order and should be filled immediately once the market price *goes through* and thus becomes *worse than* the

price specified by the customer. "Worse than" means above the specified price for an order to buy, and below the specified price for an order to sell. As the name suggests, a stop order is often used to liquidate an existing position after losses reach a certain point.

The following examples illustrate how these order types are executed under different market situations:

Example 2.1: A contract is trading at $3.50 when a customer submits a market order to buy. The order will be filled at $3.50.

Example 2.2: A contract is trading at $3.50 when a customer submits a market order to sell. The order will be filled at $3.50.

Example 2.3: A contract is trading at $3.50 when a customer submits a limit order to buy at $3.55. The limit order will be filled at $3.50, because $3.50 is a "better" buying price than $3.55.

Example 2.4: A contract is trading at $3.50 when a customer submits a limit order to sell at $3.55. The limit order will not be filled until the futures price rises to at least $3.55, because $3.55 is a "better" selling price than $3.50.

Example 2.5: A contract is trading at $3.50 when a customer submits a stop order to buy at $3.55. The stop order will not be filled until the futures price rises to at least $3.55, because $3.55 is a "worse" buying price than $3.50. In this case the trader is willing to lose at least 5 cents ($3.50 − $3.55) before the buy order is executed. Stated differently, the market must "go through" $3.55 in the wrong direction and create a loss for the customer before the stop order will be triggered, hence the term "stop loss."

Example 2.6: A contract is trading at $3.50 when a customer submits a stop order to sell at $3.55. The stop order will be filled at $3.50, because $3.50 is a "worse" selling price than $3.55.

Other common order types include:

- Cancel (CXL), which immediately cancels a previously-submitted order that has not yet been filled.
- Cancel and Replace (CRO), which immediately cancels a previously-submitted order that has not yet been filled and replaces it with a new order; it then lists the details of the new order.
- Market if Touched (MIT), which becomes a market order once the market price reaches or *touches* – but need not go through – the price specified by the customer.

The customer also may indicate how long the order remains in effect:

- Day (DAY) orders are *good* or effective only for that trading session and then expire. This is the default period if no other information is provided.
- Open (OPEN) or Good 'til Cancelled (GTC) orders remain valid until they are either filled by the broker or cancelled by the customer.

After all details of the order had been entered on the ticket, the desk clerk would read it back to the caller for confirmation, time stamp the ticket, remove the bottom page (i.e., desk copy), and hand the remaining two pages (i.e., original and broker copy) to a *runner* who immediately delivered the ticket to the firm's broker in the pit. A market order was filled immediately; otherwise the ticket was inserted into the broker's *deck* of orders and held until the necessary market conditions were met for the order to be filled, or until the order expired.

Open Outcry and Hand Signals

Pit trading is also called open outcry trading because *bids* − expressions of willingness to buy − and *offers* or *asks* − expressions of willingness to sell − were required to be called out loudly and clearly to expose each order to all traders in the pit. Typically only the quantity and the last few digits of the price were called out, because the general price level was already known from previous trades. In addition, the order in which the price and quantity were expressed, and the use of "on" for a bid and "at" for an offer, indicated whether the trader was a buyer or a seller. Bids were called out using the words "(price) on (quantity)," such as "40 on 5" to indicate the trader was willing to pay $3.40 for 5 contracts in a market trading at the $3 level. Offers were called out "(quantity) at (price)," such as "10 at 60" to indicate the trader was willing to sell 10 contracts at $3.60 in a market trading at the $3 level.

With so many traders shouting bids and offers at the same time, the noise level in a pit could be quite high, so traders in open outcry trading also used hand signals to indicate prices and quantities, shown in Figure 2.5. A trader would hold out one hand with the palm facing out to indicate their willingness to sell, or facing in to indicate their willingness to buy. The fingers on that hand were used to indicate the quantity and the last digit of the price, alternating back and forth between the two signals. The other hand would hold order tickets or trading cards and a pen, and would be waved about to help attract attention to the trader and their quote.

Suppose Trader 1 called out "10 at 60" to indicate their willingness to sell 10 contracts at $3.60. If Trader 2 agreed to both the quantity and price, Trader 2 would call out "Buy 10 at 60" to indicate their acceptance of Trader 1's offer. Trader 1 then would acknowledge both Trader 2's acceptance and the completed transaction by calling out "Done" and signal by making a fist.

Now suppose Trader 2 wanted only 5 of the 10 contracts offered at that price. Trader 2 would call out "Buy 5 at 60" to indicate their partial acceptance of Trader 1's offer. Trader 1 would acknowledge Trader 2's partial acceptance, and then would proceed to sell the remaining 5 contracts by calling out "5 at 60." Trader 2 also could have countered by bidding a lower price, such as "55 on 10" for a bid of $3.55 on 10 contracts. Trader 1 then would either accept or decline Trader 2's bid.

Finally, suppose Trader 2 and Trader 3 both called out "Buy 10 at 90" to accept Trader 1's offer. Trader 1 could split the trade and give 5 contracts to Trader 2 and 5 contracts to Trader 3. Alternatively, Trader 1 might decide that one of the bidders was just a bit quicker and award them all 10 contracts.

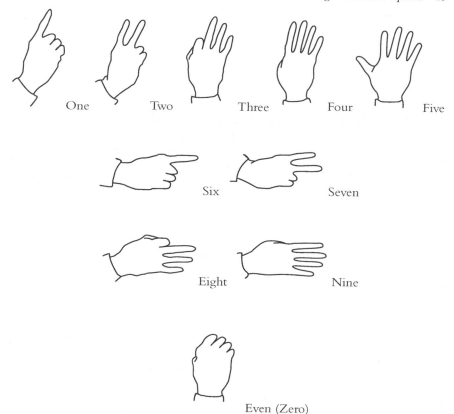

One   Two   Three   Four   Five

Six   Seven

Eight   Nine

Even (Zero)

Figure 2.5 Hand Signals

Price Reporting

The price of each trade, plus changes in the bid and offer prices, was monitored by a *pit reporter* stationed at a terminal in the trading pit. Each time the traded price changed, the reporter entered the new price into the *price reporting system*. A new price also would be entered each time there was a better (higher) bid, or a better (lower) offer relative to the last reported price. The new prices were displayed on *wall boards* that displayed prices on the trading floor, and at the same time were transmitted outside the exchange to quote vendors and news services which in turn distributed these prices to subscribers.

Each time a transaction was completed, both (or all) parties recorded the details of the trade. A broker wrote the quantity, commodity code and contract month, price, badge acronym, and clearing firm of the opposite trader(s) on the order ticket. Then the broker initialed the ticket, removed the broker copy, and gave the original to a runner. The runner immediately delivered the ticket to the desk where it was time stamped, and then the information on the ticket was entered into the clearing system.

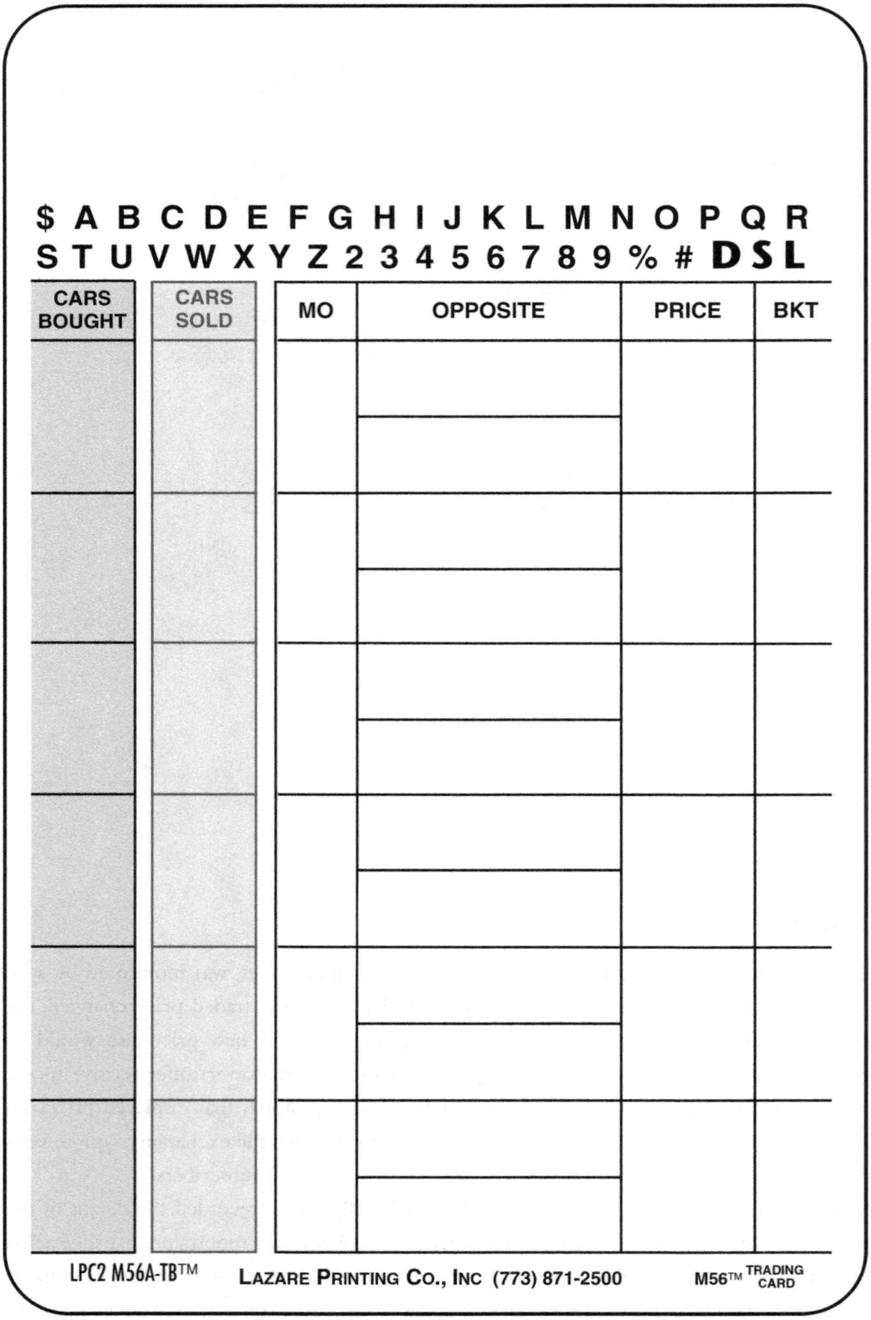

$ A B C D E F G H I J K L M N O P Q R
S T U V W X Y Z 2 3 4 5 6 7 8 9 % # **D S L**

CARS BOUGHT	CARS SOLD	MO	OPPOSITE	PRICE	BKT

LPC2 M56A-TB™   LAZARE PRINTING CO., INC (773) 871-2500   M56™ TRADING CARD

Figure 2.6 Trading Card for Recording Trade Information. Actual size 3.5 × 5.5 inches
Image courtesy of Lazare Printing Co., Inc.

A floor speculator did not have an order ticket, since order tickets were used only for customer orders. Instead, the floor speculator recorded the same information – quantity, commodity code and contract month, price, badge acronym, and clearing firm of the opposite trader(s) – on a trading card, shown in Figure 2.6. These trading cards were collected periodically during the trading session, time stamped, and the information on the cards was entered into the clearing system.

A trade was processed, or *cleared*, if all the information entered by the buying trader and the selling trader – quantity, commodity code and contract month, price, badge acronyms, and clearing firms – matched entirely. Any discrepancies resulted in an *out-trade* and that trade was not processed until the discrepancy was resolved by the two parties, typically at an out-trade session the following morning before the market opened for trading. The vast majority of discrepancies – for example, a "5" that looked like a "6" – were easily resolved: one party accepted responsibility, the error was corrected, and the trade was then cleared. In other cases there was no clear solution to the dispute, so the two parties might simply agree to split the difference. In rare cases when the two parties could not agree, the matter was resolved by an arbitration panel.

Pit trading is simple, flexible, and has low initial cost. However, pit trading is prone to errors and trading capacity is limited, resulting in high ongoing cost. As the futures and options markets grew in size and importance, these drawbacks became increasingly important as barriers to continued expansion.

Electronic Trading

The Role of Technology

Beginning around 1990, electronic trading became feasible because computers and related technology had advanced to the point that many parts of the trading process could be automated. This prompted several exchanges around the world to introduce electronic trading as a solution to the disadvantages of pit trading. European and Asian exchanges, which tended to be smaller and newer than American exchanges, were the first to make the conversion to electronic trading. Several new exchanges started as all-electronic venues and never had pits or trading floors. U.S. exchanges, which were the largest and oldest, were slower to adapt. Reasons for this delay included resistance from the trading floor population, many of whom were also exchange member/owners; massive investments in (and often the development of) technology capable of handling large volumes of trading at extremely high levels of reliability; and the conversion from membership organizations to stockholder-owned corporations, in which the sale of shares provided the funding for the necessary technology.

The conversion to electronic trading proceeded rapidly, and by the mid-2000s the majority of futures trading in the US was conducted on electronic platforms. Options trading is more complex, so the transition process has been somewhat slower, but by the mid-2010s the majority of options trading in the US was conducted on electronic platforms.

Components of Electronic Trading

All electronic trading systems have at least four components: a central limit order book, a matching engine, a front end for order entry, and a set of customer protection features.

Central Limit Order Book

A *central limit order book* is the listing of all bids and offers at each possible price, along with the corresponding quantities and other information. From our discussion of pit trading, recall that floor brokers held decks of order tickets. If all these decks for all the brokers in a particular market were combined, the result would be the central limit order book. Unlike pit trading, where the contents of a broker's deck were strictly confidential, the order book in electronic trading is visible to the entire market. This provides market participants with useful information about the collective willingness of everyone in the market to buy or sell at various prices, and the number of contracts waiting to be bought or sold at each price.

In the hypothetical order book shown in Table 2.1, the market is trading at $3.50 bid, $3.5025 ask. Prices move in minimum increments or *ticks* of $.0025, or ¼ cent. The *bid-ask spread* also happens to be $0.0025 (¼ cent), which is the cost of buying and immediately selling (or selling and immediately buying) a contract. The bid-ask spread is commonly used as a measure of market liquidity, with a narrow or "tight" bid-ask spread indicative of a liquid market.

Table 2.1 Hypothetical Order Book

Bid quantity	Price	Ask quantity
	3.52	0
	3.5175	1
	3.5150	8
	3.5125	23
	3.51	61
	3.5075	112
	3.5050	89
	3.5025	12
35	3.50	
61	3.4975	
127	3.4950	
54	3.4925	
19	3.49	
13	3.4875	
5	3.4850	
2	3.4825	

In the ask column on the right side of the order book – recall from the order ticket used in pit trading that "buy" was on the left and "sell" was on the right – there are 12 contracts waiting to be sold at $3.5025, 89 contracts waiting to be sold at $3.5050, and 112 contracts waiting to be sold at $3.5075. A market order to buy 100 contracts would pay $3.5025 for the first 12 contracts and $3.5050 for the next 88 contracts, for an average price of $3.5047.

A limit order to buy 100 contracts at a price of $3.5050 "or better" would have the same result; a limit order to buy 100 contracts at a price of $3.5025 would buy only the 12 contracts at $3.5025, because buying at $3.5050 is not "better" than buying at $3.5025. A stop order to buy 100 contracts at $3.5050 would be filled once the market "goes through" $3.5050, beginning at $3.5075 and going up in price until all 100 contracts have been bought.

Matching Engine

The *matching engine*, as the name suggests, is the software that matches bids and offers at the same price. This matching process uses various algorithms to determine which contracts in the queue are used to fill incoming orders, and the markets for different commodities may use different matching algorithms. Possible algorithms include:

- First In, First Out (FIFO) – Strict price/time priority, so the earliest bid (or offer) at a particular price is the first to be matched with an incoming offer (or bid).
- Pro Rata – Takes an equal share from each order at a particular price.
- All or None (AON) – Matched with a single order for the same (or larger) quantity.

For example, suppose there are standing bids for 80 contracts, all at the same price:

- 10 contracts (oldest bid)
- 50 contracts (second-oldest bid)
- 11 contracts (third-oldest bid)
- 4 contracts (fourth-oldest bid)
- 5 contracts (fifth-oldest bid; also the newest bid)

Next, a matching offer at that price comes into the market for 40 contracts. If first in, first out is the matching algorithm, the oldest bid (10 contracts) and 30 contracts from the second-oldest bid are used. If pro rata is the matching algorithm, 5 contracts from the oldest bid, 25 contracts from the second-oldest bid, 5 (or 6, depending on the rounding rule employed by the algorithm) contracts from the third-oldest bid, 2 contracts from the fourth-oldest bid, and 2 (or 3, again depending on the rounding rule employed by the algorithm) contracts from the fifth-oldest bid are used. If all or none is the matching algorithm, 40 contracts from the second-oldest bid are used. In general, the owner of the incoming order will be indifferent regarding the matching algorithm used, but the owners of the standing orders will be very interested in how this allocation process is handled.

Front End

The *front end* is the software that allows a trader to enter and manage orders, and serves as the interface between the trader and the matching engine. This software is available with various features and is often provided by brokerage firms to their customers. At a minimum, a front-end package will allow the trader to select the commodity and contract month, number of contracts to be traded, whether to buy or sell, and order type (market, limit, stop, etc.). More advanced versions may show the trader's current position, account balance, and latest prices in one or more markets. Some front ends also show the order book, provide news feeds, and show graphic renditions of recent price activity. More sophisticated versions allow traders to develop strategies and test them on historical data before implementing them. An example of the order entry screen for a front end is shown in Figure 2.7.

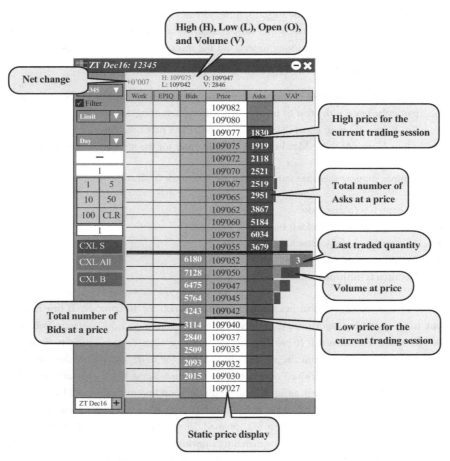

Figure 2.7 Hypothetical Order Book Showing Prices and Quantities
Image courtesy of Trading Technologies International, Inc. All rights reserved.

Customer Protection Features

In electronic trading there are no humans at any point in the trading process to intervene and prevent potentially serious mistakes. Recall from our earlier description of pit trading that there were several individuals – the brokerage firm representative who phoned the order to the trading floor, the desk clerk who received the order and wrote the ticket, the broker in the pit who executed the trade – who physically handled each order, could spot unusual instructions and/or potential problems, and frequently prevented customers from making costly errors. In contrast, customers in an electronic trading environment submit their orders directly, and their orders are filled instantaneously, so serious errors can occur very quickly, often with tragic consequences.

In one infamous trading disaster that occurred in 2005, a customer at the Tokyo Stock Exchange wanted to sell 1 share at a price of 610,000 Japanese Yen. Instead, the customer mistakenly entered an order for 610,000 shares at a price of 1 Yen, resulting in a loss of 27 billion Yen for the customer and their brokerage firm. This type of mistake is commonly referred to as a *fat finger error*, in which trading details are input incorrectly. Today, system-level controls at most exchanges prevent many of these types of customer errors from being executed.

Credit controls are used to prevent a customer from trading beyond their financial capacity. In one common type of credit control, a customer is prevented from making any trades if losses exceed a certain amount. There also may be *trading limits* established by the brokerage firm that restrict the number of contracts that a customer is allowed to trade in a single order or within a trading day. These trading limits are in addition to, and are much lower than, the *position limits* imposed on all traders by exchanges and regulators.

The widespread use of computerized trading programs, which identify trading opportunities and submit buy and sell orders, has introduced the potential for *runaway trading*. In one of the simplest forms, a "bug" in the software might cause the program to submit the same order over and over again, irrespective of market conditions or the logic coded into the program. In one such case in 2012, a software glitch caused Knight Capital Group to lose $440 million in 30 minutes. This event prompted many firms to install a "kill switch" so their automated trading programs can be interrupted manually when such problems arise.

Benefits vs. Costs of Electronic Trading

Electronic trading is not without problems. In addition to the potential for costly mistakes, the technology is complex with high initial costs and high ongoing costs for the necessary support, maintenance, and upgrades to keep everything running smoothly. However, electronic trading offers a number of important advantages that far outweigh the disadvantages. Out-trades have become a thing of the past, because orders that do not match simply are not executed. Trading has become much faster, simpler and cheaper, and customers now have direct access to the markets. Customers also can view the order book and observe the numbers of standing bids and offers at each price, which can be highly useful when making trading decisions. Finally, electronic trading provides much greater capacity, both in terms of handling large volumes of trades and in processing trades more quickly. These features have led to unprecedented growth and allowed trading volumes to reach levels that would have been unimaginable just a few years ago.

3 Understanding and Interpreting Futures Prices

In Chapter 1 we noted that all terms and conditions for a futures contract except the price are established beforehand, so the price is the only feature to be negotiated between the buyer and seller. In this chapter we will explore how futures prices are quoted and how these prices can be interpreted.

How Futures Prices Are Quoted

Futures Prices and Summary Price Measures

Recall from Chapter 2 that a price is generated and recorded each time a futures trade is completed. A price is also generated and recorded each time there is a better (higher) bid or a better (lower) offer relative to the last reported price. Consequently, over the course of a trading session there may be thousands of prices that reflect the market price for a commodity at particular points in time. Each of these prices and the time at which it occurs is recorded in a *time and sales* report. These thousands of prices from a single trading session can be summarized into seven measures that together give an indication of price activity and market trend:

- *Open,* which is the first price (or prices) recorded as the market opens for trading. The open may be a traded price, a bid price, or an ask price, and depending on the particular market may be the very first price of the session or a range of prices over a span of time such as the first 30 seconds of trading.
- *High,* which is the highest price recorded during the trading session. The high may be a *traded price,* at which a transaction actually took place, or a *bid price,* at which a buyer was willing to trade but there was no willing seller.
- *Low,* which is the lowest price recorded during the trading session. The low may be a traded price, at which a transaction actually took place, or an *ask price,* at which a seller was willing to trade but there was no willing buyer.
- *Last,* which is the most recent price recorded during the trading session while the market is still open and may be a traded price, a bid price, or an ask price. After the market closes, the last is usually replaced by the closing price.

- *Close*, which is the final price (or prices) recorded as the market closes for trading. T] close may be a traded price, a bid price, or an ask price, and depending on the particul market may be the very last price of the session or a range of prices over a span of time such as the final 30 seconds of trading.

- *Settle*, or *daily settlement price*, which is calculated and reported as a single number – never a range – shortly after the end of the trading session. Depending on the particular market, the settlement price is based on the trading activity during a span of time such as the final 30 seconds of trading. The method for calculating the settlement price varies from market to market, but it is often a volume-weighted average of the prices during the closing period. The settlement price is used to value all open positions at the end of the day, and also serves as the reference point for calculating the price *change* in the next trading session.

- *Change*, which compares a particular price to the settlement price from the previous trading session. Prices from the current trading session (i.e., Tuesday) are compared to the settlement price from the previous trading session (i.e., Monday) to measure whether the market has moved up or down and by how much. An example of these summary prices is shown in Figure 3.1.

Month	Options	Charts	Last	Change	Prior Settle	Open	High	Low	Volume	Hi / Low Limit	Updated
DEC 2016	OPT		340'6	-2'6	343'4	343'2	345'0	339'0	185,910	365'2 / 315'2	16:40:47 CT 11 Nov 2016
MAR 2017	OPT		349'2	-2'6	352'0	351'4	353'4	347'4	116,084	374'0 / 324'0	16:40:46 CT 11 Nov 2016
MAY 2017	OPT		356'6	-2'4	359'2	359'0	360'6	355'0	25,150	381'4 / 331'4	16:40:48 CT 11 Nov 2016
JUL 2017	OPT		364'0	-2'4	366'4	366'4	367'4	362'2	14,725	389'0 / 339'0	16:40:45 CT 11 Nov 2016
SEP 2017	OPT		370'6	-2'4	373'2	373'2	374'2	369'2	4,201	395'6 / 345'6	16:40:48 CT 11 Nov 2016
DEC 2017	OPT		379'6	-2'2	382'0	382'0	383'2	378'0	5,610	404'4 / 354'4	16:40:48 CT 11 Nov 2016
MAR 2018	OPT		389'0	-2'4	391'4	392'0	392'0	387'6	255	414'2 / 364'2	16:40:48 CT 11 Nov 2016
MAY 2018	OPT		393'6	-3'0	396'6	394'4	394'4	393'6	144	420'0 / 370'0	16:40:48 CT 11 Nov 2016
JUL 2018	OPT		399'4	-1'4	401'0	399'0	399'4	397'2	340	424'2 / 374'2	16:40:48 CT 11 Nov 2016

Figure 3.1 Corn Futures Prices from November 11, 2016
Courtesy of CME Group

Tick Size and Contract Size

All prices – open, high, low, last/close, settle, and change, as well as all prices for transactions, bids, and offers – are quoted as multiples of the tick, or minimum price increment. The tick size varies from one commodity to the next, just as the *unit of measurement* – bushel, pound, barrel, index point, etc. – varies from one commodity to the next, but the tick is typically much smaller than the price increment used in commercial transactions of that commodity. Using smaller increments facilitates trading by reducing the amount that buyers and sellers must "give away" to the other side to complete a trade, resulting in greater liquidity.

Futures contracts represent a specific quantity of a commodity, which is referred to as the *contract size* and expressed in the unit of measurement for that commodity. The contract size varies from one commodity to the next – 5,000 bushels, 40,000 pounds, 1,000 barrels, and so forth – but typically corresponds to the quantity traditionally used in commercial transactions of that commodity. This number of units is sometimes referred to as the *multiplier* because the price change multiplied by the contract size equals the change in the value of one futures contract.

For example, a price change of ¼ cent ($.0025) per bushel – the tick for corn, oats, wheat, and soybeans – multiplied by 5,000 bushels (the contract size for corn, oats, wheat, and soybeans) equals 1,250 cents or $12.50 per contract. Similarly, a price change of $.00025 per pound – the tick for live cattle and lean hogs – multiplied by 40,000 pounds (the contract size for live cattle and lean hogs) equals $10.00 per contract. Likewise, a price change of $.01 per barrel – the tick for crude oil – multiplied by 1,000 barrels (the contract size for crude oil) equals $10.00 per contract.

The tick for corn, oats, wheat, and soybean futures traditionally is reported in multiples of ⅛ of cent. Corn, oats, and wheat are the oldest futures contracts in the US, dating back to the 1870s, when prices were transmitted via telegraph. To minimize the number of keystrokes required to transmit a particular price, a shorthand notation was developed that used only the numerator of the fraction and separated this digit from the rest of the price by an apostrophe, dash, or other character – for example, 353'6 for 353⅝ cents, which is equivalent to $3.53¾. Over time, the "odd" ticks (⅛, ⅜, ⅝, ⅞) were eliminated and only the "even" ticks (²⁄₈, ⁴⁄₈, ⁶⁄₈, and 0, abbreviated as '2, '4, '6, and '0 respectively) were used. This pricing convention was later applied to soybeans when they were introduced in the 1930s.

A different shorthand was adopted for livestock futures, which were introduced in the 1960s. The tick for live cattle, lean hogs, and feeder cattle is $.00025 per pound, which is equivalent to .025 cents per pound or $.025 per hundredweight (abbreviated as "cwt" and equal to 100 pounds, the traditional measure of weight in the livestock markets). A hypothetical sequence of livestock prices increasing in 1-tick increments would be 83.300, 83.325, 83.350, and 83.375 cents per pound. In an effort to reduce the number of characters, the trailing "0" or "5" was – and still is – frequently omitted, so these prices commonly appear as 83.30, 83.32, 83.35, and 83.37 respectively.

Commodity Codes and Month Codes

In yet another step to reduce keystrokes, commodity names were reduced to a single, unique letter called a *ticker symbol* or *commodity code* – for example, C for corn, O for oats, and W for wheat. Similarly, expiration month names were designated by a single, unique letter. Since

Table 3.1 Month Codes and Corresponding Calendar Months

Code	Calendar month	Code	Calendar month
F	January	N	July
G	February	Q	August
H	March	U	September
J	April	V	October
K	May	X	November
M	June	Z	December

many of the letters were already being used for commodity codes, the letters shown in Table 3.1 were chosen for *month codes*. For example, CZ was used to represent the December futures contract for corn: C for corn and Z for December.

Later on, as more futures contracts were added and the supply of single-letter codes was depleted, two-letter and eventually three-letter commodity codes (and letter–number combinations) were developed. In addition, as futures contracts were listed for more distant expiration dates, the last digit of the expiration year was added to distinguish between futures contracts expiring in the same month but different years, such as CLH7 for March 2017 crude oil futures and CLH8 for March 2018 crude oil futures. Although the telegraph was replaced long ago, this concise method for expressing futures prices, commodity names, and expiration dates is still used today.

Contract Expiration

Futures contracts are legal agreements, and just as any other legal agreement between two parties has a date at which it becomes effective, each futures contract has a definite ending date which is established in advance by the exchange. Among other things, this definite ending date means the buyer and seller cannot hold a futures contract forever. On or before the ending date, the futures contract turns into a legal obligation for the seller to obtain and deliver the commodity specified in the contract (or in some cases the value of the commodity in dollars – more on this in Chapter 4), and for the buyer to receive and pay for the commodity specified in the contract. To avoid this legal obligation to make or take delivery, the seller and buyer must liquidate their respective futures positions, with the seller effectively "buying back" and the buyer effectively "selling back" the futures contract. The difference between the selling price and buying price equals the profit or loss realized by each party.

Another way that futures contracts are like other legal agreements is that a futures contract does not exist before the buyer and seller agree to enter into the contract, and it does not exist after the contract expires or after the buyer and seller liquidate their positions and exit the agreement. Unlike other financial instruments such as stocks or bonds for which there is a fixed number or dollar amount of a security, the number of futures contracts for a particular commodity at a particular time is limited only by the willingness of buyers and sellers to trade with each other. A futures contract is created each time a new buyer and a new seller make a transaction, so at any time prior to expiration the amount of a commodity represented by futures contracts is unrelated to – and frequently exceeds – the amount of the underlying commodity actually in existence. This is possible because futures contracts are derivatives and not the actual commodity.

Because futures contracts are standardized, a seller wishing to "buy back" the futures contract created in an earlier sale, or a buyer wishing to "sell back" a futures contract created in an earlier purchase, does not need to find the original buyer or original seller and get them to agree to reverse the original transaction. Instead, a seller or buyer can trade with anyone, because all terms and conditions of the new futures contract are identical to those of the original futures contract, except the price. This is the reason why all futures contracts for the same commodity and expiration date are fungible, or interchangeable.

Long and Short Positions

A person can first buy a contract – called *going long* or taking a *long position* – and then sell the same contract later to liquidate the long position, or a person can first sell a contract – called *going short* or taking a *short position* – and then buy the same contract later to close out the short position. While it might seem strange that a person can sell or "short" something they don't own, taking a particular futures position, long or short, is not dependent upon a person's holdings of the underlying commodity. This is possible because futures contracts are derivatives and not the actual commodity, and a futures contract is created each time a new buyer and a new seller make a transaction, irrespective of whether either (or neither) party owns the commodity.

Measures of Trading Activity

Volume and Open Interest

A futures contract is created each time a new buyer and a new seller make a transaction to enter the market. Conversely, a futures contract is eliminated each time an existing long and an existing short both make a transaction to exit the market. These points lead to two important measures of futures market activity, *volume* and *open interest*. Volume is simply the number of contracts traded (i.e., bought or sold) over some period of time such as a day or a month, and is a measure of trading activity. Volume is often used as an indirect measure of market liquidity, since more volume makes it easier to buy and sell, all else the same.

Open interest is the number of contracts outstanding or in existence at some point in time, much like a snapshot of the market. It is a measure of market size at some point in time such as the end of a day or end of a month. Because each futures contract consists of a long position and a short position, open interest equals the total number of longs for a particular market, as well as the total number of shorts for a particular market. This is not the same as the number of buyers or sellers, since an individual trader may hold multiple long or short positions.

When a trade occurs, volume always increases by the number of contracts transacted. However, a trade may cause open interest to increase, or decrease, or remain unchanged, depending on whether the buyer and seller had pre-existing positions prior to the trade. The following series of examples will demonstrate this point.

Trading Impact on Volume and Open Interest

Suppose a futures market consists of just four traders: Trader A, Trader B, Trader C, and Trader D. At the beginning of a particular trading session they hold these positions:

- Trader A is long 12 contracts.
- Trader B is short 5 contracts.
- Trader C is short 15 contracts.
- Trader D is long 8 contracts.

The open interest is 20 contracts: 12 long (for Trader A) plus 8 long (for Trader D), or equivalently 5 short (for Trader B) plus 15 short (for Trader C). The volume is zero for this trading session because trading has not yet begun. Also notice that the total number of longs must always equal the total number of shorts, because each contract has both a buyer and a seller.

Example 3.1: From this starting point, suppose that Trader A sells 3 contracts to Trader B; therefore Trader B buys 3 contracts from Trader A. The four traders' holdings are now:

- Trader A is long 9 contracts. They began with 12 longs and added 3 shorts, so 12–3 = 9.
- Trader B is short 2 contracts. They began with 5 shorts and added 3 longs, so 5–3 = 2.
- Trader C is short 15 contracts (unchanged).
- Trader D is long 8 contracts (unchanged).

The open interest is now 17 contracts: long 9 (for Trader A) plus long 8 (for Trader D), or equivalently short 2 (for Trader B) plus short 15 (for Trader C), and the change in open interest is −3 because it was originally 20 contracts and is now 17 contracts. The volume for this trading session is 3 contracts, because 3 contracts (i.e., 3 shorts plus 3 longs) were transacted between Trader A and Trader B. Notice that the volume is not 6 contracts, because each contract consists of both a long and a short.

Also notice that a trader cannot hold long positions and short positions in the same expiration month of the same contract simultaneously. Long positions offset short positions and vice versa, so a trader must be long, or short, or *flat* (i.e., no market position, either long or short).

Example 3.2: From the same starting point (i.e., Trader A is long 12 contracts, Trader B is short 5 contracts, Trader C is short 15 contracts, and Trader D is long 8 contracts), instead suppose that Trader A buys 3 contracts from Trader B; therefore Trader B sells 3 contracts to Trader A. The four traders' holdings are now:

- Trader A is long 15 contracts. They began with 12 longs and added 3 longs, so 12 + 3 = 15.
- Trader B is short 8 contracts. They began with 5 shorts and added 3 shorts, so 5 + 3 = 8.

- Trader C is short 15 contracts (unchanged).
- Trader D is long 8 contracts (unchanged).

The open interest is now 23 contracts: long 15 (for Trader A) plus long 8 (for Trader D), or equivalently short 8 (for Trader B) plus short 15 (for Trader C), and the change in open interest is +3 because it was originally 20 contracts and is now 23 contracts. The volume for this trading session is 3 contracts, because 3 contracts were transacted between Trader A and Trader B.

Example 3.3: From the same starting point (i.e., Trader A is long 12 contracts, Trader B is short 5 contracts, Trader C is short 15 contracts, and Trader D is long 8 contracts), this time suppose that Trader A sells 3 contracts to Trader D; therefore Trader D buys 3 contracts from Trader A. The four traders' holdings are now:

- Trader A is long 9 contracts. They began with 12 longs and added 3 shorts, so 12–3 = 9.
- Trader B is short 5 contracts (unchanged).
- Trader C is short 15 contracts (unchanged).
- Trader D is long 11 contracts. They began with 8 longs and added 3 longs, so 8 + 3 = 11.

The open interest is still 20 contracts: long 9 (for Trader A) plus long 11 (for Trader D), or equivalently short 5 (for Trader B) plus short 15 (for Trader C), and the change in open interest is 0 or unchanged because it was originally 20 contracts and is now 20 contracts. The volume for this trading session is 3 contracts, because 3 contracts were transacted between Trader A and Trader D. Notice in this example that Trader A effectively transferred 3 longs to Trader D, so the total open interest is unchanged.

Example 3.4: From the same starting point (i.e., Trader A is long 12 contracts, Trader B is short 5 contracts, Trader C is short 15 contracts, and Trader D is long 8 contracts), suppose that a new Trader E enters the market and has no contracts long or short. Also suppose that Trader A sells 3 contracts to this new Trader E; therefore Trader E buys 3 contracts from Trader A. The five traders' holdings are now:

- Trader A is long 9 contracts. They began with 12 longs and added 3 shorts, so 12 − 3 = 9.
- Trader B is short 5 contracts (unchanged).
- Trader C is short 15 contracts (unchanged).
- Trader D is long 8 contracts (unchanged).
- Trader E is long 3 contracts. They began with 0 longs and 0 shorts, so 0 + 3 = 3.

The open interest is still 20 contracts: long 9 (for Trader A) plus long 8 (for Trader D) plus long 3 (for Trader 3), or equivalently short 5 (for Trader B) plus short 15 (for Trader C), and the change in open interest is 0 or unchanged because it was originally 20 contracts and is now 20 contracts. The volume for this trading session is 3 contracts, because 3 contracts were transacted between Trader A and Trader E. Notice in this example that Trader A effectively transferred 3 longs to new Trader E, so once again the total open interest is unchanged.

Example 3.5: From the same starting point (i.e., Trader A is long 12 contracts, Trader B is short 5 contracts, Trader C is short 15 contracts, and Trader D is long 8 contracts), suppose that Trader A sells 3 contracts: 1 contract to Trader C, 1 contract to Trader D, and 1 contract to new Trader E who has no contracts long or short. Therefore Trader C, Trader D, and Trader E each buy 1 contract from Trader A. The five traders' holdings are now:

- Trader A is long 9 contracts. They began with 12 longs and added 3 shorts, so 12 − 3 = 9.
- Trader B is short 5 contracts (unchanged).
- Trader C is short 14 contracts. They began with 15 shorts and added 1 long, so 15 − 1 = 14.
- Trader D is long 9 contracts. They began with 8 longs and added 1 long, so 8 + 1 = 9.
- Trader E is long 1 contract. They began with 0 longs and 0 shorts, so 0 + 1 = 1.

The open interest is now 19 contracts: long 9 (for Trader A) plus long 9 (for Trader D) plus long 1 (for Trader 3), or equivalently short 5 (for Trader B) plus short 14 (for Trader C); the change in open interest is −1 because it was originally 20 contracts and is now 19 contracts. The volume for this trading session is 3 contracts, because 3 contracts were transacted between Trader A and Traders C, D, and E.

From these five examples, a 3-contract transaction always results in 3 contracts of volume, but the impact on open interest varies depending on the traders' beginning positions. Open interest may decrease by 3 contracts (Example 3.1), or increase by 3 contracts (Example 3.2), or be unchanged (Examples 3.3 and 3.4), or decrease by 1 contract (Example 3.5). Other examples using these five traders could be constructed that cause open interest to decrease by 2 contracts, or increase by 1 contract, or increase by 2 contracts.

Stated differently, a 3-contract transaction may increase open interest by as much as 3 contracts, or decrease open interest by as much as 3 contracts. The actual impact on open interest depends on whether the 3-contract trade creates new contracts, or liquidates existing contracts, or simply transfers existing contracts, or some combination of these three possible actions.

Other Relationships between Volume and Open Interest

In addition to measuring market activity and size, volume and open interest can be used as indicators of trader behavior. If traders as a group are increasing their holdings in a particular market, then much of the volume will translate into higher open interest, and high volumes will be accompanied by rising open interest. Conversely, if traders as a group are decreasing their holdings in a particular market, then much of the volume will translate into lower open interest, and high volumes will be accompanied by falling open interest. If traders as a group are simply transferring their positions to other traders, then high volumes will be accompanied by relatively stable open interest. Alternatively, if traders as a group are *rolling* or switching their positions from one contract month to another within the same commodity, then the change in open interest in one contract month will be matched by a change in the other contract month that is roughly equal in size but opposite in direction.

In general, volume and open interest tend to be highest for contract months closest to expiration, and lowest for contracts furthest from expiration, all else being the same. This occurs because there is greater interest and urgency associated with sooner-to-occur prices than with later-to-occur prices, all else the same. Likewise, daily price changes tend to be greatest in the contract months closest to expiration, all else the same. This occurs because day-to-day changes in supply and demand conditions for the underlying markets will have the biggest impact on the contract months that are closest to expiration, where there is less time for buyers and sellers to adjust.

Interpreting Price Differences: Time, Space, and Form

For any commodity, price differences generally can be explained by differences in time, space, and form.

Price Differences Due to Time: Carrying Costs

The price for a commodity at some later date (i.e., Time 2) normally will be higher than the price at some earlier date (i.e., Time 1), all else the same. The difference between the Time 1 price and the Time 2 price reflects the cost of storage (i.e., warehouse space), interest on the cost of the commodity, and insurance on the replacement value of the commodity for that period of time. These are collectively referred to as *carrying costs* or the *cost of carry* because it represents the cost to "carry" the commodity in inventory. If the price difference between Time 1 and Time 2 is greater than the cost of carry, then it would be profitable to buy the commodity at Time 1, simultaneously contract to sell the commodity at Time 2, and store the commodity from Time 1 until Time 2. For example, if the forward (or futures) price at Time 1 is $3.00, the forward (or futures) price at Time 2 is $4.00, and the cost of carry for the period of time between Time 1 and Time 2 is $0.70, then a trader could receive a risk-free profit of $0.30 by buying the commodity for $3.00, contracting to sell it for $4.00, and paying $0.70 of carrying costs. Markets typically do not offer risk-free profits for *arbitrage*, or buying and selling the same commodity between two different markets, so the cost of carry is the upper bound on price differences over two points in time. Notice in this example that the *arbitrageur*, or person conducting the arbitrage, owns the commodity only from Time 1 to Time 2; they do not own the commodity prior to Time 1 or after Time 2.

If the price difference is less than the cost of carry, then it may be possible to reverse the arbitrage process described above, and sell the commodity at Time 1, simultaneously contract to buy the commodity at Time 2, and avoid storing the commodity from Time 1 to Time 2. Notice that in this approach the arbitrageur does not own the commodity from Time 1 to Time 2, but must own the commodity before Time 1 and will own the commodity again after Time 2. This is much different from the first arbitrage scenario, but it illustrates how a commodity owner can use the arbitrage process to retain ownership and avoid carrying costs. Building on the previous example, if the forward price at Time 1 is $3.00, the forward price at Time 2 is $3.50, and the cost of carry for the period of time between Time 1 and Time 2 is $0.70, then a trader who needs the commodity at Time 2 could save $0.20 by contracting to buy the commodity at Time 2, instead of owning it at Time 1 and storing it until Time 2.

Carrying Costs and Convenience Yield

In practice, the difference between the Time 1 price and the Time 2 price is generally positive but less than *full carry*, or the full amount of the carrying cost, due to the convenience and certainty of having the commodity on hand. This *convenience yield* acts as a negative component in the cost of carry calculation, and causes inventory holders to require less reimbursement to carry a commodity from Time 1 to Time 2 than otherwise would be the case. For example, suppose that a company uses 100,000 units of a commodity per month. It routinely carries an inventory of 5,000 units, regardless of the carrying cost, as a reserve against unexpected supply disruptions that would force the company to shut down. Holding 5% (= 5,000 units ÷ 100,000 units) of its inventory at zero carrying cost, and the remaining 95% at the full carrying cost, is equivalent to carrying the full 100,000 units at 95% of full carry.

The Forward Curve

Forward Curve for a Normal Market

Suppose that we plot the prices for all futures contract months of a particular commodity. The result would be a line known as the *forward curve* because it shows prices at various points "forward" in time. The forward curve is normally upward sloping, where the upward slope reflects positive carrying costs. An upward sloping forward curve is also known as a *normal market* because this is the typical situation; another term for this is a *contango market*. Higher prices at later points in time encourage sellers to wait until later to sell, while lower prices at earlier points in time encourage buyers to make their purchases now. The forward curve, with its opposite signals to buyers and sellers, helps the market to balance supply and demand over time, thereby avoiding surpluses at certain times and shortages at others. An example of a normal forward curve is shown in Figure 3.2.

Generally speaking, the larger the supply relative to the demand, the more steeply upward sloping the forward curve will be. The slope of the forward curve represents the average price change per month, and shows how much the market is offering sellers to wait and sell later rather than now. Stated differently, a steeper positive slope indicates that the market is offering to reimburse more of the seller's carrying costs, and is encouraging them to move the commodity into storage. Recall that full carry is the upper bound on carrying costs, so full carry also determines the steepest positive slope for the forward curve. Markets approach full carry when the supply is large relative to demand, so a steeper curve reflects a more *bearish* or negative near-term price outlook for the commodity, all else the same.

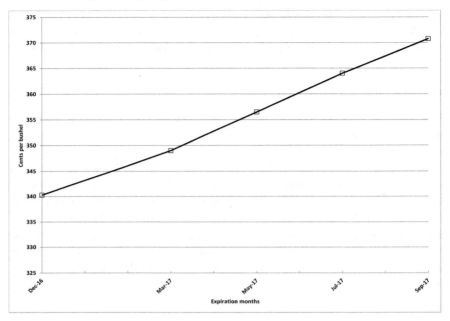

Figure 3.2 Forward Curve for Corn Futures as of November 11, 2016

Forward Curve for an Inverted Market

Under different conditions the forward curve may be downward sloping, where the downward slope represents negative carrying costs. Recall that convenience yield acts as a negative component in the cost of carry calculation. This negative impact causes the forward curve to have a less positive slope than would otherwise be the case. In extreme cases, such as a supply shortage due to a crop failure or other disaster, the convenience yield can be so large (and negative) that it exceeds the combined (positive) costs of storage, interest, and insurance. The result is a downward sloping forward curve, where the downward slope reflects negative carrying costs. A downward sloping forward curve is also known as an *inverted market* because this is an atypical situation; another term for this is *backwardation* or a *backwardated market*. Higher prices at earlier points in time encourage sellers to sell now, while lower prices at later points in time encourage buyers to wait until later to make their purchases. Immediate needs are generally more urgent and price-sensitive than future needs, because the additional time allows buyers to adjust consumption or find substitutes, and allows sellers to adjust production. An example of an inverted forward curve is shown in Figure 3.3.

Generally speaking, the larger the demand relative to the supply, the more steeply downward-sloping (i.e., inverted) the forward curve will be. Recall that the slope of the forward curve represents the average price change per month. In the case of a downward-sloping forward curve, a steeper negative slope shows how much the market is penalizing sellers to wait rather than sell now. A zero slope indicates that the market is reimbursing none of the

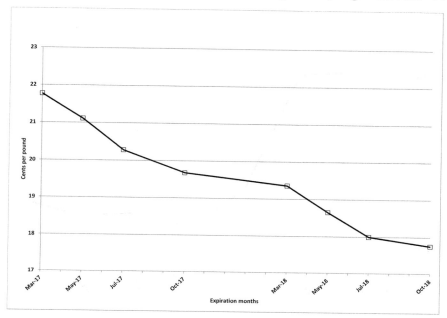

Figure 3.3 Forward Curve for Sugar #11 Futures as of November 11, 2016

seller's carrying costs, so as the slope becomes more negative the seller pays an increasingly greater penalty for holding onto the commodity. Unlike positive carrying costs which have an upper bound, negative carrying costs have no lower bound, so the penalty on the seller is potentially unlimited. Markets become inverted when the supply is small relative to the demand, so a steeper negative slope is sometimes equated with a more *bullish* or positive near-term price outlook for the commodity, all else the same.

Effects of Seasonality

Many commodities – crude oil and gold, for example – are produced and consumed more or less continuously throughout the year, so the forward curve is relatively smooth. Other commodities are produced seasonally – for example, corn which in the US is produced (i.e., harvested) once a year in the fall – or consumed seasonally – for example, natural gas which experiences heaviest usage during the winter residential heating season. For these seasonal commodities, the forward curve may exhibit a sharp break at the beginning and end of the peak supply or demand period.

Forward Curve for Nonstorable Commodities

The commodities we have discussed to this point – crude oil, gold, corn, and natural gas – are *storable*, so prices at different points in time are connected by carrying costs, and the forward

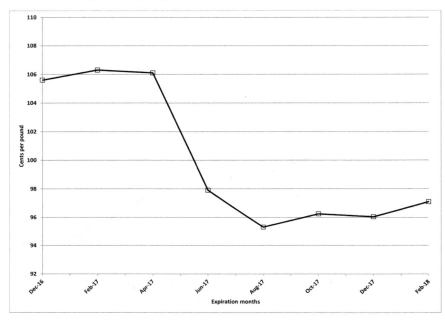

Figure 3.4 Forward Curve for Live Cattle Futures as of November 11, 2016

curve can be used to stimulate movement into and out of storage. This is not the case for all commodities. Some commodities are perishable – livestock and dairy products in particular – and cannot be stored without suffering quality losses. Other commodities – electricity is a notable example – are produced on demand. Still others – such as temperature and precipitation contracts – are highly time-specific and do not reflect market conditions in other periods. These *nonstorable* commodities have unique supply conditions at each point in time, so the price at one time is largely independent of the price at other times. Consequently, the forward curve for a nonstorable commodity may have an irregular shape, with dips in some months and bulges in others. Furthermore, because supplies are inelastic and cannot be shifted easily from one period to another, the market must adjust demand – via the price – to match the available supply. For all of these reasons, prices for nonstorables tend to be more volatile than for storables, all else the same. An example of a forward curve for a nonstorable commodity is shown in Figure 3.4.

Price Differences Due to Space: Transportation Costs

Locational Price Differentials

The price for a commodity at Location A cannot differ from the price at Location B, all else the same, by more than the cost to transport the commodity from the lower-priced location to the higher-priced location. If the price difference is greater than the transportation cost, then it would be profitable to buy the commodity at lower-priced Location A, simultaneously contract to sell it at higher-priced Location B, and immediately transport it from Location A to Location B. From the previous section, markets typically do not offer risk-free profits for buying and selling the same commodity between two different markets, so the cost of transportation is the upper bound on price differences between two locations, or points over space.

Locational price differences are sensitive to transportation disruptions – trucking delays, railcar shortages, flooding on waterways, port strikes, and so forth. Such disruptions interfere with the economic linkages that connect prices at different locations, and in extreme cases can cause prices to become disconnected. The same result can occur when two locations are separated by a physical barrier, such as a mountain range or a border between two unfriendly countries. Tariffs, duties, inspection requirements, and other political barriers can have the same economic impact as a physical barrier, by increasing the cost of moving the commodity between Location A and Location B.

Locational Premiums and Discounts

Futures contracts typically specify a "par" location which serves as the reference point for valuing the contract. Additional locations may be listed at fixed premiums or discounts to the par location, generally to facilitate the delivery process in some fashion. If these fixed premiums or discounts differ from the actual price differentials, the futures price will not reflect market conditions, and the usefulness of the futures contract for price discovery and risk management will be reduced.

For example, if the premium is too large (or the discount is too small) for a particular location, then the effective futures price for that location will be too high relative to the market price for that location. This could result in more futures deliveries at that location than otherwise would be the case, because the futures price plus the premium (or minus the discount) would be higher than the market price. If sufficiently high, this also could lead to distortions in the prices at other locations.

Conversely, if the premium is too small (or the discount is too large) for a particular location, then the effective futures price for that location will be too low relative to the market price for that location. This could result in fewer futures deliveries at that location than otherwise would be the case, because the futures price plus the premium (or minus the discount) would be lower than the market price. Ultimately this could defeat the purpose of allowing deliveries at that location, because the premiums or discounts would make those deliveries uneconomic.

Price Differences Due to Form: Processing Costs

Input–Output and Quality Differentials

The prices for two related commodities, Commodity X and Commodity Y, all else the same, cannot differ by more than the cost to transform Commodity X into Commodity Y. If the price difference is greater than the transformation cost, then it would be profitable to buy

Commodity X, immediately convert it, and sell it as Commodity Y at a profit. From the previous sections, markets typically do not offer risk-free profits for buying and selling the same commodity between two different markets, so the processing cost is the upper bound on the price difference for two related commodities, or two different forms of the same commodity. In this scenario, Commodity X may be an input for Commodity Y, or Commodity X may be a different quality of the same commodity as Commodity Y.

In the case of an input–output relationship, the difference between the output price and the input price will reflect the processing costs to convert the input into the output. In the case of a quality difference for two grades or qualities of the same commodity, the price difference will reflect the cost to upgrade the lower-quality commodity to the higher-quality commodity, for example by removing impurities or other negative quality components. Otherwise, the price difference will reflect the cost associated with substituting the lower-quality commodity for the higher-quality commodity, expressed in terms of the change in the value of the final product. If these quality differentials are fixed, then the same problems associated with locational differentials which were discussed in the previous section also apply to quality differentials. If the premium is too large (or the discount is too small) for a particular quality, the effective futures price for that quality will be too high relative to the rest of the market, and there will be excessive deliveries and possibly distortions in the underlying market. If the premium is too small (or the discount is too large) for a particular quality, then the effective futures price for that quality will be too low relative to the rest of the market, and deliveries will be uneconomic.

Actual processing costs are seldom known except to the processors themselves, but they can be estimated from historical price differentials. When the actual processing cost exceeds the difference between input and output prices, or when the loss in final product quality exceeds the price difference between the two different qualities of inputs, processing activity generally ceases and the differential eventually stabilizes or widens. Thus, the processing cost or quality loss is the lower bound on the price difference between two related commodities.

Spreads: Processing, Intra-Commodity, and Inter-Commodity

Economically important price relationships among related commodities are commonly known as *spreads*. Input–output relationships using futures contracts include the soybean crush (soybeans as the input vs. soybean meal and soybean oil as the outputs), the crude oil crack (crude oil as the input vs. gasoline and heating oil/diesel fuel as the outputs), and the cattle crush (feeder cattle and corn as the inputs vs. live cattle as the output). These spreads will be discussed in more detail in Chapter 9.

Intra-commodity price relationships between different types of the same commodity are quite common, and wheat is a prime example. The US has three different wheat futures contracts, each for a different class of wheat with different milling and baking properties. The Chicago futures contract is for soft red winter wheat, which is used primarily for cookies, crackers, and other "flat" products. The Kansas City futures contract is for hard red winter wheat, which is used primarily for bread and other baked goods that "rise." The Minneapolis

Contract Unit	5,000 bushels (~ 127 Metric Tons)
Price Quotation	Cents per bushel
Trading Hours	Sunday – Friday, 7:00 p.m. – 7:45 a.m. CT and Monday – Friday, 8:30 a.m. – 1:20 p.m. CT
Minimum Price Fluctuation	1/4 of one cent per bushel ($12.50 per contract)
Product Code	CME Globex: ZC CME ClearPort: C Clearing: C TAS: ZCT
Listed Contracts	March (H), May (K), July (N), September (U) & December (Z)
Settlement Method	Deliverable
Termination Of Trading	The business day prior to the 15th calendar day of the contract month.
Trade At Marker Or Trade At Settlement Rules	Trading at settlement is available for first 3 listed futures contracts, nearby new-crop December contract (if not part of the first 3 outrights), first to second month calendar spread, second to third month calendar spread, and nearest Jul-Dec spread when available (when July is listed); and are subject to the existing TAS rules. The Last Trade Date for CBOT Grain and Oilseed TAS products will be the First Position Day (FPD) of the front-month contract (FPD is the second to last business day in the month prior to the nearby contract month). Trading in all CBOT Grain TAS products will be 19:00-07:45 and 08:30-13:15 Chicago time. All resting TAS orders at 07:45 will remain in the book for the 08:30 opening, unless cancelled. TAS products will trade a total of four ticks above and below the settlement price in ticks of the corresponding futures contract (0.0025), off of a "Base Price" of 0 to create a differential (plus or minus 4 ticks) versus settlement in the underlying product on a 1 to 1 basis. A trade done at the Base Price of 0 will correspond to a "traditional" TAS trade which will clear exactly at the final settlement price of the day.
Settlement Procedures	Corn Settlement Procedures
Position Limits	CBOT Position Limits
Exchange Rulebook	CBOT 10
Price Limit Or Circuit	Price Limits
Vendor Codes	Quote Vendor Symbols Listing
Last Delivery Date	Second business day following the last trading day of the delivery month.
Grade And Quality	Through December 2018: #2 Yellow at contract Price, #1 Yellow at a 1.5 cent/bushel premium, #3 Yellow at a 1.5 cent/bushel discount. As of March 2019: #2 Yellow at contract Price, #1 Yellow at a 1.5 cent/bushel premium, #3 Yellow at a discount between 2 and 4 cents/bushel depending on broken corn and foreign material and damage grade factors.

Figure 3.5 Corn Futures Contract Summary Specifications as of November 11, 2016

Reprinted here with the permission of Chicago Mercantile Exchange Inc. ("CME"). CME disclaims all liability for any errors or omissions. Current rules should be consulted in all cases concerning contract specifications.

futures contract is for hard red spring wheat, which is used for breads and higher-quality baked goods. Each class can be substituted to a limited degree before it adversely affects the quality of the final product. There also are futures contracts on two grades of crude oil, West Texas Intermediate (WTI) and Brent, which have somewhat different refining properties.

Inter-commodity price relationships between different but related commodities also are quite common. Wheat may be substituted for corn in livestock feeding rations, depending on the species of animal. Beef (live cattle) and pork (lean hogs) may be interchangeable among consumers, depending on personal tastes, relative prices, and other factors. Gold and silver share some common industrial uses, and may be substitutes among certain investors. Natural gas and various petroleum products derived from crude oil may be used interchangeably in power generation, and as feedstocks (i.e., inputs) in manufacturing certain petrochemicals (i.e., outputs). Each user will apply their own metrics to determine at what price Commodity X may be substituted for Commodity Y and vice versa.

Combinations of Time, Space, and Form

Until now we have treated each attribute – time, space, and form – separately, but in practice a set of commodities may have differences in multiple areas. Each attribute is largely independent of the others, so the respective differences can be added to obtain the total or net impact on the value of the commodity in question. For example, suppose that Commodity A and Commodity B are related, but their prices are for different times (i.e., May for Commodity A and July for Commodity B), different locations (i.e., Chicago for Commodity A and New Orleans for Commodity B), and different qualities (i.e., US #1 for Commodity A and US #2 for Commodity B). By combining the carrying cost from May to July, the transportation cost from Chicago to New Orleans, and the quality differential between US #1 and US #2, the maximum difference between the price for Commodity A and Commodity B can be determined.

Each futures contract specifies a particular date for expiration, a particular location at which delivery or final settlement occurs, and a particular quality of the commodity to be delivered or valued at final settlement. These *par specifications* ensure that a futures price reflects a specific set of economic attributes for that commodity and provides clarity regarding what that futures price represents. The par specifications for the corn futures contract are summarized in Figure 3.5.

Few if any commercial buyers or sellers of a commodity use the same scheduling (time), location (space), or quality (form) characteristics as those specified in the futures contract. Likewise, few if any traders who use commodities for investment purposes have the same personal preferences as those specified in the futures contract. Instead, futures markets reflect the price of a specific *benchmark* commodity about which everyone in the marketplace is familiar. This benchmark futures price can be connected to each individual's unique pricing needs by the *basis*, which will be covered extensively beginning in Chapter 7.

4 Margins, Clearing, Delivery, and Final Settlement

A futures trade begins with the payment of *margin*, or collateral, to guarantee a trader's financial performance. These funds are deposited in a special account which can be used only for margin purposes. An important difference between futures contracts and other financial instruments is that daily gains and losses are not simply bookkeeping entries: the actual funds are added to or removed from a trader's account at the end of each trading session. Stated differently, futures gains and losses are *realized* gains and losses; in futures trading there are no unrealized or "paper" gains and losses. In this chapter we will examine how the margining process operates, the role of the clearing house, and the final settlement procedures used for futures contracts.

Margins in Futures Trading

Initial Margin, Maintenance Margin, and Margin Calls

Both buyers and sellers are required to post an *initial margin* when a futures position is established. This initial margin is typically between 5% and 10% of the full value of the futures contract. For example, for a 5,000-bushel corn futures contract at a price of $3.50 per bushel, the full value of the contract is $17,500 (= 5,000 bushels × $3.50 per bushel), so the initial margin would be between $875 (= 5% × $17,500) and $1,750 (= 10% × $17,500). At the end of each trading session, each trader's gains (or losses) for that day are credited to (or debited from) their margin account balance. If their losses cause the margin account balance to drop below the *maintenance margin* level, the trader receives a *margin call* and is required to deposit additional funds. Notice that the trader must restore the account balance not simply to the maintenance level, but to the higher initial margin level. These additional funds generally must be deposited by the start of the next trading session, or the trader's position(s) will be liquidated. Conversely, excess funds over and above the amount needed to meet maintenance margin requirements may be withdrawn by the trader, just as if the margin account were a bank account.

Margin levels are established for each commodity by the *clearing house*, which is part of the exchange. Nearly all exchanges worldwide use SPAN, or **S**tandard **P**ortfolio **AN**alysis of

Risk, to determine these margin requirements. In practice, SPAN is used to determine the maintenance margin level for a particular contract, and then the initial margin requirement is set at 110% of the maintenance level. Consequently, losing 10% of the initial margin will result in a margin call, all else the same. Using our example from above, if the initial margin for a corn futures contract is $1,000, then a $100 loss on a futures position – equivalent to a loss of $0.02 per bushel (= $100 ÷ 5,000 bushels per contract) – would trigger a margin call.

SPAN calculates the worst possible one-day loss that a position might experience with a 99% probability under a range of different market conditions. A one-day loss is appropriate because all positions are valued at the current market price, or *marked to market*, at the end of each trading day, and because traders are required to deposit additional funds when their account balances fall below the maintenance margin levels. Market volatility is the primary variable used by SPAN. Margin levels are reviewed at least daily and may be adjusted intraday as market conditions dictate. For example, if there is an event that causes a market to suddenly become more volatile, margins can be increased to ensure that sufficient funds will be available to cover that day's potential losses.

The Clearing House and Clearing Firms

The clearing house collects margins from *clearing firms*, which typically are large brokerage firms that provide clearing as a service to their futures customers. Clearing firms must hold additional capital and meet additional financial requirements, over and above the amounts required of regular brokerage firms. The clearing house does not deal directly with individual traders; instead, the clearing house collects margins from the clearing firms, and each clearing firm then collects margins from each of its customers. Margins may be posted in the form of cash (in US dollars as well as certain foreign currencies), US Treasury and government agency debt, letters of credit from major banks, and select securities such as blue-chip stocks. The list of acceptable financial instruments and assets varies over time, and there may be a *haircut* or discount applied to certain items to ensure that sufficient funds can be obtained if those items must be sold immediately.

The Clearing House as Central Counterparty

The clearing house inserts itself between the buyer and seller in every trade. For example, Figure 4.1 shows a simplified transaction between a buyer (long) and a seller (short) of a futures contract. If the futures price increases, the long has a gain and the short has a corresponding loss. The "loser" pays the "winner," so funds are transferred directly from the losing position (short) to the winning position (long), represented by the top arrow in Figure 4.1. Conversely, if the futures price decreases, the short has a gain and the long has a corresponding loss. The loser pays the winner, so in this case funds are transferred directly from the losing position (long) to the winning position (short), represented by the bottom arrow in Figure 4.1. Notice that in this scenario the two parties deal directly with one another, without any intermediaries.

In contrast, Figure 4.2 shows the clearing house positioned between the long and the short, in which all transfers of funds occur through the clearing house. In most cases the transfer of funds from loser to winner is a simple pass-through operation. But if the losing party fails to provide the necessary funds, the clearing house will pay the winner and then pursue payment from the loser. Thus, the clearing house *guarantees financial performance* by the losing party and eliminates *customer default risk* from the futures trading process. Because of its position in the middle of all transactions, the clearing house is often described as a *central counterparty* or "the buyer to every seller and the seller to every buyer."

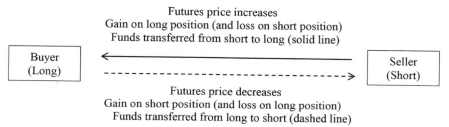

Futures price increases
Gain on long position (and loss on short position)
Funds transferred from short to long (solid line)

Futures price decreases
Gain on short position (and loss on long position)
Funds transferred from long to short (dashed line)

Figure 4.1 Direct Exchange of Cash Flows Between Buyer and Seller

Futures price increases
Gain on long position (and loss on short position)
Funds transferred from short to long via clearing house (solid lines)

Futures price decreases
Gain on short position (and loss on long position)
Funds transferred from long to short via clearing house (dashed lines)

Figure 4.2 Exchange of Cash Flows Between Buyer and Seller with Clearing House as Intermediary

In practice, the clearing house typically causes the failing party's clearing firm to fulfill these obligations on behalf of its customer, and the clearing house steps in only if the clearing firm is unwilling or unable to act. Consequently, the buyer's and seller's clearing firms are also involved in each transaction, as shown in Figure 4.3.

In the event that the failing party's clearing firm also fails to perform, a series of backup provisions, commonly referred to as a *clearing waterfall*, come into play. The clearing house might draw on its own financial reserves, or funds contributed by the other clearing firms might be tapped, or the other clearing firms might be assessed to make up the shortfall, with the specific action(s) taken depending on the particular situation. In addition, the defaulting clearing firm's customer accounts would be transferred to one or more other clearing firms.

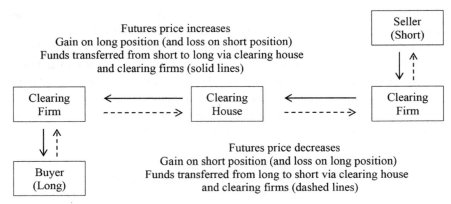

Figure 4.3 Exchange of Cash Flows Between Buyer and Seller with Clearing House and Both Clearing Firms as Intermediaries

Each margin or trading account is held on the books of a brokerage firm, formally known as a *futures commission merchant* (FCM). An FCM may be a clearing firm, or it may be a non-clearing FCM in which case it will have an agreement with a clearing firm to guarantee its trades. Each account is *segregated* from the accounts of all other traders, and from the FCM's own funds. These segregated funds protect each trader from the actions of all other traders, so if one trader goes bankrupt the accounts of all other traders are unaffected.

The Daily Settlement Process

At the end of each trading day, the clearing house calculates the total gains or losses for all accounts held by each clearing firm. These gains and losses are netted into a single amount for each clearing firm. Some firms will have positive net daily margin balance changes (i.e., total gains exceed total losses for all accounts held by the firm) and other firms will have negative net daily margin balance changes (i.e., total losses exceed total gains for all accounts held by the firm). The clearing house then issues *pays and collects* to all clearing firms, by which funds are collected from "losing firms" with negative net daily margin balance changes (i.e., pays) and transferred to "winning firms" with positive daily net margin balance changes (i.e., collects). These amounts are also known as *variation margin* because they represent the combined variation in all margin account balances held by each firm. Each clearing firm then conducts a similar process for all accounts under its control, transferring funds from losing accounts to winning accounts at the end of each trading day.

Each futures contract is a closed system in which total gains equal total losses, before adjustments for commissions and other trading expenses, which are deducted by each FCM after all margin funds have been transferred. Because total gains equal total losses for each futures contract, it is also true that total gains equal total losses for all futures contracts combined. Futures trading is often referred to a *zero-sum game* because for every dollar lost by one trader, a dollar is gained by another trader and vice versa. Similarly, for every dollar paid by one clearing firm, a dollar is collected by another clearing firm, so the sum total of each day's pays and collects is zero.

Margin Account Example

The following hypothetical example illustrates the margining process for an individual trader. Suppose that a trader decides to take a short position in corn futures. Assume that the initial margin for corn futures is $1,000 per contract and the maintenance margin is $900 per contract, so the trader simultaneously deposits $1,000 in their account and places a market order to sell 1 contract, which is filled at $3.51 per bushel.

Day 1 Results: At the end of Day 1 the daily settlement price is $3.49. The trader has a gain of $0.02 per bushel (= $3.51 price of short position on Day 1 − $3.49 Day 1 settlement price). This is equivalent to a profit of $100 (= $0.02 per bushel × 5,000 bushels per contract) on the trader's 1-contract short position for Day 1. The $100 profit from Day 1 is added to the $1,000 beginning balance for the trader's account, so the trader's new margin account balance at the end of Day 1 is $1,100. This amount is above the $900 maintenance level, so the trader does not receive a margin call. Notice that the trader could withdraw the first day's profit of $100, or any amount up to $200 (= $1,100 Day 1 balance − $900 maintenance margin), without receiving a margin call. Instead, the trader chooses to keep the additional funds in their margin account.

Day 2 Results: On Day 2, the daily settlement price is $3.54½ per bushel, for a change of +$0.05½ per bushel. Recall that the price change is calculated using the settlement price from the previous trading session, so +$0.05½ = $3.54½ settlement price on Day 2 − $3.49 settlement price on Day 1. By convention, the daily price change (i.e., gain or loss) is expressed in terms of a long position. However, the trader has a short position, so this $0.05½ price increase results in a $0.05½ per bushel loss on the trader's short position.

This loss of $0.05½ per bushel is equivalent to a loss of $275 (= −$0.05½ per bushel 5,000 bushels per contract) on the trader's 1-contract short position for Day 2. The $275 loss from Day 2 is deducted from the trader's $1,100 balance at the end of Day 1, so the trader's new margin account balance at the end of Day 2 is $825. This amount is below the $900 maintenance level, so the trader receives a margin call and must deposit additional funds immediately to bring the account balance back to the initial margin level of $1,000 − not the $900 maintenance margin level − or their short position will be liquidated. The trader is responsible for any additional losses (or gains) that might occur between the time a margin call is issued and the time additional funds are deposited or the position is liquidated. Notice that the remaining margin account balance of $825 at the end of Day 2 is sufficient to cover a further $0.16½ per bushel (= $825 ÷ 5,000 bushels per contract) price increase before the trader's account balance reaches zero, not including commissions and other trading expenses. A considerable safety factor is built into the margining system, both to prevent individual traders from losing their entire account balances and to protect clearing firms and others from the failure of an individual trader.

Day 3 Results: The trader decides to meet the margin call and deposits $175 to bring the account balance back up to the $1,000 initial margin level. On Day 3, the daily settlement price is $3.57½ per bushel and the daily change is +$0.03, where the price change is calculated using the settlement price from the previous trading session. The trader has a short position, so this $0.03 per bushel price increase results in a $0.03 per bushel loss on the trader's short position.

This loss of $0.03 per bushel is equivalent to a loss of $150 (= −$0.03 per bushel × 5,000 bushels per contract) on the trader's 1-contract short position for Day 3. The $150 loss from Day 3 is deducted from the $1,000 balance after meeting the margin call, so the trader's new margin account balance at the end of Day 3 is $850. Once again, this amount is below the $900 maintenance level, so the trader receives a margin call and must deposit additional funds to bring the account balance back to the initial margin level of $1,000. The trader meets the margin call, this time by depositing an additional $150.

Day 4 Results: On Day 4, the daily settlement price is $3.44 per bushel, −$0.13½. The trader has a short position, so this $0.13½ per bushel price decrease results in a $0.13½ per bushel gain on the trader's short position. This gain of $0.13½ per bushel is equivalent to a gain of $675 (= +$0.13½ per bushel × 5,000 bushels per contract) on the trader's 1-contract short position for Day 4. The $675 gain from Day 4 is added to the $1,000 balance after meeting the second margin call, so the trader's new margin account balance at the end of Day 4 is $1,675. This is above the $900 maintenance level, so the trader does not receive a margin call. Notice that the trader could withdraw any amount up to $775 (= $1,675 Day 4 balance − $900 maintenance margin) without receiving a margin call. Instead, the trader chooses to keep the additional funds in their margin account.

Day 5 Results: On Day 5 the trader decides to liquidate the short position and places a limit order to buy 1 futures contract at a price of $3.43 or better, which is $0.01 below the daily settlement price on Day 4. This turns out to be the price at which the order is filled, and it results in an additional $0.01 per bushel gain on the trader's short position. This gain of $0.01 per bushel is equivalent to a gain of $50 (= +$0.01 per bushel × 5,000 bushels per contract) on the trader's 1-contract short position for Day 5. The $50 gain from Day 5 is added to the $1,675 balance at the end of Day 4, so the trader's new margin account balance at the end of Day 5 is $1,725.

Final Profit and Loss: The gross profit on this trade, ignoring commissions and other trading expenses, is $0.08 per bushel (= $3.51 short price on Day 1 − $3.43 long price on Day 5). This amount is equal to the sum of the daily profit-and-loss or *P and L* values (= +$0.02 from Day 1 − $0.05½ from Day 2 − $0.03 from Day 3 + $0.13½ from Day 4 + $0.01 from Day 5). It is also equal to the sum of the margin account deposits and withdrawals, where (−) is a deposit and (+) is a withdrawal (= −$1,000 per contract initial deposit at beginning of Day 1 + $0 at end of Day 1 − $175 at end of Day 2 − $150 at end of Day 3 + $0 at end of Day 4 + $1,725 withdrawal on Day 5 = $400 per contract; and then $400 per contract ÷ 5,000 bushels per contract = $0.08 per bushel).

Final Settlement via Delivery

The Physical Delivery Process

For most of the history of futures trading, a futures contract required delivery of the underlying commodity at some point at or near the end of the contract's life. This delivery feature is the reason why the contract month or expiration month is commonly referred to as the *delivery month*. In the delivery process, the futures contract is replaced by the underlying commodity on a certain date specified in the contract. Once delivery is underway, neither party is allowed to make an offsetting trade to liquidate their position. The seller is obligated to provide the commodity meeting the requirements specified in the contract, and the buyer is obligated to make full payment (i.e., 100% margin vs. the typical 5% to 10%) for the commodity. Because of this dramatic increase in responsibilities for both parties, virtually all futures positions are liquidated or *traded out* prior to delivery.

The purpose of delivery is to force together the futures price and the *spot* or *cash* price for the actual, physical commodity through a process called *convergence*. The long will refuse to pay a higher price for the underlying commodity through the futures delivery process than they could pay in the cash market. This refusal by the long puts downward pressure on the futures price if it is higher than the corresponding cash price. Similarly, the short will refuse to accept a lower price for the underlying commodity through the futures delivery process than they could receive in the cash market. This refusal by the short puts upward pressure on the futures price if it is lower than the corresponding cash price. These refusals by both buyer and seller cause futures prices to move toward the cash price as delivery approaches, and by the expiration date any difference between the futures price and cash price normally will be too small to arbitrage profitably.

Delivery as Arbitrage

Delivery is also known as *cash-futures arbitrage* because it uses offsetting positions in the cash market and the futures market to eliminate any discrepancies between cash prices and futures prices. At expiration, if the futures price is greater than the cash price, traders will sell futures, simultaneously buy the underlying commodity in the cash market, and use the commodity to make delivery on their short futures positions. Selling in the futures market puts downward pressure on futures prices, while at the same time buying in the cash market puts upward pressure on cash prices. These opposite forces help to bring together the futures price and the cash price.

In the opposite situation, where the futures price is less than the cash price, traders will buy futures, simultaneously sell the underlying commodity in the cash market, take delivery on their long futures positions and use the commodity received in delivery to meet their cash market obligations. Buying in the futures market puts upward pressure on futures prices, while at the same time selling in the cash market puts downward pressure on cash prices, and these opposite forces help to bring together the futures price and the cash price.

Notice that in both situations, traders buy the underpriced position and sell the overpriced position. This activity allows traders to capitalize on a profit opportunity and capture this price difference. But more importantly in terms of market performance, delivery forces the cash and futures prices closer together, causes the futures market to more closely reflect the cash market, and improves the price discovery and risk management functions of the futures market.

Steps in the Delivery Process

Delivery occurs only when the difference between the futures price and the cash price is large enough to make it economically feasible to make or take delivery. The delivery process is not intended to be used for routine purchases or sales. Instead, it is designed to be used solely to force convergence in cases when it has not already occurred.

The delivery process is initiated by the short, because the short is the party most likely to already have, or to be in a position to obtain, the underlying commodity. The short submits a *delivery notice* to the clearing house, and the clearing house then assigns this notice to a trader holding a long position. Traditionally this assignment is made to the *oldest long*, based on the date the long's position was established. However, some markets use random assignment in which the delivery may be assigned to any long position, irrespective of when the position was established.

Soon after assignment, the long must deposit funds with the clearing house equal to the full value of the futures position. Until this time, both buyer and seller have been able to trade on margins equal to just 5–10% of the contract value. Now the buyer must post 100% of the contract value, typically within one business day of assignment. Similarly, the seller must provide the required quantity and quality of the commodity, at the required location, at the date and time specified in the contract. Failure of one or both parties to fulfill their obligations results in a default, so clearing firms closely monitor the delivery activity of their customers and encourage customers without commercial interests – in other words, those who are not in a position to readily make or take delivery of the commodity – to liquidate their positions prior to the start of the delivery process. For example, farmers typically have possession of the cash commodity, but if they do not also have access to the necessary delivery facilities, they are not able to make delivery.

The clearing house also closely monitors deliveries and acts as an escrow agent, ensuring that both parties satisfy all delivery requirements before the commodity and the respective funds are exchanged. Delivery of physical commodities often involves grading, inspection, weighing, and other evaluation by an independent third party such as a government agency or a private laboratory. In some cases, the delivery process requires the commodity to be physically transferred from one point to another. In other cases, a *delivery instrument* – such as a warehouse receipt or loadout certificate – is exchanged. This eliminates the need to move the commodity, and instead the commodity remains in storage at the delivery facility but with a new owner. In still other cases, such as foreign currencies, delivery is accomplished via wire transfer, with dollars wired to the seller's bank account and a similar amount of foreign currency wired to the buyer's bank account. Each delivery process is tailored to the specific commodity and uses common trade practices wherever possible.

Final Settlement via Cash Settlement

The physical delivery process can be costly, time-consuming, and complicated, with many uncertainties for both buyers and sellers. In 1981, the advent of stock index futures led to the introduction of *cash settlement* as a final settlement method for certain futures contracts. A stock index is a collection of individual common stocks in varying amounts; for example, the S&P 500 contains the shares of 500 different companies. Buying and transferring 500 different stocks, often involving fractional shares, all in a timely fashion, would be highly impractical. Instead, at some pre-established date and time, all futures contracts for a partic-ular contract month are closed out and settled, or *marked-to-market*, to some independently-determined value for that commodity – in this case, the S&P 500 index. Buyers and sellers then make final settlement in cash (dollars), hence the term "cash settlement."

In general, trading ends for a cash-settled contract and the final settlement price is deter-mined and announced soon afterwards. If the final cash settlement price is lower than the daily settlement price on the last trading day, there will be a gain for the shorts and a loss for the longs. The clearing house transfers this difference from longs to shorts in the same man-ner as a normal daily settlement. Conversely, if the final cash settlement price is higher than the daily settlement price on the last trading day, there will be a gain for the longs and a loss for the shorts, and the clearing house transfers this difference from shorts to longs.

Cash settlement is well-suited to financial products that have publicly available values which are widely followed and can be independently calculated and verified. It is also used for some physical commodities, particularly perishable products and other items that cannot be delivered easily.

5 Market Regulation

Futures markets are generally considered to be the closest real-world examples of the perfect competition model. Although futures prices are arrived at by the law of supply and demand, this does not imply that futures markets are unregulated. In fact, the US derivatives industry is highly regulated, and it is important to understand the various rules, regulations, and laws that govern futures trading and related activities. In this chapter we will look at how these markets are regulated, with a special emphasis on how the regulatory process affects market participants and the trading process.

Futures as Contracts

In Chapter 2 we introduced the concept of futures as *contracts*. A futures contract is an obligation to make delivery (for the seller) or take delivery (for the buyer) of a commodity at some future date, with the price of the commodity established today. The word "obligation" underscores the point that futures contracts are legally enforceable agreements. The buyer has recourse if the seller refuses to deliver the commodity, and the seller has recourse if the buyer refuses to pay for it.

Establishing the price now, and exchanging the commodity later, is different from most transactions in which the money and the goods are exchanged simultaneously. At one time these types of transactions were commonly called "cash and carry" (not to be confused with cash and carry arbitrage, which is another term for physical delivery) because the buyer would pay for the commodity (cash) and leave with the goods (carry). This phrase was later shortened to simply cash, and is synonymous with spot, a shortened version of "on the spot" that indicates the here-and-now nature of most everyday transactions.

From Chapter 1, recall that a forward contract also is an obligation to make delivery or take delivery of a commodity at some future date, with the price of the commodity established today. The key difference between forwards and futures is that with forwards, all terms and conditions can be negotiated and customized to meet the needs of the buyer and seller. With futures, all terms and conditions are standardized except the price, so there is only one thing for futures buyers and sellers to negotiate. The standardized terms and conditions of a futures contract are known as the *contract specifications* and they define both the commodity traded by the futures contract and how the contract is intended to operate. Complete specifications for the corn futures contract as of November 11, 2016 are presented in Appendix 5.1 at the end of this chapter.

Contract Specifications

Par Quality

The specifications of every futures contract include the commodity being traded and the quality of that commodity. Most commodities have official grades and standards which are established and maintained either by a government agency or by an industry group. For example, the US Department of Agriculture (USDA) defines the names and sets the corresponding requirements for the quality classifications of many agricultural commodities: No. 2 yellow corn, Choice beef, Grade A milk, and so forth. In the petroleum markets, many standards are defined by the American Petroleum Institute (API) and use testing procedures developed by ASTM (formerly the American Society for Testing and Materials). Futures contracts adopt the measurements and methods used by the industry, and typically use the common or *benchmark* quality for a commodity as the par or "base" quality specified by the futures contract. This ensures that the futures price closely reflects the cash commodity price experienced by most buyers and sellers.

Premiums and Discounts for Quality Variations

In some cases, there may be more than one quality level that can be delivered. When there are multiple grades and the prices differ, it may be necessary to apply a quality premium or discount to one or more grades as a way to equalize prices across all quality levels, as was discussed in Chapter 3. Better-than-par grades are assigned premiums, and worse-than-par grades are assigned discounts. Without these quality differentials, sellers could deliver the lowest allowable quality but still receive the par price. Buyers then would reduce the amount they would be willing to pay for futures contracts, and eventually the futures price would reflect the lowest deliverable quality, rather than the par grade. This situation is often referred to as the *cheapest to deliver* problem.

Quantity

A futures contract also specifies the quantity of the commodity that must be delivered, commonly referred to as the *contract size*. This size is often a transportation-based quantity such as a truckload or railcar, or some multiple of that quantity, that is commonly used in commercial transactions. For example, three railroad boxcars – which were used long before the introduction of covered hopper cars – would hold 1,000 bushels of grain. Similarly, a livestock semi-trailer truck can carry 40,000 to 50,000 pounds of cattle or hogs.

Delivery Location

The delivery point(s) may be a single location, multiple separate locations, or an entire region. When there is more than one location and the prices differ, it may be necessary to apply a locational premium or discount to one or more locations as a way to equalize prices across all delivery points. This is similar to the use of premiums and discounts for multiple qualities described above, and is frequently used to avoid a locational version of the cheapest to deliver problem.

Delivery Date

The date and timing of delivery is another critical detail, and the delivery schedule varies widely among futures contracts, usually based on practices in the cash market for that commodity. Some contracts have delivery periods of only a few days, while others use an entire month. Some contracts allow delivery to occur while trading in that contract month is still underway, while others allow delivery only after trading in that contract month has ended. Some contracts have delivery occur in the "named" month (i.e., deliveries for the March contract occur in March), others have delivery occur in the following month (i.e., deliveries for the March contract occur in April), and still others have delivery occur in both months (i.e., deliveries for the March contract begin in March and end in April). Regardless of when delivery occurs, the delivery schedule is spelled out in the contract, along with the specific steps that must be followed by both parties and the corresponding deadlines that must be met.

Cash Settlement vs. Physical Delivery

Many of the descriptions to this point have explained contract specifications in terms of the delivery process. However, as was covered in Chapter 4, many futures contracts today rely on cash settlement. In cash settlement, the contract rules specify a price series for a specific quality of a commodity at a specific location, with final settlement on a specific date. The source(s) of the prices used in the cash settlement index and the calculation process, if any, are also described in detail. Often this description includes the steps to be taken in case there are revisions or delays in the release of prices used for cash settlement purposes.

Position Limits

The rules for futures contracts generally include *position limits*, which set the maximum number of contracts that an individual can own or control at various times during the life of the contract. Position limits are an important tool for preventing manipulation, and are based on the principle that individuals holding larger positions potentially have greater impact on prices, all else the same. Sometimes two or more individuals may attempt to circumvent these limits by holding separate positions that are below the limit, but when combined would be above the limit. Although each account is separately owned, the positions follow the same trading directions and are effectively controlled by a single person – hence the distinction between "own" and "control" at the beginning of this paragraph. Multiple persons doing smaller amounts of the same type of trading can have the same market impact as one person doing all of the trading. Consequently the individual positions are *aggregated* or combined and treated for position limit purposes as if all of the positions belong to one person.

There are three main types of position limits, with separate values for each. The *spot month* limit is the maximum number of contracts, long or short, that can be held during the delivery or expiration month of a maturing contract, and is the most restrictive of all the position limits. The *single month* or *non-spot* month limit is the maximum number of contracts, long or short, that can be held in each of the other contract months that are available for trading. The *all-months-combined* or *aggregate* limit is the maximum number of contracts, net long or short, that can be held in the spot month and all of the individual non-spot months combined. Because the all-months-combined limit is a net value, if long positions are held in one or more contract months and short positions are held in one or more other contract months, then the longs and shorts will offset, and only the difference will apply toward the all-months-combined limit. Instead of position limits, some futures contracts in larger markets use *position accountability*. Under position accountability, traders are not restricted to a fixed number of contracts, but those holding large positions above a certain size must provide information about their trading activity to regulators upon request.

Spot Limits

Spot month limits are the most restrictive because futures prices are most susceptible to manipulation during the delivery or expiration period. It is also during the delivery or expiration period that the underlying cash market is most susceptible to distortions in the futures market. The spot month limit is based on the *deliverable supply*, or the quantity of the commodity which meets the quality and other requirements on the futures contract. As the name suggests, deliverable supply must be in proximity to the futures contract delivery point(s) and available for delivery on the futures contract. When futures deliveries exceed deliverable supplies, a situation known as a *short squeeze* may result in which owners of short futures positions are unable to obtain the commodity for delivery purposes. Owners of long futures positions then may be able to "squeeze" or force the owners of short futures positions to bid up the futures price in order to liquidate their positions and avoid a default on their delivery obligations. This can distort the futures price, and can also distort the price of the underlying cash commodity if sufficient supplies are diverted from commercial channels and used instead for futures delivery purposes. True short squeezes cannot occur in cash settled contracts, but other types of problems may arise that can distort the cash settlement index.

Non-Spot Limits

Non-spot limits apply to contract months other than the spot month. The connection between the number of contracts held in a non-spot month and potential impact on either the futures price or the cash price is much less strong than for the spot month, largely because there is much more time until delivery occurs on that contract. Consequently, non-spot position limits tend to be substantially larger than spot limits, all else the same. Some observers argue that non-spot limits serve no useful anti-manipulation purpose because it is virtually impossible to distort prices outside the delivery period. In this view, the primary function of non-spot limits is to ensure the orderly liquidation of positions as the contract approaches delivery and expiration.

All-Months-Combined Limits

All-months-combined limits, which apply to both spot and non-spot months, serve a somewhat different purpose. For commodities with a seasonal production schedule, including most crops, a given deliverable supply may be used to meet the spot-month needs of all contract months within the same production cycle. Because the deliverable supplies of the separate contract months are interconnected, there is a need to impose a limit on related contract months. For commodities which are produced continuously, such as energy and metals, and especially for perishable, nonstorable commodities such as livestock and dairy, the connection between the deliverable supplies of separate contract months is much weaker. For some of these commodities, the deliverable supply in one period may be independent of the deliverable supply in another, and consequently many of the futures contracts for continuously-produced commodities do not have all-months-combined limits. Non-spot and all-months-combined limits typically are based on the open interest of the futures contract, so these limits are set in proportion to the market's size and trading capacity, rather than deliverable supply.

Position Limits for Hedgers

Position limits apply to all market participants, not just speculators. Although these limits are often called "speculative position limits," in fact hedgers also must abide by position limits. This can lead to problems because hedgers often have cash positions that exceed the number of futures contracts allowed by the position limits. However, in most markets a bona fide hedger may apply for a *hedging exemption* which – if approved – provides the hedger with a custom-tailored set of position limits. These customized limits are based on the size of the hedger's cash market position, the timing of the hedger's expected cash market purchases or sales, and the futures market's ability to handle these larger positions without experiencing disruptions.

Reportable Levels

In addition to position limits and position accountability, all futures markets also have *reportable levels* above which traders – hedgers and speculators alike – must file weekly reports with the exchange and with the federal regulator. These reportable levels facilitate

CORN – CHICAGO BOARD OF TRADE
Disaggregated Commitments of Traders – Futures Only, December 27, 2016

Code-002602

(CONTRACTS OF 5,000 BUSHELS)

	Open Interest	Producer/Merchant/Processor/User Long	Producer/Merchant/Processor/User Short	Swap Dealers Long	Swap Dealers Short	Swap Dealers Spreading	Managed Money Long	Managed Money Short	Managed Money Spreading	Other Reportables Long	Other Reportables Short	Other Reportables Spreading	Nonreportable Long	Nonreportable Short
Positions														
All	1,231,462	305,691	540,774	261,693	3,607	12,425	163,648	273,250	63,799	178,037	58,581	105,195	140,974	173,831
Old	1,096,404	257,766	476,872	246,591	3,576	4,688	154,925	261,315	59,126	168,693	65,929	80,757	123,858	144,141
Other	135,058	47,925	63,902	20,681	5,610	2,158	12,682	15,894	714	30,100	13,408	3,682	17,116	29,690

Changes in Commitments from: December 20, 2016

	Open Interest	PM Long	PM Short	Swap Long	Swap Short	Swap Spreading	MM Long	MM Short	MM Spreading	Other Long	Other Short	Other Spreading	NonRep Long	NonRep Short
	4,026	19,309	-13,684	-7,633	-383	-829	-117	13,959	3,024	-13,379	8,712	-1,982	5,633	-4,791

Percent of Open Interest Represented by Each Category of Trader

	Open Interest	PM Long	PM Short	Swap Long	Swap Short	Swap Spreading	MM Long	MM Short	MM Spreading	Other Long	Other Short	Other Spreading	NonRep Long	NonRep Short
All	100.0	24.8	43.9	21.3	0.3	1.0	13.3	22.2	5.2	14.5	4.8	8.5	11.4	14.1
Old	100.0	23.5	43.5	22.5	0.3	0.4	14.1	23.8	5.4	15.4	6.0	7.4	11.3	13.1
Other	100.0	35.5	47.3	15.3	4.2	1.6	9.4	11.8	0.5	22.3	9.9	2.7	12.7	22.0

Number of Traders in Each Category

	Open Interest	PM Long	PM Short	Swap Long	Swap Short	Swap Spreading	MM Long	MM Short	MM Spreading	Other Long	Other Short	Other Spreading
All	706	219	299	23	4	17	49	70	43	98	73	101
Old	698	214	284	23	4	13	48	71	39	102	79	83
Other	400	52	228	13	7	6	15	12	4	38	55	18

Percent of Open Interest Held by the Indicated Number of the Largest Traders

	By Gross Position				By Net Position			
	4 or Less Traders		8 or Less Traders		4 or Less Traders		8 or Less Traders	
	Long	Short	Long	Short	Long	Short	Long	Short
All	12.5	12.3	19.9	19.0	11.8	11.5	18.7	17.5
Old	13.5	13.3	21.5	20.4	13.2	12.6	21.0	18.4
Other	26.0	15.7	39.7	25.0	25.3	15.2	38.9	24.0

Figure 5.1 Disaggregated Commitments of Traders Report for Corn Futures as of December 27, 2016

US Commodity Futures Trading Commission

monitoring of traders holding larger positions, and provide a type of "early warning system" about individuals and entities that are accumulating large numbers of futures contracts.

At the federal level, these reportable data are compiled each week and published in the *Commitments of Traders* report; an example for corn futures is presented in Figure 5.1. This report provides a contract-by-contract summary of the types of traders – Producer/ Merchant/Processor/User (i.e., commercial hedgers), Swap Dealers, Managed Money, and Other Reportables – and the number of long and short positions held by the reportable traders in each category. These data are also presented in terms of the percent of open interest represented by each category, the number of reporting traders in each category, and the percent of open interest held by the 4 largest and 8 largest traders in each category. Week-to-week changes in the market composition – in other words, the types of traders and their holdings, both long and short – provide a detailed view of each market and are closely watched by market participants for possible explanations about recent price changes and clues about future market direction. The Commitments of Traders report will be discussed in detail in Chapter 12.

Minimum Price Increment

All futures prices have a minimum price increment, or tick, that is a small fraction of the typical price change observed in the cash market. For grain futures the tick is $0.0025 (i.e., ¼ cent) per bushel, for livestock contracts it is $0.00025 per pound ($0.025 per cwt), for petroleum contracts it is typically $0.01 per barrel or $0.0001 per gallon, and so forth. The tick size can be multiplied by the contract size to find the *tick value*, or change in the value of a futures contract from a one-tick change in the price. Using the tick values above, a 5,000-bushel grain contract has a tick value of $12.50 per contract, a 40,000-pound livestock contract has a tick value of $10 per contract, a 1,000-barrel oil contract has a tick value of $10 per contract, and a 42,000-gallon gasoline contract has a tick value of $4.20.

Daily Price Limits

Many futures contracts have *daily price limits* to restrict the amount that prices can move up or down in a single trading session. Daily price limits are designed to prevent extreme price moves up or down, and to interrupt trading when prices are exceptionally volatile. These price limits are based on the previous trading day's settlement price, in much the same way that daily price changes are calculated.

When the market moves either *limit-up* or *limit-down*, trading stops until prices move back within the daily limits. If prices remain *locked limit* at one of these extremes for the rest of the session, trading resumes the next trading day with new maximum and minimum prices based on the settlement price from the limit-up or limit-down trading session. Some markets also have *expandable limits* or *telescoping price limits*, so the limits can increase when prices are more volatile and contract when less volatile. Whatever the method used, it is important that these price limits not be unduly restrictive and cause an excessive number of limit-up or limit-down sessions. If properly set, there should be only a few limit-move sessions per year.

Expiration Date and Last Trading Date

Every futures contract has an expiration date, when the buyer and seller must complete their obligations. Details about the last trading day – which may or may not be the same as expiration day – as well as delivery or cash settlement procedures, trading hours, contract months, listing cycles, and various other date-related matters, may be contained in the futures contract, or they may appear in a separate exchange document.

In addition to developing and maintaining contract specifications, exchanges are responsible for much of the behind-the-scenes infrastructure necessary for a successful marketplace. The exchanges perform these functions not only because it is their interest to do so, but also because it is mandated by the regulatory system that governs these markets.

Regulation by Exchanges

Exchanges are designated as *first-line regulators* because most regulatory issues can be quickly and effectively addressed at this level. Each exchange is responsible for developing and enforcing its own rules as a *self-regulatory organization* (SRO). These responsibilities include designing and maintaining the specifications for the contracts offered for trading; developing and enforcing the trading practices used for those contracts; and a wide range of other details covered in the exchange rulebook, the clearing house manual, and various other exchange documents.

As part of its responsibilities as a self-regulatory organization, each exchange is required by federal law to:

- operate and maintain competitive, open, and efficient markets;
- prevent market manipulation;
- ensure the financial integrity of all transactions;
- collect and disseminate market information;
- protect customers from abusive practices;
- resolve disputes fairly and equitably; and
- fulfill a number of other *core principle* obligations.

Exchanges must receive *prior approval* from the federal regulator to conduct business, to start trading in a newly-listed contract, to stop trading in an already-listed contract, to change the specifications of an already-listed contract, and to do virtually anything else that affects the status quo.

The guiding principle behind limiting changes to the specifications of an already-listed contract can be summarized as, "You can't change the rules in the middle of the game." Once buyers and sellers have established positions in a contract, it would be unfair to make any changes that affect the contract's price or performance. Only in rare situations is it possible to make changes to a contract month with nonzero open interest. For this reason, most contract modifications are implemented on newly-listed contract months, or on already-listed contract months which do not yet have any open interest.

Regulation by the Federal Government

The *Commodity Futures Trading Commission* (CFTC) is the primary federal regulator of the US futures and options industry, and is the entity from which exchanges must receive prior approval. The CFTC oversees the futures exchanges, formally known as *designated contract markets* (DCMs), and supervises their activities. It also supervises the activities of clearing houses, clearing firms, brokerage firms (formally known as futures commission merchants or FCMs), and certain individual market participants such as traders with large positions. The CFTC coordinates its activities with other US financial market regulators, and with regulatory agencies in other countries.

Legislative History

The CFTC began as the Grain Futures Commission, which was authorized by the Grain Futures Act in 1922. At the time, all futures markets were based on grains and other crops. As noted earlier, livestock futures did not appear until the 1960s, futures on currencies, interest rates, and energy were not introduced until the 1970s, and stock index futures were not launched until the 1980s. The Grain Futures Commission was established as an agency within the US Department of Agriculture (USDA), and the Grain Futures Act was the first major effort to regulate the futures markets at the federal level.

Although limited in scope, the Grain Futures Act introduced a number of important regulatory concepts. It required all futures trading to take place on exchanges, rather than off-exchange "bucket shops" where orders to buy and sell were little more than bets on prices. It also established the first requirements to become a DCM, and contained provisions to suspend or revoke an exchange's designation. In addition, it implemented a large trader reporting system, based on the principle that large traders are more likely to have an influence on prices than small traders, all else the same.

The Grain Futures Commission became the Commodity Exchange Authority in 1936, following passage of the Commodity Exchange Act. Chapter 1 of the Commodity Exchange Act describes the purpose of futures markets as follows:

(a) Findings

The transactions subject to this chapter are entered into regularly in interstate and international commerce and are affected with a national public interest by providing a means for managing and assuming price risks, discovering prices, or disseminating pricing information through trading in liquid, fair and financially secure trading facilities.

(7 USC §5).

"Managing price risks" using futures is known as *hedging* and "assuming price risks" using futures is called *speculation*, while "discovering prices" or *price discovery* is the use of supply and demand to find the price. Price discovery and risk management are generally considered the two most important economic functions of futures markets, while speculation supplies liquidity to the hedging process and enhances the price discovery process by removing inefficiencies. "Disseminating pricing information" is important because futures prices can be useful in pricing the underlying commodity and other related commodities.

Regulation and the Perfect Competition Model

As noted at the beginning of this chapter, futures prices are obtained through a process resembling the perfect competition model: large numbers of buyers and sellers with no individual large enough to influence the price, homogeneous products, low barriers to entry and exit, and all decisions driven by profit maximization. The perfect competition model also helps identify the types of commodities suitable for futures trading. Thin long-run profit margins, a critical need to control costs, and volatile prices make commodity-based industries particularly well-suited for using futures markets. This is the reason why so many commodities have futures contracts, and why futures contracts were first developed for commodities.

Regulatory Purpose

Chapter 1 of the Commodity Exchange Act also describes the purpose of regulating these markets:

(b) Purpose

It is the purpose of this chapter to serve the public interests described in subsection (a) of this section through a system of effective self-regulation of trading facilities, clearing systems, market participants and market professionals under the oversight of the Commission. To foster these public interests, it is further the purpose of this chapter to deter and prevent price manipulation or any other disruptions to market integrity; to ensure the financial integrity of all transactions subject to this chapter and the avoidance of systemic risk; to protect all market participants from fraudulent or other abusive sales practices and misuses of customer assets; and to promote responsible innovation and fair competition among boards of trade, other markets and market participants.

(7 USC §5).

Commodities are often necessities for individuals or businesses – food, fiber, energy, metals – and their prices tend to be sensitive to small changes in supply and demand, making it important to "deter and prevent price manipulation" and provide fair prices for producers and consumers. It is also essential to "ensure the financial integrity of all transactions . . . and the avoidance of systemic risk" to ensure that buyers and sellers are not disadvantaged and the macro economy is not disrupted. The very nature of commodity markets, with wide swings in prices that can quickly produce large profits and losses, makes it necessary to "protect all market participants from fraudulent or other abusive sales practices and misuses of customer assets." Recognizing the need to "promote responsible innovation and fair competition" represents a balanced approach to regulation that meets the needs of all parties.

Creation of the Commodity Futures Trading Commission

In 1974, the Commodity Exchange Act was amended by Commodity Futures Trading Act. It moved the Commodity Exchange Authority out of the USDA and established it as the Commodity Futures Trading Commission, an independent regulatory agency. The CFTC was modelled after the Securities and Exchange Commission (SEC), the primary federal regulator of the securities markets. Futures are financial instruments but they are not securities, so futures and futures-based instruments are under the jurisdiction of the CFTC, not the SEC.

Authority and Jurisdiction

The Commodity Futures Trading Act gave the CFTC exclusive authority over the trading of, and the markets for, futures and options on futures. However, the CFTC shares authority with the SEC on futures and options contracts on common stocks including stock indexes. The CFTC also shares jurisdiction with the SEC, Federal Reserve, and Treasury Department on futures and options contracts for debt instruments (bonds, notes, and bills). The CFTC does not have any regulatory authority over the underlying cash markets for commodities, or over forward contracts on those commodities, except in cases where positions in cash markets or forwards are used to manipulate futures prices. The Commodity Futures Trading Act also gave responsibility to the exchanges for setting futures margins, unlike securities markets where margins are set by the Federal Reserve and enforced by the SEC.

Organization

There are five CFTC commissioners, who are appointed by the President and approved by the Senate to staggered five-year terms. These five consist of a Chairperson selected by the President, two commissioners selected by Republicans, and two commissioners selected by Democrats. The CFTC also has approximately 700 staff at offices in Washington DC, Chicago, Kansas City, and New York. The agency is funded entirely by Congressional appropriations; all fees and fines collected by the CFTC are turned over to the US Treasury.

For the first 25 years of its existence, CFTC regulations based on the Commodity Futures Trading Act were largely proscriptive, describing in detail what was or was not allowed. This led to frequent "gray areas" that required judgment calls by CFTC staff and commissioners. In addition, as the futures markets grew in size, and as innovation led to new types of contracts, questions arose that the CFTC's existing legal and regulatory framework was not designed to address. Amending laws and updating regulations is a time-consuming process, leading to growing concerns that US futures markets were at a competitive disadvantage to overseas exchanges.

In 2000, the Commodity Futures Modernization Act (CFMA) extensively revised the Commodity Exchange Act. It replaced much of the proscriptive language with a system of *core principles* or broad guidelines to guide decisions and permit flexibility. In 2010, largely in response to the 2007–2008 financial crisis, the Dodd-Frank Wall Street Reform and Consumer Protection Act (Dodd-Frank) added language to the Commodity Exchange Act regarding *swaps*, which are customized futures- or option-like instruments traded off-exchange. Dodd-Frank gave the CFTC primary regulatory responsibility for swaps, which until then had been largely unregulated.

Self-Regulation by the Industry

The Commodity Futures Trading Act also established the National Futures Association (NFA), an organization modelled after the National Association of Securities Dealers (NASD), since renamed the Financial Industry Regulatory Authority (FINRA). NFA was authorized in 1974, founded in 1976, and registered by the CFTC in 1981 as the official self-regulatory organization of the futures industry.

NFA is responsible for testing, registering, and regulating traders, commodity brokers, commodity brokerage firms, commodity investment funds, and other customer-facing commodity trading entities. Its responsibilities include:

- administering the National Commodity Futures Examination, commonly known as the Series 3 exam;
- monitoring advertising, telephone solicitations, disclosure statements, and claims made to current and prospective customers;
- auditing the financial status of commodity brokers, brokerage firms, and commodity investment funds; and
- providing arbitration services to resolve disputes.

Membership in NFA is mandatory for all exchanges, FCMs, and other customer-facing firms and individuals in the US. The association is funded by annual dues paid by its members, a fee paid by each exchange based on the number of contracts traded, and a fee paid by customers on each *round-turn*, or complete buy-and-sell transaction.

As stated above, virtually all customer-facing individuals involved in commodity futures trading activities must register with NFA. This excludes individuals who engage in commodity trading for commercial purposes, such as a merchandiser who hedges the purchases and sales of a grain elevator, or an individual who trades futures for their own personal account. The registration process includes fingerprinting of the applicant, a criminal background check, and a passing score on the Series 3 exam. The first part of the exam tests an individual's knowledge about how these markets operate, trading methodology, and applications for risk management and investment purposes. The second part covers regulatory matters, dispute resolution, and disciplinary procedures.

Applications in Other Sectors and Countries

Futures were one of the few parts of the financial system that did not experience serious problems during the 2007–2008 financial crisis. This fact was noted by Congress as they were drafting the Dodd-Frank Act, and led them to borrow a number of features from the futures markets – centralized clearing, margins and margin calls, periodic mark-to-market settlements, and position limits – and apply them to other parts of the US financial sector. The three-part regulatory system – exchanges, government, and industry – used by the US has also worked effectively during non-crisis periods, and this basic structure has been adopted to various degrees by a number of other countries.

Appendix 5.1

Chapter 10
Corn Futures

10100.   SCOPE OF CHAPTER

This chapter is limited in application to Corn futures. The procedures for trading, clearing, inspection, delivery and settlement of Corn futures not specifically covered herein or in Chapter 7 shall be governed by the general rules of the Exchange.

10101.   CONTRACT SPECIFICATIONS

Each futures contract shall be for 5,000 bushels of No. 2 yellow corn at par, No. 1 yellow corn at 1½ cents per bushel over contract price, or No. 3 yellow corn at 1½ cents per bushel under contract price. Every delivery of corn may be made up of the authorized grades for shipment from eligible regular facilities provided that no lot delivered shall contain less than 5,000 bushels of any one grade from any one shipping station.

10102.   TRADING SPECIFICATIONS

Trading in Corn futures is regularly conducted in five months – September, December, March, May, and July. The number of months open for trading at a given time shall be determined by the Exchange.

10102.A.   Trading Schedule

The hours for trading of Corn futures shall be determined by the Exchange.

On the last day of trading in an expiring future, the close of the expiring future shall begin at 12 o'clock noon and trading shall be permitted thereafter for a period not to exceed one minute. Quotations made during this one minute period shall constitute the close.

10102.B.   Trading Unit

The unit of trading shall be 5,000 bushels of corn.

10102.C.   Price Increments

The minimum fluctuation for Corn futures shall be ¼ cent per bushel ($12.50 per contract), including spreads.

10102.D.   Daily Price Limits

Daily price limits for Corn futures are reset every six months. The first reset date would be the first trading day in May based on the following: Daily settlement prices are collected for the nearest July contract over 45 consecutive trading days before and on the business day prior to April 16th. The average price is calculated based on the collected settlement prices and then multiplied by seven percent. The resulting number, rounded to the nearest 5 cents per bushel, or 20 cents per bushel, whichever is higher, will be the new initial price limit for Corn futures and will become effective on the first trading day in May and will remain in effect through the last trading day in October.

The second reset date would be the first trading day in November based on the following: Daily settlement prices are collected for the nearest December contract over 45 consecutive trading days before and on the business day prior to October 16th. The average price is calculated based on the collected settlement prices and then multiplied by seven percent. The resulting number, rounded to the nearest 5 cents per bushel, or 20 cents per bushel, whichever is higher, will be the new initial price limit for Corn futures and will become effective on the first trading day in November and will remain in effect through the last trading day in next April.

There shall be no trading in Corn futures at a price more than the initial price limit above or below the previous day's settlement price. Should two or more corn futures contract months within the first five listed non–spot contracts (or the remaining contract month in a crop year, which is the September contract) settle at limit, the daily price limits for all contract months shall increase by 50 percent the next business day, rounded up to the nearest 5 cents per bushel. If no Corn futures contract month settles at the expanded limit the next business day, daily price limits for all contract months shall revert back to the initial price limit the following business day. There shall be no price limits on the current month contract on or after the second business day preceding the first day of the delivery month.

10102.E.   Position Limits, Exemptions, Position Accountability and Reportable Levels

The applicable position limits and/or accountability levels, in addition to the reportable levels, are set forth in the Position Limit, Position Accountability and Reportable Level Table in the Interpretations & Special Notices Section of Chapter 5.

A Person seeking an exemption from position limits for bona fide commercial purposes shall apply to the Market Regulation Department on forms provided by the Exchange, and the Market Regulation Department may grant qualified exemptions in its sole discretion.

Refer to Rule 559 for requirements concerning the aggregation of positions and allowable exemptions from the specified position limits.

10102.F.   Limit on Holdings of Registered and Outstanding Shipping Certificates

No person, at any time, shall own or control more than 600 registered and outstanding Corn Shipping Certificates issued by facilities designated by the Exchange as regular to issue shipping certificates for Corn. The 600 certificate maximum shall include mini-sized Corn certificates such that each mini-sized certificate represents the equivalent of one-fifth of a full- sized certificate.

If a person stops Corn certificates for delivery in a quantity that would cause such person to exceed the 600 certificate limit, the person must cancel, retender or sell the quantity of certificates in excess of 600 not later than the following business day.

A person seeking an exemption from this limit for bona fide commercial purposes shall apply to the Market Regulation Department on forms provided by the exchange, and the Market Regulation Department may grant qualified exemptions in its sole discretion.

Refer to Rule 559 for requirements concerning aggregation of accounts and allowable exemptions from position limits. The same standards that apply to allowable exemptions and aggregation of positions for position limit purposes shall also apply to limit on holdings of registered and outstanding shipping certificates.

10102.G.   Termination of Trading

No trades in Corn futures deliverable in the current month shall be made after the business day preceding the 15th calendar day of that month. Any contracts remaining open after the last day of trading must be either:

(a)   Settled by delivery no later than the second business day following the last trading day (tender on business day prior to delivery).

(b)   Liquidated by means of a bona fide Exchange of Futures for Related Position, no later than the business day following the last trading day.

10103.   RESERVED

10104.   GRADES / GRADE DIFFERENTIALS

Upon written request by a taker of delivery at the time loading orders are submitted, a futures contract for the sale of corn shall be performed on the basis of United States origin only.

A contract for the sale of corn for future delivery shall be performed on the basis of the grades officially promulgated by the Secretary of Agriculture as conforming to United States Standards at the time of making the contract. If no such United States grades shall have been officially promulgated, then such contract shall be performed on the basis of the grades established by the Department of Agriculture of the State of Illinois, or the standards established by the Rules of the Exchange in force at the time of making the contract.

CORN DIFFERENTIALS

No. 1 Yellow Corn (maximum 15% moisture)	at 1½ cents per bushel over contract price
No. 2 Yellow Corn (maximum 15% moisture)	at contract price
No. 3 Yellow Corn (maximum 15% moisture)	at 1½ cents per bushel under contract price

10105.   LOCATION DIFFERENTIALS

Corn for shipment from regular shipping stations located within the Chicago Switching District or the Burns Harbor, Indiana Switching District may be delivered in satisfaction of Corn futures contracts at contract price, subject to the differentials for class and grade outlined above.

Corn for shipment from regular shipping stations located within the Lockport-Seneca Shipping District may be delivered in satisfaction of Corn futures contracts at a premium of 2 cents per bushel over contract price, subject to the differentials for class and grade outlined above.

Corn for shipment from regular shipping stations located within the Ottawa-Chillicothe Shipping District may be delivered in satisfaction of Corn futures contracts at a premium of 2½ cents per bushel over contract price, subject to the differentials for class and grade outlined above.

Corn for shipment from regular shipping stations located within the Peoria-Pekin Shipping District may be delivered in satisfaction of Corn futures contracts at a premium of 3 cents per bushel over contract price, subject to the differentials for class and grade outlined above.

10106.   DELIVERY POINTS

Corn shipping certificates shall specify shipment from one of the warehouses or shipping stations currently regular for delivery and located in one of the following territories:

A.   Chicago and Burns Harbor, Indiana Switching District — When used in these Rules, the Chicago Switching District will be that area geographically defined by Tariff ICC WTL 8020-Series and that portion of the Illinois Waterway at or above river mile 304 which includes the Calumet Sag Channel and the Chicago Sanitary & Ship Canal. When used in these Rules, Burns Harbor, Indiana Switching District will be that area geographically defined by the boundaries of Burns Waterway Harbor at Burns Harbor, Indiana which is owned and operated by the Indiana Port Commission.

B.   Lockport-Seneca Shipping District — When used in these Rules, the Lockport-Seneca Shipping District will be that portion of the Illinois Waterway below river mile 304 at the junction of the Calumet Sag Channel and the Chicago Sanitary & Ship Canal and above river mile 244.6 at the Marseilles Lock and Dam.

C.   Ottawa-Chillicothe Shipping District — When used in these Rules, the Ottawa-Chillicothe Shipping District will be that portion of the Illinois Waterway below river mile 244.6 at the Marseilles Lock and Dam and at or above river mile 170 between Chillicothe and Peoria, IL.

D.   Peoria – Pekin Shipping District — When used in these Rules, the Peoria-Pekin Shipping District will be that portion of the Illinois Waterway below river mile 170 between Chillicothe and Peoria, IL and at or above river mile 151 at Pekin, IL.

**10107.   REGISTRATION AND DELIVERY OF CORN SHIPPING CERTIFI-
CATES AND DELIVERY PAYMENT**

10107.A.   Registration and Delivery of Corn Shipping Certificates

(Refer to Rule 712., Delivery and Registration, and Rule 713., Delivery
Procedures.)

10107.B.   Delivery Payment

Delivery payment shall be made utilizing the electronic delivery system via
the Clearing House's online system. Delivery Payment will be made during the
6:45 a.m. collection cycle, or such other time designated by the Clearing House.
Thus, the cost of delivery will be debited or credited to a clearing firm's settlement
account. Buyers obligated to accept delivery must take delivery and make Delivery Payment and sellers obligated to make delivery must make delivery during
the 6:45 a.m. settlement process, or such other time designated by the Clearing
House, on the day of delivery, except on banking holidays when delivery must
be taken or made and Delivery Payment made during the 6:45 a.m. settlement
process, or such other time designated by the Clearing House, on the next banking business day. Adjustments for differences between contract prices and delivery
prices established by the Clearing House shall be made with the Clearing House
in accordance with its rules, policies and procedures.

10108.   PREMIUM CHARGES

To be valid for delivery on futures contracts, all shipping certificates covering corn
under obligation for shipment must indicate the applicable premium charge. No
shipping certificates shall be valid for delivery on Corn futures contracts unless
the premium charges on such corn shall have been paid up to and including the
18th calendar day of the preceding month, and such payment is endorsed on
the shipping certificate. Unpaid accumulated premium charges at the posted rate
applicable to the facility shall be allowed and credited to the buyer by the seller up
to and including the date of delivery.

The premium charges on corn shall not exceed 16.5/100 of one cent per bushel
per day.

**10109.   REGULARITY OF WAREHOUSES AND ISSUERS OF SHIPPING
CERTIFICATES**

10109.A.   Regularity Requirements

In addition to the conditions set forth in Rule 703.A., Conditions for Approval,
the following shall constitute requirements and conditions for regularity:

1.   The operator of a shipping station issuing corn shipping certificates shall limit
the number of shipping certificates issued to an amount not to exceed:

  a.   20 times his registered total daily rate of loading barges, or in the case of
the Chicago, Illinois and Burns Harbor, Indiana Switching Districts, his
registered storage capacity; and

  b.   a value greater than 50 percent of the operator's net worth.

2. The shipper issuing corn shipping certificates shall register his total daily rate of loading barges at his maximum 8 hour load out capacity in an amount not less than:

    a. One barge per day at each shipping station within the Locport-Seneca Shipping District, within the Ottawa-Chillicothe Shipping District, and within the Peoria-Pekin Shipping District; and

    b. three barges per day at each shipping station in the Chicago, Illinois and Burns Harbor, Indiana Switching Districts.

3. Shippers located in the Chicago, Illinois and Burns Harbor, Indiana Switching Districts shall be connected by railroad tracks with one or more railway lines.

10109.B. Location

For the delivery of corn, regular facilities may be located within the Chicago Switching District or within the Burns Harbor, Indiana Switching District or within the Lockport-Seneca Shipping District or within the Ottawa-Chillicothe Shipping District or within the Peoria-Pekin Shipping District.

No such regular facility within the Chicago Switching District shall be declared regular unless it is conveniently approachable by vessels of ordinary draft and has customary shipping facilities. Ordinary draft shall be defined as the lesser of (1) channel draft as recorded in the Lake Calumet Harbor Draft Gauge, as maintained by the Corps of Engineers, U.S. Army, minus one foot, or (2) 20 feet.

Delivery in Burns Harbor must be made from regular facilities providing water loading facilities and maintaining water depth equal to normal seaway draft of 27 feet.

In addition, deliveries of corn may be made from regular elevators or shipping stations within the Burns Harbor Switching District PROVIDED that:

(a) When corn represented by shipping certificates is ordered out for shipment by a barge, it will be the obligation of the party making delivery to protect the barge freight rate from the Chicago Switching District (i.e. the party making delivery and located in the Burns Harbor Switching District will pay the party taking delivery an amount equal to all expenses for the movement of the barge from the Chicago Switching District, to the Burns Harbor Switching District and the return movement back to the Chicago Switching District).

If inclement weather conditions make the warehouse or shipping station located in the Burns Harbor Switching District unavailable for barge loadings for a period of five or more calendar days, the party making delivery will make grain available on the day following this five calendar day period to load into a barge at one mutually agreeable water warehouse or shipping station located in the Chicago Switching District; PROVIDED that the party making delivery is notified on the first day of that five-day period of inclement weather that the barge is available for movement but cannot be moved from the Chicago Switching District to the Burns Harbor Switching District, and is requested on the last day of this five calendar day period in which the barge cannot be moved.

(b) When corn represented by shipping certificates is ordered out for shipment by vessel, and the party taking delivery is a recipient of a split delivery of grain between a warehouse or shipping station located in Burns Harbor and a warehouse or shipping station in Chicago, and the grain in the Chicago warehouse or shipping station will be loaded onto this vessel, it will be the obligation of the party making delivery at the request of the party taking delivery to protect the holder of the shipping certificates against any additional charges resulting from loading at one berth in the Burns Harbor Switching District and at one berth in the Chicago Switching District as compared to a single berth loading at one location. The party making delivery, at his option, will either make the grain available at one water warehouse or shipping station operated by the party making delivery and located in the Chicago Switching District for loading onto the vessel, make grain available at the warehouse or shipping station in Burns Harbor upon the surrender of shipping certificates issued by other regular elevators or shipping stations located in the Chicago Switching District at the time vessel loading orders are issued, or compensate the party taking delivery in an amount equal to all applicable expenses, including demurrage charges, if any, for the movement of the vessel between a berth in the other switching district. On the day that the grain is ordered out for shipment by vessel, the party making delivery will declare the regular warehouse or shipping station in which the grain will be available for loading.

Delivery within the Lockport-Seneca Shipping District or within the Ottawa-Chillicothe Shipping District or within the Peoria-Pekin Shipping District must be made at regular shipping stations providing water loading facilities and maintaining water depth equal to the draft of the Illinois River maintained by the Corps of Engineers.

10109.C. Barge Load-Out Procedures for Corn

(Refer to Rule 703. C., Load-Out, and the Interpretations to Chapter 7).

10110. BILLING

10110.A. Corn (Chicago Delivery)

The Chicago shipper is not required to furnish transit billing on corn represented by shipping certificate deliveries in Chicago, Illinois. Delivery shall be flat.

10110.B. Corn (Burns Harbor Delivery)

When corn represented by shipping certificates delivered in Burns Harbor is ordered out for shipment by rail, it will be the obligation of the party making delivery to protect the Chicago rail rate, if lower, which would apply to the owner's destination had a like kind and quantity of corn designated on the shipping certificates been loaded out and shipped from a regular shipping station located in the Chicago Switching District. If corn is loaded out and shipped to an industry in the Chicago Switching District, the party making delivery will protect the minimum crosstown switch charge in the Chicago Switching District.

When rail loading orders are submitted, the party taking delivery shall state in writing if he elects to receive the applicable rail rates from Burns Harbor or Chicago. If the party taking delivery specifies Burns Harbor, the party making delivery will load rail cars at the Burns Harbor shipping station and will not be required to protect the Chicago rates.

If the party taking delivery specifies Chicago rates, the party making delivery will declare on the day that the corn is ordered out for shipment by rail, the shipping station at which the corn will be made available, which is operated by the party making delivery and is located either in the Burns Harbor or the Chicago Switching Districts. If the declared shipping station is located in the Chicago Switching District, the party making delivery will provide only that billing specified in Rule 10110.A.

However, if the declared shipping station is located in Burns Harbor and the rail rate from Chicago or the minimum Chicago crosstown switch charge requires protection, the party making delivery will compensate the party taking delivery. The compensation shall be in an amount equivalent to the difference of the freight charges from Burns Harbor and the freight charges which would be applicable had the corn been loaded at and shipped from a shipping station located in the Chicago Switching District to the owner's destination.

6 Hedging with Futures

In Chapter 5, price discovery and risk management were described as the two most important economic functions of futures markets. Our discussion thus far has focused on price discovery and how buyers and sellers – the forces of demand and supply – interact to arrive at a futures price. We now shift our focus to risk management and how futures can be used to manage the risks of volatile prices that are an inherent part of commodity markets.

The Role of Correlation

In active, liquid futures markets the futures price will be highly correlated with the cash price. Recall from Chapter 4 that in the final settlement process, the futures contract is replaced by the underlying commodity when the contract uses physical delivery, or by some index value when the contract uses cash settlement. If the futures price is below the cash price or index, a trader can buy the cheaper futures contract and exchange it at expiration for the more expensive commodity or index. This will encourage futures buying that puts upward pressure on the futures price. Conversely, if the futures price is above the cash price or index, a trader can sell the more expensive futures contract and exchange it for the cheaper commodity or index at expiration. This will encourage futures selling that puts downward pressure on the futures price. These upward and downward forces cause the futures price to *converge* to the cash price or index value as expiration approaches. These same forces also cause the day-to-day changes in the futures price to more closely follow the day-to-day changes in the cash price or index value as expiration approaches. Because of this high correlation between the cash price (or index value) and the futures price, a futures market position can be used as a temporary substitute for a cash market position. This substitution is particularly useful when a position in the underlying commodity will be taken at a later date, because the hedger can effectively establish or *lock in* the buying or selling price months or even years prior to the actual cash market transaction.

   A *hedge* uses a futures position in combination with a cash position to manage price risk, where the gains on one position offset the losses on the other. Stated differently, a hedge uses the cash flows from a futures position to offset the cash flows from a cash market position and vice versa. Notice that hedging involves positions in both cash and futures, not just one or the other. Also notice that the purpose of hedging is to stabilize the net price paid or received, not to generate a gain from a favorable price move. These points will be illustrated using the following examples.

Hedging Against a Price Increase

Loss on Cash Position, Gain on Futures Position

We begin with a scenario involving a hypothetical consumer, or user, who buys a commodity and therefore is exposed to the risk of rising prices:

Example 6.1: A processor buys and uses corn as part of its normal operations. It expects corn prices to rise over the next several months, but it doesn't have either the funds or the storage space to buy cash corn now and store it for several months. Instead, it buys corn futures now to lock in the price. At some later date it buys cash corn, and simultaneously sells corn futures to liquidate its futures position. Assume the processor was right about the market direction, and the cash price increased from $3.50 per bushel to $4.50 per bushel.

To calculate the outcome of this hedge, the processor creates a table with separate columns for the cash position and the futures position. Each time a pricing decision is made, the information is recorded in a separate row of the table including the date, the positions taken (long or short), the respective prices, and other relevant information. At the bottom of the table the processor uses one row for the gain or loss, and a second row for the net price paid. The partially completed table with only the cash positions appears as Table 6.1–Partial.

Table 6.1 Results for Long Hedge: Rising Prices (Partial)

	Cash	Futures
Time 1:	[Short at $3.50]	
Time 2:	Long at $4.50	
Gain (Loss):	−$1.00	
Net Price:		

Notice that the processor is shown as having a short position at Time 1, with the position and price in brackets. The Time 1 position is implied by the Time 2 position. The Time 2 position is long because the processor buys cash corn at Time 2. Consequently the Time 1 cash position is short, and the brackets around the Time 1 position denote this as an implicit position, because no sale of cash corn occurred at Time 1.

Stated differently, if the processor did nothing else at Time 1, it would incur a loss of $1.00 per bushel; in other words, it would pay $1.00 more at Time 2 than at Time 1. Although the processor did not actually sell cash corn at Time 1, nevertheless its cash position effectively was short because a higher cash price at Time 2 would result in a loss, and a lower cash price at Time 2 would result in a gain, all else the same. Since there was no actual cash transaction at Time 1, the cash position and price at Time 1 are shown in brackets. In contrast, there was an actual cash transaction at Time 2 when the processor bought cash corn, so the Time 2 cash position and price are shown without brackets.

Now suppose that at Time 1 the processor hedged by simultaneously taking an offsetting long futures position. This is called a *long hedge* because the hedger uses a long futures position. Also suppose that the futures price was $3.50 at Time 1 and $4.50 at Time 2. In this and all other examples in this chapter we will assume that the quantities represented by the cash and futures positions were identical, so all calculations can be expressed in terms of the price per unit (i.e., dollars per bushel). To determine the outcome of the hedge, the processor updated the table with the futures positions and prices, and then calculated the futures gain/ loss and the net price. The completed table appears as Table 6.1.

Table 6.1 Results for Long Hedge: Rising Prices

	Cash	Futures
Time 1:	[Short at $3.50]	Long at $3.50
Time 2:	Long at $4.50	Short at $4.50
Gain (Loss):	−$1.00	+$1.00
Net Price:	$4.50 actual cash purchase price − $1.00 futures gain = $3.50 net purchase price	

In this example, the $1.00 increase in the value of the futures position exactly offset the $1.00 decrease in the value of the cash position, giving the processor the same net price ($3.50) it would have paid if it had bought the cash corn at Time 1 (ignoring transaction and carrying costs). Stated differently, the $1.00 gain on the futures position was subtracted from the $4.50 purchase price of the cash corn, reducing the processor's net price to $3.50. This is called a *perfect hedge* because the change in the futures price perfectly matches the change in the cash price. This rarely happens in practice, but the perfect hedge is useful for demonstration purposes, so it will be used for all examples in this chapter.

Gain on Cash Position, Loss on Futures Position

There is no guarantee that the price will behave as expected after the hedge is placed, as demonstrated in the next example. We begin with the same initial scenario involving the processor, but now the price moves in the opposite direction:

Example 6.2: A processor buys and uses corn as part of its normal operations. It expects corn prices to rise over the next several months, but it doesn't have either the funds or the storage space to buy cash corn now and store it for several months. Instead, it buys corn futures now to lock in the price. At some later date it buys cash corn, and simultaneously sells corn futures to liquidate its futures position. Assume the processor was wrong about the market direction, and the cash price decreased from $3.50 per bushel to $2.50 per bushel.

As before, the processor creates a table with separate columns for the cash position and the futures position. Each time a pricing decision is made, the information is recorded in a separate row of the table including the date, the positions taken (long or short), and the respective prices. The partially completed table with only the cash positions appears as Table 6.2–Partial.

Table 6.2 Results for Long Hedge: Falling Prices (Partial)

	Cash	Futures
Time 1:	[Short at $3.50]	
Time 2:	Long at $2.50	
Gain (Loss):	+$1.00	
Net Price:		

Notice that once again the processor is shown as having a short position at Time 1, with the position and price in brackets. The Time 1 position is implied by the Time 2 position, because no sale of cash corn occurred at Time 1.

Stated differently, if the processor did nothing else at Time 1, it would have a gain of $1.00 per bushel; in other words, it would pay $1.00 less at Time 2 than at Time 1. Although the processor did not actually sell cash corn at Time 1, nevertheless its cash position effectively was short for the reasons described in Example 6.1.

Now suppose that at Time 1 the processor hedged by simultaneously taking an offsetting long futures position to create a long hedge. Also suppose that the futures price was $3.50 at Time 1 and $2.50 at Time 2; keep in mind that at Time 1 the processor had no idea whether the price would go up or down. To determine the outcome of the hedge, the processor updated the table with the futures positions and prices, and calculated the futures gain/loss and the net price. The completed table appears as Table 6.2.

Table 6.2 Results for Long Hedge: Falling Prices

	Cash	Futures
Time 1:	[Short at $3.50]	Long at $3.50
Time 2:	Long at $2.50	Short at $2.50
Gain (Loss):	+$1.00	−$1.00
Net Price:	$2.50 actual cash purchase price + $1.00 futures loss = $3.50 net purchase price	

In this example, the $1.00 decrease in the value of the futures position exactly offset the $1.00 gain in the value of the cash position, giving the processor the same net price ($3.50) it would have paid if it had bought the cash corn at Time 1 (ignoring transaction and carrying costs). Stated differently, the $1.00 loss on the futures position was added to the $2.50 purchase price of the cash corn, increasing the processor's net price to $3.50.

In hindsight, it might seem that the processor in this example would have been better off by not hedging. However, recall that at Time 1, when the hedge was placed, the processor expected prices to rise but it did not know for sure whether the price would go up or down. In Example 6.2, the price went down and hedging caused the processor to forfeit the price decrease. In Example 6.1, the price went up and hedging protected the processor from the price increase; but in both cases the processor had the same $3.50 net purchase price. Hedging substitutes price stability for the possibility of better prices and the risk of worse prices. Stated differently, hedging locked in a net price of $3.50, regardless of whether prices went up or down.

No Gain or Loss on Cash Position, No Gain or Loss on Futures Position

The same $3.50 net price also would have occurred if prices had remained stable, as demonstrated in the next example using the same initial scenario involving the processor:

Example 6.3: A processor buys and uses corn as part of its normal operations. It expects corn prices to rise over the next several months, but it doesn't have either the funds or the storage space to buy cash corn now and store it for several months. Instead, it buys corn futures now to lock in the price. At some later date it buys cash corn, and simultaneously sells corn futures to liquidate its futures position. Assume the cash price was unchanged at $3.50 per bushel.

As in the previous two examples, the processor creates a table with separate columns for the cash position and the futures position. Each time a pricing decision is made, the information is recorded in a separate row of the table with the date, the positions taken (long or short), and the respective prices. The partially completed table with only the cash positions appears as Table 6.3–Partial.

Table 6.3 Results for Long Hedge: Stable Prices (Partial)

	Cash	Futures
Time 1:	[Short at $3.50]	
Time 2:	Long at $3.50	
Gain (Loss):	$0.00	
Net Price:		

If the processor did nothing else at Time 1, it would have no gain or loss, and would pay the same $3.50 price at Time 2 as it would have paid at Time 1. Although the processor did not actually sell cash corn at Time 1, nevertheless its cash position effectively was short, for the reasons described above.

Table 6.3 Results for Long Hedge: Stable Prices

	Cash	Futures
Time 1:	[Short at $3.50]	Long at $3.50
Time 2:	Long at $3.50	Short at $3.50
Gain (Loss):	$0.00	$0.00
Net Price:	$3.50 actual cash purchase price ± $0.00 futures gain/loss = $3.50 net purchase price	

Now suppose that at Time 1 the processor hedged by simultaneously taking an offsetting long futures position to create a long hedge. Also suppose that the futures price was $3.50 at Time 1 and $3.50 at Time 2. To determine the outcome of the hedge, the processor updated the table with the futures positions and prices, and calculated the futures gain/loss and the net price. The completed table appears as Table 6.3.

In this example, there is no change in the value of either the cash position or the futures position, so the processor paid the same cash price at Time 2 as it would have paid at Time 1 (ignoring transaction and carrying costs). Stated differently, the futures position had no impact on the purchase price of the cash corn, so the net price was $3.50.

Stabilizing the Net Purchase Price

Notice that in all three examples under this scenario the net purchase price was $3.50, regardless of whether the price between Time 1 and Time 2 increased (as in Example 6.1), or decreased (as in Example 6.2), or was unchanged (as in Example 6.3). The results would have been the same for any price change up or down, or for no price change, underscoring the point that hedging locks in the net price.

Each of these three examples is a long hedge in which a long futures position is used to protect the hedger from the effects of a price increase. Because the hedger is effectively short cash corn, the hedger is sometimes described as being a *natural short* and therefore requires an offsetting long futures position as the hedging instrument. Also notice how the long futures position in all three examples is used as a temporary substitute for a cash commodity purchase (i.e., a long cash position) at a later point in time. The processor was unable to buy the cash corn at Time 1, so instead it bought a corn futures contract. Then at Time 2 it replaced the long futures position with a long cash position.

Hedging Against a Price Decrease

Loss on Cash Position, Gain on Futures Position

Examples 6.1, 6.2, and 6.3 all were based on the same basic scenario: a user of the commodity planned to make a purchase at some later date and wanted to lock in the current price, rather than risk the possibility of paying a higher price later. In a similar fashion, hedges can be constructed to protect a hedger from the effects of a price decrease, by using a short futures position as a temporary substitute for a cash commodity sale at a later point in time. We now introduce a new scenario involving a hypothetical producer who sells a commodity and therefore is exposed to the risk of falling prices:

Example 6.4: A farmer grows and sells corn as part of their normal operations. They believe that corn prices might drop over the course of the growing season, but they are unable to sell cash corn right now because the crop has not yet been harvested. Instead, they sell corn futures now to lock in the price. At some later date, after harvest, they sell cash corn and simultaneously buy corn futures to liquidate their futures position. Assume the farmer was right about the market direction, and the cash price decreased from $3.50 per bushel to $3.00 per bushel.

To calculate the outcome of this hedge, the farmer creates a table with separate columns for the cash position and the futures position. Each time a pricing decision is made, the information is recorded in a separate row of the table including the date, the positions taken (long or short), the respective prices, and other relevant information. At the bottom of the table the farmer designates one row for the gain or loss, and a second row for the net price received. The partially completed table with only the cash positions appears as Table 6.4–Partial.

Table 6.4 Results for Short Hedge: Falling Prices (Partial)

	Cash	Futures
Time 1:	[Long at $3.50]	
Time 2:	Short at $3.00	
Gain (Loss):	−$0.50	
Net Price:		

Notice that the farmer is shown as having a long position at Time 1, with the position and price in brackets. The Time 1 position is implied by the Time 2 position. The Time 2 position is short because the processor sells cash corn at Time 2. Consequently the Time 1 cash position is long, and the brackets around the Time 1 position denote this as an implicit position, because no purchase of cash corn occurred at Time 1.

Stated differently, if the farmer did nothing else at Time 1, they would incur a loss of $0.50 per bushel; in other words, they would receive $0.50 less at Time 2 than at Time 1. Although the farmer did not actually buy cash corn at Time 1, nevertheless their position effectively was long because a lower cash price at Time 2 would result in a loss, and a higher cash price at Time 2 would result in a gain, all else the same. Since there was no actual transaction at Time 1, the cash position and price at Time 1 are shown in brackets. In contrast, there was an actual cash transaction at Time 2 when the farmer sold cash corn, so the Time 2 cash position and price are shown without brackets.

Now suppose that at Time 1 the farmer hedged by simultaneously taking an offsetting short futures position. This is called a *short hedge* because the hedger uses a short futures

Table 6.4 Results for Short Hedge: Falling Prices

	Cash	Futures
Time 1:	[Long at $3.50]	Short at $3.50
Time 2:	Short at $3.00	Long at $3.00
Gain (Loss):	−$0.50	+$0.50
Net Price:	$3.00 actual cash sale price + $0.50 futures gain = $3.50 net sale price	

position. Also suppose that the futures price was $3.50 at Time 1 and $3.00 at Time 2. To determine the outcome of the hedge, the farmer updated the table with the futures positions and prices, and calculated the futures gain/loss and the net price. The completed table appears as Table 6.4.

In this example, the $0.50 increase in the value of the futures position exactly offset the $0.50 decrease in the value of the cash position, giving the farmer the same net price ($3.50) they would have received if they had sold the cash corn at Time 1 (ignoring production constraints and interest). Stated differently, the $0.50 gain on the futures position was added to the $3.00 sale price of the cash corn, increasing the farmer's net price to $3.50.

Gain on Cash Position, Loss on Futures Position

There is no guarantee that the price will behave as expected after the hedge is placed, as demonstrated in the next example. We begin with the same initial scenario involving the farmer, but now the price moves in the opposite direction:

Example 6.5: A farmer grows and sells corn as part of their normal operations. They believe that corn prices might drop over the course of the growing season, but they are unable to sell cash corn right now because the crop has not yet been harvested. Instead, they sell corn futures now to lock in the price. At some later date, after harvest, they sell cash corn and simultaneously buy corn futures to liquidate their futures position. Assume the farmer was wrong about the market direction, and the cash price increased from $3.50 per bushel to $4.00 per bushel.

As before, the farmer creates a table with separate columns for the cash position and the futures position. Each time a pricing decision is made, the information is recorded in a separate row of the table including the date, the positions taken (long or short), and the respective prices. The partially completed table with only the cash positions appears as Table 6.5–Partial.

Notice that once again the farmer is shown as having a long position at Time 1, with the position and price in brackets. The Time 1 position is implied by the Time 2 position, because no purchase of cash corn occurred at Time 1.

Table 6.5 Results for Short Hedge: Rising Prices (Partial)

	Cash	Futures
Time 1:	[Long at $3.50]	
Time 2:	Short at $4.00	
Gain (Loss):	+$0.50	
Net Price:		

Stated differently, if the farmer did nothing else at Time 1, they would have a gain of $0.50 per bushel; in other words, they would receive $0.50 more at Time 2 than at Time 1. Although the farmer did not actually buy cash corn at Time 1, nevertheless their position effectively was long for the reasons described in Example 6.4.

Now suppose that at Time 1 the farmer hedged by simultaneously taking an offsetting short futures position to create a short hedge. Also suppose that the futures price was $3.50 at Time 1 and $4.00 at Time 2; keep in mind that at Time 1 the farmer had no idea whether the price would go up or down. To determine the outcome of the hedge, the farmer updated the table with the futures positions and prices, and calculated the futures gain/loss and the net price. The completed table appears as Table 6.5.

Table 6.5 Results for Short Hedge: Rising Prices

	Cash	Futures
Time 1:	[Long at $3.50]	Short at $3.50
Time 2:	Short at $4.00	Long at $4.00
Gain (Loss):	+$0.50	−$0.50
Net Price:	$4.00 actual cash sale price − $0.50 futures loss = $3.50 net sale price	

In this example, the $0.50 decrease in the value of the futures position exactly offset the $0.50 gain in the value of the cash position, giving the farmer the same net price ($3.50) they would have received if they had sold the cash corn at Time 1 (ignoring production constraints and interest). Stated differently, the $0.50 loss on the futures position was deducted from the $4.00 purchase price of the cash corn, decreasing the farmer's net price to $3.50.

In hindsight, it might seem that the farmer in this example would have been better off by not hedging. However, recall that at Time 1 when the hedge was placed, the farmer expected prices to fall, but they did not know for sure whether the price would go up or down. In Example 6.5 the price went up and hedging caused the farmer to forfeit the price increase; in Example 6.4 the price went down and hedging protected the farmer from the price decrease; but in both cases the farmer had the same $3.50 net sale price. Hedging substitutes price stability for the possibility of better prices and the risk of worse prices. Stated differently, hedging locked in a net price of $3.50, regardless of whether prices went up or down.

No Gain or Loss on Cash Position, No Gain or Loss on Futures Position

The same $3.50 net price also would have occurred if prices had remained stable, as demonstrated in the next example using the same initial scenario involving the farmer:

Example 6.6: A farmer grows and sells corn as part of their normal operations. They believe that corn prices will drop over the course of the growing season, but they are unable to sell cash corn right now because the crop has not yet been harvested. Instead, they sell corn futures now to lock in the price. At some later date, after harvest, they sell cash corn and simultaneously buy corn futures to liquidate their futures position. Assume the cash price was unchanged at $3.50 per bushel.

As in the previous two examples, the farmer creates a table with separate columns for the cash position, and the futures position. Each time a pricing decision is made, the information is recorded in a separate row of the table including the date, the positions taken (long or short), and the respective prices. The partially completed table with only the cash positions appears as Table 6.6–Partial.

Table 6.6 Results for Short Hedge: Stable Prices (Partial)

	Cash	Futures
Time 1:	[Long at $3.50]	
Time 2:	Short at $3.50	
Gain (Loss):	$0.00	
Net Price:		

If the farmer did nothing else at Time 1, they would have no gain or loss, and would receive the same $3.50 price at Time 2 as they would have received at Time 1. Although the farmer did not actually buy cash corn at Time 1, nevertheless their cash position effectively was long for the reasons described above.

Now suppose that at Time 1 the farmer hedged by simultaneously taking an offsetting short futures position to create a short hedge. Also suppose that the futures price was $3.50 at Time 1 and $3.50 at Time 2. To determine the outcome of the hedge, the farmer updated the table with the futures positions and prices, and calculated the futures gain/loss and the net price. The completed table appears as Table 6.6.

Table 6.6 Results for Short Hedge: Stable Prices

	Cash	Futures
Time 1:	[Long at $3.50]	Short at $3.50
Time 2:	Short at $3.50	Long at $3.50
Gain (Loss):	$0.00	$0.00
Net Price:	$3.50 actual cash sale price ± $0.00 futures gain/loss = $3.50 net sale price	

In this example, there is no change in the value of either the cash position or the futures position, so the farmer received the same cash price at Time 2 as they would have received at Time 1 (ignoring production constraints and interest). Stated differently, the futures position had no impact on the sale price of the cash corn, so the net price was $3.50.

Stabilizing the Net Sale Price

Notice that in all three examples under this scenario the net sale price was $3.50, regardless of whether the price between Time 1 and Time 2 decreased (as in Example 6.4), or increased (as in Example 6.5), or was unchanged (as in Example 6.6). The results would have been the same for any price change up or down, or for no price change, underscoring the point that hedging locks in the net price.

Each of these three examples is a short hedge, in which a short futures position is used to protect the hedger from the effects of a price decrease. Because the hedger is effectively long cash corn, the hedger is sometimes described as being a *natural long* and therefore requires an offsetting short futures position as the hedging instrument. Also notice how the short futures position in all three examples is used as a temporary substitute for a cash commodity sale (i.e., a short cash position) at a later point in time. The farmer was unable to sell the cash corn at Time 1, so instead they sold a corn futures contract. Then at Time 2 they replaced the short futures position with a short cash position.

All six of the hedging examples presented in this chapter have a number of important real-world shortcomings. For one, the cash prices and futures prices were identical; this rarely happens. For another, the cash prices and futures prices changed by exactly the same amounts; this also rarely happens. However, as long as cash prices and futures prices are highly (if not perfectly) correlated, hedging will be effective.

More on the Role of Correlation: An Example from the Corn Market

The essential role of correlation can be demonstrated with a real-world example using cash corn prices in east central Illinois from December 15, 2011 through December 14, 2012. This one-year period was selected because prices were extremely volatile during the 2012 growing season, and the last day of the period corresponds to the last trading day for December 2012 corn futures.

Figure 6.1 shows how cash prices moved mostly sideways in a band between $6.00 and $7.00 until July, when an extended period of hot, dry weather put the growing crop in jeopardy. Prices then climbed above $8.00 and remained at that level until September. Once harvest was underway, prices drifted lower and then moved mostly sideways in a band between $7.00 and $8.00 for the remainder of the period.

Similarly, Figure 6.2 shows how December 2012 corn futures prices moved mostly sideways in a band between $5.00 and $6.00 until July. Prices then jumped to the $8.00 level and remained there until September, when they edged lower, and then moved mostly sideways around the mid-$7.00 level for the remainder of the period.

Cash prices and futures prices during this period traded at similar but not identical levels, and followed similar but not identical paths. When the cash and futures prices are plotted on the same graph, these differences appear as a gap between the two solid lines in Figure 6.3. The dollar value of this gap is plotted as the dotted line in Figure 6.3; notice that the right-hand scale has been adjusted to accommodate negative values that occurred in November. If cash and futures prices were equal, there would be no gap and the two solid lines would be superimposed one on top of the other. If the difference between cash and futures prices were constant, the gap between the two solid lines in Figure 6.3 would be uniform and the dotted line would be straight and horizontal.

Cash prices and futures prices can be highly correlated without the difference between them being zero or constant. In the case of the cash prices and futures prices in Figure 6.3, the correlation coefficient is +.966. Cash prices and futures prices for the same commodity tend to be highly correlated, all else the same.

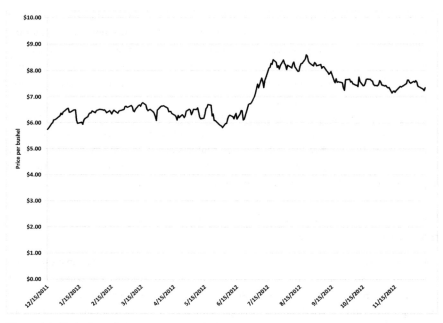

Figure 6.1 Cash Corn Prices, East Central Illinois

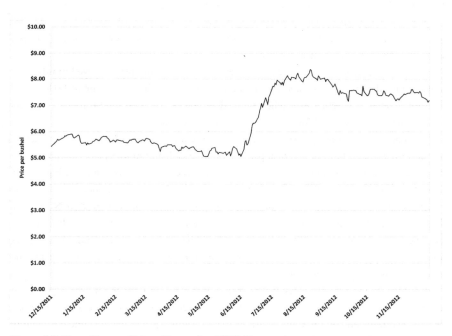

Figure 6.2 Corn Futures Prices, December 2012 Contract

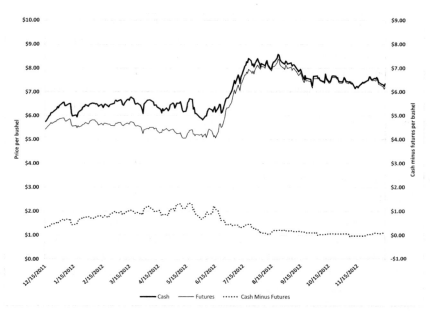

Figure 6.3 Cash Corn Prices, East Central Illinois, Corn Futures Prices, December 2012 Contract, and Cash Minus Futures

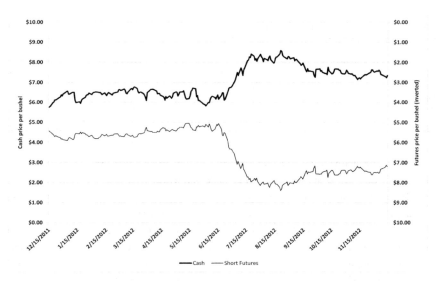

Figure 6.4 Long Cash Corn, East Central Illinois and Short Corn Futures, December 2012 Contract

Suppose a hedger has a long position in cash corn and a short position in corn futures, such as the farmer in Examples 6.4, 6.5, and 6.6. The prices for a long position in cash corn correspond to the heavy solid line in Figure 6.3. However, the prices for a short futures position are opposite (i.e., upside-down) those represented by the light solid line representing a long futures position in Figure 6.3. When these futures prices are inverted to reflect a short futures position, as in Figure 6.4, the offsetting effects of a short position and a long position become apparent. It then follows that for any commodity, holding opposite positions in cash and futures will stabilize the net price for the hedger.

Price Changes vs. Prices Levels: The Importance of Returns

The focus of this chapter – like the focus of most hedgers – is on prices and specifically on price levels, which are easy to observe, monitor, and interpret. But the feature that allows a hedge to perform effectively is not price itself, but *price change* or *return*, where the return is expressed in dollars and cents. This should not be confused with the rate of return, which would be expressed as a percentage.

From Examples 6.1, 6.2, and 6.3 with the processor, and Examples 6.4, 6.5, and 6.6 with the farmer, the cancelling-out effects of the hedges were due to equal-size and opposite-sign (i.e., + or −) price changes in cash and futures, and not the identical price levels used in all six examples. To illustrate this point, suppose that the futures prices in Example 6.4 had been at a substantially different price level – say, $100 higher – than the cash prices. Table 6.7 shows what the hedging results would have looked like.

Table 6.7 Results for Short Hedge: Falling Prices, and Futures Prices $100 Higher than Cash Prices

	Cash	*Futures*
Time 1:	[Long at $3.50]	Short at $103.50
Time 2:	Short at $3.00	Long at $103.00
Gain (Loss):	−$0.50	+$0.50
Net Price:	$3.00 actual cash sale price + $0.50 futures gain = $3.50 net sale price	

Despite the dramatically different cash and futures price levels used in Table 6.7, the outcome is identical to the result shown in Table 6.4, which used the same cash and futures price levels. The point of this example is to show that similar price levels for cash and futures is unimportant; similar price changes (i.e., returns) is what really matters for an effective hedge. Stated differently, the hedger is concerned about price changes, not price levels. It then follows that instead of using the correlation of cash and futures prices, a better gauge of potential hedging performance is the correlation of cash price changes and futures price changes. The correlation coefficient for the daily changes in cash and futures for December 15, 2011 through December 14, 2012 is +.889.

Notice how the Cash Minus Futures line in Figure 6.3 is much more stable than either the Cash price line or the Futures price line. The Cash Minus Futures line represents the *basis*. The basis is calculated as the cash price minus the futures price, or

Basis = Cash − Futures   (Equation 6.1)

The basis is simply the gap between the cash price and the futures price shown in Figure 6.3. Notice that basis values may be either positive or negative. If the basis is positive, as is the case most of the time in Figure 6.3, the futures price is less than the cash price; if the basis is negative, as is the case during most of November in Figure 6.3, the futures price is greater than the cash price. Basis behavior determines hedging performance, and for most commodities the basis is less volatile and more predictable than either the cash price or the futures price. In Chapter 7 we will take a closer look at the connection between hedging and the basis.

7 Hedging and the Basis

> The previous chapter demonstrated long hedging and short hedging with futures, and introduced the concept of the basis. In all those examples, the cash price and the futures price changed by identical amounts, so the price changes were perfectly correlated. In this chapter we will examine how hedging performance is affected when cash and futures prices change by different amounts – in other words, when the correlation of cash price changes and futures price changes is less than perfect – and how hedging performance is directly related to basis behavior.

Hedging and Basis Changes

Actual Values and Expected Values

Recall Table 6.1 from Chapter 6, in which a processor used a long futures position to hedge a short position in cash corn. The cash price and the futures price both increased by $1.00 per bushel.

Table 6.1 Results for Long Hedge: Rising Prices

	Cash	Futures
Time 1:	[Short at $3.50]	Long at $3.50
Time 2:	Long at $4.50	Short at $4.50
Gain (Loss):	−$1.00	+$1.00
Net Price:	$4.50 actual cash purchase price − $1.00 futures gain = $3.50 net purchase price	

To measure and evaluate basis behavior we need to add a column to this table for the basis values. We also incorporate the basis formula:

Basis = Cash − Futures   (Equation 6.1)

into the column headings to assist us with our basis calculations. This modified version of Table 6.1 will be designated as Table 7.1.

Table 7.1 Results for Long Hedge: Rising Prices, Basis Zero and Unchanged

	Cash	−	Futures	=	Basis
Time 1:	[Short at $3.50]		Long at $3.50		$0.00
Time 2:	Long at $4.50		Short at $4.50		$0.00
Gain (Loss):	−$1.00		+$1.00		$0.00
Net Price:	$4.50 actual cash purchase price − $1.00 futures gain = $3.50 net purchase price				

We also need to introduce the concepts of actual values and expected values. The *actual cash price* and the corresponding *actual basis* are the values that the hedger actually experiences, and for which actual dollars and actual commodities are exchanged. In Table 7.1, the hedger's actual cash price is $4.50; this is the price that the processor actually pays for cash corn.

The *expected cash price* and the corresponding *expected basis* are the values that the hedger expects to occur at some later date, and which serve as estimates for planning purposes. In Table 7.1, the hedger's expected cash price is $3.50; this is the price that the processor expects to pay at Time 2 when the actual cash transaction occurs. Sometimes these expected values are called the *target price* and the *target basis*, respectively, to underscore the fact that these values are goals, not results. The expected cash price and expected basis are selected by the hedger. They might be the values which exist at Time 1, and which the hedger hopes are still available at Time 2 when the actual transaction occurs, or they might be predicted values based on a formal forecast or an average of historical values. The difference between what the hedger expects and what the hedger actually experiences is an important measure of how well the hedge performs.

Basis Behavior and the Correlation of Returns

Recall from Chapter 6 that cash and futures prices are rarely the same, and rarely change by exactly the same amounts. These points were illustrated with an example from 2012, in which cash and futures prices were highly but not perfectly correlated, and basis values were relatively but not perfectly stable. In a real-world hedging situation it is highly unlikely that the gains and losses from the cash and futures positions will be exactly equal in size but opposite in sign (i.e., + or −). Stated differently, the cash returns and futures returns almost always will be less than perfectly positively correlated (i.e., $\rho < +1.0$) if the cash and futures positions are both long or both short, so the returns almost always will be less than perfectly negatively correlated (i.e., $\rho > -1.0$) if one position is long and the other position is short.

Correlation and the correlation coefficient are useful concepts for understanding the effects of offsetting long and short positions in a hedge, but they are not very useful for measuring the financial impact. For such a bottom-line, profit-and-loss assessment we need a dollars-and-cents measure, and this is why basis behavior is so important. The correlation of cash returns and futures returns for a hedge is rarely perfect, so the *basis change* is rarely zero. Over the life of a hedge the basis typically will become either *stronger* (i.e., more positive or less negative) or *weaker* (i.e., less positive or more negative).

Long Hedging and Basis Behavior

Rising Prices, Positive Initial Basis, and Basis Strengthens

To show how basis changes affect hedging results when prices are rising, we will present a series of variations on Table 7.1. We begin with Table 7.1A, which shows an initial basis of +$0.50 (rather than zero) that strengthens by $0.10 (rather than remains unchanged) over the life of the hedge.

Table 7.1A Results for Long Hedge: Rising Prices, Basis Positive and Strengthens

	Cash	−	Futures	=	Basis
Time 1:	[Short at $3.50]		Long at $3.00		+$0.50
Time 2:	Long at $4.50		Short at $3.90		+$0.60
Gain (Loss):	−$1.00		+$0.90		−$0.10
Net Price:	$4.50 actual cash purchase price − $0.90 futures gain = $3.60 net purchase price				

The gain on the futures position ($0.90) is subtracted from the actual cash purchase price ($4.50), which reduces the net purchase price to $3.60. The actual cash purchase price represents an outflow of funds; conversely, the futures gain represents an inflow of funds. Because these flows are in opposite directions, the futures gain must be subtracted from the actual cash purchase price to find the net price paid. Alternatively, the net purchase price shown at the bottom of Table 7.1A can be calculated by combining the expected cash price and the basis change:

$3.50 expected cash purchase price + $0.10 basis loss = $3.60 net purchase price

Notice that the basis loss ($0.10) is added to the expected cash purchase price ($3.50), which increases the net purchase price to $3.60. The expected cash purchase price represents an outflow of funds; the basis loss also represents an outflow of funds. Because these flows are in the same direction, the basis loss must be added to the expected cash purchase price to find the net price paid. Regardless of the calculation method used, the increase in the basis from +$0.50 to +$0.60 results in a $0.10 increase in the net purchase price. Consequently, a stronger (i.e., more positive or less negative) basis is harmful to a long hedger, all else the same.

Rising Prices, Positive Initial Basis, and Basis Weakens

Next, we again use an initial basis of +$0.50, but in this case the basis weakens (rather than strengthens) by $0.10 over the life of the hedge (see Table 7.1B).

Table 7.1B Results for Long Hedge: Rising Prices, Basis Positive and Weakens

	Cash	−	Futures	=	Basis
Time 1:	[Short at $3.50]		Long at $3.00		+$0.50
Time 2:	Long at $4.50		Short at $4.10		+$0.40
Gain (Loss):	−$1.00		+$1.10		+$0.10
Net Price:	$4.50 actual cash purchase price − $1.10 futures gain = $3.40 net purchase price				

As in Table 7.1A, the gain on the futures position ($1.10) is subtracted from the cash purchase price ($4.50), which reduces the net purchase price to $3.40. Once again, the actual cash purchase price represents an outflow of funds; conversely, the futures gain represents an inflow of funds. Because these flows are in opposite directions, the futures gain must be subtracted from the actual cash purchase price to find the net price paid. Alternatively, the net purchase price shown at the bottom of Table 7.1B can be calculated by combining the expected cash price and the basis change:

$3.50 expected cash purchase price − $0.10 basis gain = $3.40 net purchase price

Notice that the basis gain ($0.10) is subtracted from the expected purchase price ($3.50), which reduces the net purchase price to $3.40. The expected cash purchase price represents an outflow of funds; the basis gain represents an inflow of funds. Because these flows are in opposite directions, the basis gain must be subtracted from the expected cash purchase price to find the net price paid. For either calculation method, the decrease in the basis from +$0.50 to +$0.40 results in a $0.10 decrease in the net purchase price, so a weaker (i.e., less positive or more negative) basis is helpful to a long hedger, all else the same.

From these two examples, it appears that a long hedger is helped by a weaker basis and harmed by a stronger basis, all else the same. But this tentative conclusion is based only on examples using a positive initial basis, so next we will look at examples using a negative initial basis.

Rising Prices, Negative Initial Basis, and Basis Strengthens

To determine whether the impact of a changing basis differs when the beginning basis is negative, we begin with an initial basis of −$0.50, which strengthens by $0.10 over the life of the hedge (see Table 7.1C).

Table 7.1C Results for Long Hedge: Rising Prices, Basis Negative and Strengthens

	Cash	−	Futures	=	Basis
Time 1:	[Short at $3.50]		Long at $4.00		−$0.50
Time 2:	Long at $4.50		Short at $4.90		−$0.40
Gain (Loss):	−$1.00		+$0.90		−$0.10
Net Price:	$4.50 actual cash purchase price − $0.90 futures gain = $3.60 net purchase price				

The gain on the futures position ($0.90) is subtracted from the actual cash purchase price ($4.50), which reduces the net purchase price to $3.60, same as in Table 7.1A. The actual cash purchase price represents an outflow of funds; conversely, the futures gain represents an inflow of funds. Because these flows are in opposite directions, the futures gain must be subtracted from the actual cash purchase price to find the net price paid. Alternatively, the net purchase price shown at the bottom of Table 7.1C can be calculated by combining the expected cash price and the basis change:

$3.50 expected cash purchase price + $0.10 basis loss = $3.60 net purchase price

The basis loss ($0.10) is added to the expected cash purchase price ($3.50), which increases the net purchase price to $3.60, same as in Table 7.1A. The expected cash purchase price represents an outflow of funds; the basis loss also represents an outflow of funds. Because these flows are in the same direction, the basis loss must be added to the expected cash purchase price to find the net price paid. Once again, we find that a stronger (i.e., more positive or less negative) basis is harmful to a long hedger, all else the same.

Rising Prices, Negative Initial Basis, and Basis Weakens

We also examine the results for a negative initial basis (−$0.50), which weakens (by $0.10) over the life of the hedge (see Table 7.1D).

Table 7.1D Results for Long Hedge: Rising Prices, Basis Negative and Weakens

	Cash	−	Futures	=	Basis
Time 1:	[Short at $3.50]		Long at $4.00		−$0.50
Time 2:	Long at $4.50		Short at $5.10		−$0.60
Gain (Loss):	−$1.00		+$1.10		+$0.10
Net Price:	$4.50 actual cash purchase price − $1.10 futures gain = $3.40 net purchase price				

The gain on the futures position ($1.10) is subtracted from the cash purchase price ($4.50), which reduces the net purchase price to $3.40, identical to the result in Table 7.1B. The actual cash purchase price represents an outflow of funds; conversely, the futures gain represents an inflow of funds. Because these flows are in opposite directions, the futures gain must be subtracted from the actual cash purchase price to find the net price paid. Alternatively, the net purchase price shown at the bottom of Table 7.1D can be calculated by combining the expected cash price and the basis change:

$3.50 expected cash purchase price − $0.10 basis gain = $3.40 net purchase price

The basis gain ($0.10) is subtracted from the expected cash purchase price ($3.50), which reduces the net purchase price to $3.40, and which once again is exactly the same result as in Table 7.1B. The expected cash purchase price represents an outflow of funds; the basis gain represents an inflow of funds. Because these flows are in opposite directions, the basis gain must be subtracted from the expected cash purchase price to find the net price paid.

The results from Tables 7.1C and 7.1D agree with our results from Tables 7.1A and 7.1B, specifically that a long hedger is helped by a weaker basis and harmed by a stronger basis, all else the same. However, these findings are based only on examples using rising prices, so we need to examine hedging results with a stronger or weaker basis during a period of falling prices.

To determine the impact of basis changes on hedging results when prices are falling, we begin by adding a column for the basis values to Table 6.2 from Chapter 6. This modified version of Table 6.2 will be designated as Table 7.2.

Table 7.2 Results for Long Hedge: Falling Prices, Basis Zero and Unchanged

	Cash	−	Futures	=	Basis
Time 1:	[Short at $3.50]		Long at $3.50		$0.00
Time 2:	Long at $2.50		Short at $2.50		$0.00
Gain (Loss):	+$1.00		−$1.00		$0.00
Net Price:	$2.50 actual cash purchase price + $1.00 futures loss = $3.50 net purchase price				

Falling Prices, Positive Initial Basis, and Basis Strengthens

We then further modify this example so there is an initial basis of +$0.50 (rather than zero), and the basis strengthens by $0.10 (rather than remains unchanged) over the life of the hedge (see Table 7.2A).

Table 7.2A Results for Long Hedge: Falling Prices, Basis Positive and Strengthens

	Cash	−	Futures	=	Basis
Time 1:	[Short at $3.50]		Long at $3.00		+$0.50
Time 2:	Long at $2.50		Short at $1.90		+$0.60
Gain (Loss):	+$1.00		−$1.10		−$0.10
Net Price:	$2.50 actual cash purchase price + $1.10 futures loss = $3.60 net purchase price				

Alternatively, the net purchase price shown at the bottom of Table 7.2A can be calculated by combining the expected cash price and the basis change:

$3.50 expected cash purchase price + $0.10 basis loss = $3.60 net purchase price

As we observed earlier in Table 7.1A, the increase in the basis from +$0.50 to +$0.60 results in a $0.10 increase in the net purchase price. Therefore, a stronger (i.e., more positive or less negative) basis is harmful to a long hedger, all else the same.

Falling Prices, Positive Initial Basis, and Basis Weakens

Next, we use an initial basis of +$0.50 (same as in Table 7.2A), but in this case the basis weakens (rather than strengthens) by $0.10 (see Table 7.2B).

Table 7.2B Results for Long Hedge: Falling Prices, Basis Positive and Weakens

	Cash	—	Futures	=	Basis
Time 1:	[Short at $3.50]		Long at $3.00		+$0.50
Time 2:	Long at $2.50		Short at $2.10		+$0.40
Gain (Loss):	+$1.00		−$0.90		+$0.10
Net Price:	$2.50 actual cash purchase price + $0.90 futures loss =				
	$3.40 net purchase price				

Alternatively, the net purchase price shown at the bottom of Table 7.2B can be calculated by combining the expected cash price and the basis change:

$3.50 expected cash purchase price − $0.10 basis gain = $3.40 net purchase price

Notice that the decrease in the basis from +$0.50 to +$0.40 results in a $0.10 decrease in the net purchase price, which is the same result as in Table 7.1B. Therefore, a weaker (i.e., less positive or more negative) basis is helpful to a long hedger, all else the same.

Falling Prices, Negative Initial Basis, and Basis Strengthens

We also examine the results for a negative basis, using an initial basis of −$0.50, which strengthens by $0.10 over the life of the hedge (see Table 7.2C).

Table 7.2C Results for Long Hedge: Falling Prices, Basis Negative and Strengthens

	Cash	—	Futures	=	Basis
Time 1:	[Short at $3.50]		Long at $4.00		−$0.50
Time 2:	Long at $2.50		Short at $2.90		−$0.40
Gain (Loss):	+$1.00		−$1.10		−$0.10
Net Price:	$2.50 actual cash purchase price + $1.10 futures loss =				
	$3.60 net purchase price				

Alternatively, the net purchase price shown at the bottom of Table 7.2C can be calculated by combining the expected cash price and the basis change:

$3.50 expected cash purchase price + $0.10 basis loss = $3.60 net purchase price

The increase in the basis from −$0.50 to −$0.40 increases the net purchase price by $0.10. This is the same result as in Table 7.1C, so a stronger (i.e., more positive or less negative) basis is harmful to a long hedger, all else the same.

Falling Prices, Negative Initial Basis, and Basis Weakens

Finally, we also consider the results for a negative initial basis (−$0.50), which weakens (by $0.10) over the life of the hedge (see Table 7.2D).

Table 7.2D Results for Long Hedge: Falling Prices, Basis Negative and Weakens

	Cash	−	Futures	=	Basis
Time 1:	[Short at $3.50]		Long at $4.00		−$0.50
Time 2:	Long at $2.50		Short at $3.10		−$0.60
Gain (Loss):	+$1.00		−$0.90		+$0.10
Net Price:	$2.50 actual cash purchase price + $0.90 futures loss = $3.40 net purchase price				

Alternatively, the net purchase price shown at the bottom of Table 7.2D can be calculated by combining the expected cash price and the basis change:

$3.50 expected cash purchase price − $0.10 basis gain = $3.40 net purchase price

The decrease in the basis from −$0.50 to −$0.60 decreases the net purchase price by $0.10, demonstrating once again that a weaker (i.e., less positive or more negative) basis is helpful to a long hedger, all else the same.

Basis Impact on Long Hedging Results

From these long hedging examples, we see that hedging results are better than expected – in other words, the net purchase price is lower – if the basis weakens (i.e., Tables 7.1B, 7.1D, 7.2B, and 7.2D), and worse than expected – in other words, the net purchase price is higher – if the basis strengthens (i.e., Tables 7.1A, 7.1C, 7.2A, and 7.2C), regardless of whether prices are rising or falling. We can summarize these long hedging results as follows (see Table 7.3).

Table 7.3 Summary of Long Hedge Results with Basis Impact on Buyer

Table	Basis gain or loss	Expected purchase price	Actual purchase price	Change in net purchase price	Change in basis	Impact on buyer
7.1	$0.00	$3.50	$3.50	$0.00	None	n/a
7.1A	−$0.10	$3.50	$3.60	+$0.10	Stronger	Worse
7.1B	+$0.10	$3.50	$3.40	−$0.10	Weaker	Better
7.1C	−$0.10	$3.50	$3.60	+$0.10	Stronger	Worse
7.1D	+$0.10	$3.50	$3.40	−$0.10	Weaker	Better
7.2	$0.00	$3.50	$3.50	$0.00	None	n/a
7.2A	−$0.10	$3.50	$3.60	+$0.10	Stronger	Worse
7.2B	+$0.10	$3.50	$3.40	−$0.10	Weaker	Better
7.2C	−$0.10	$3.50	$3.60	+$0.10	Stronger	Worse
7.2D	+$0.10	$3.50	$3.40	−$0.10	Weaker	Better

Notice in each case how the basis gain or loss directly affects the net purchase price. A strengthening of the basis increases the net purchase price by an identical amount and results in a worse-than-expected outcome for the long hedger, while a weakening of the basis decreases the net purchase price cent-for-cent and results in a better-than-expected outcome.

Also notice that these results apply only to long hedgers. The second half of this chapter will explore the relationship between basis behavior and hedging performance for short hedgers.

Short Hedging and Basis Behavior

Recall Table 6.4 in Chapter 6, in which a farmer used a short futures position to hedge a long position in cash corn. The cash price and the futures price both decreased by $0.50 per bushel.

Table 6.4 Results for Short Hedge: Falling Prices

	Cash	Futures
Time 1:	[Long at $3.50]	Short at $3.50
Time 2:	Short at $3.00	Long at $3.00
Gain (Loss):	−$0.50	+$0.50
Net Price:	$3.00 actual cash sale price + $0.50 futures gain = $3.50 net sale price	

As before with the long hedging examples, we add a column for the basis values and incorporate the basis formula into the column headings to assist us with our basis calculations. This modified version of Table 6.4 will be designated as Table 7.4.

Table 7.4 Results for Short Hedge: Falling Prices, Basis Zero and Unchanged

	Cash	−	Futures	=	Basis
Time 1:	[Long at $3.50]		Short at $3.50		$0.00
Time 2:	Short at $3.00		Long at $3.00		$0.00
Gain (Loss):	−$0.50		+$0.50		$0.00
Net Price:	$3.00 actual cash sale price + $0.50 futures gain = $3.50 net sale price				

The expected cash price and the corresponding expected basis are the values that the hedger expects to occur at some later date, and which serve as estimates for planning purposes. In Table 7.4, the expected cash price is $3.50: this is the price that the farmer expects to receive at Time 2 when the actual cash transaction occurs. The actual cash price is $3.00: this is price that the farmer actually receives for cash corn at Time 2. The difference between what the hedger expects and what the hedger actually experiences, after futures returns have been included, or after basis changes have been taken into consideration, is an important measure of how well the hedge performs.

Falling Prices, Positive Initial Basis, and Basis Strengthens

To show how basis changes affect hedging results when prices are falling, we will present a series of variations on Table 7.4, beginning with an initial basis of +$0.50 (rather than zero), and the basis strengthens by $0.10 (rather than remains unchanged) over the life of the hedge (see Table 7.4A).

Table 7.4A Results for Short Hedge: Falling Prices, Basis Positive and Strengthens

	Cash	—	Futures	=	Basis
Time 1:	[Long at $3.50]		Short at $3.00		+$0.50
Time 2:	Short at $3.00		Long at $2.40		+$0.60
Gain (Loss):	−$0.50		+$0.60		+$0.10
Net Price:	$3.00 actual cash sale price + $0.60 futures gain = $3.60 net sale price				

The gain on the futures position ($0.60) is added to the actual cash sale price ($3.00), which increases the net sale price to $3.60. The actual cash sale price represents an inflow of funds; likewise, the futures gain represents an inflow of funds. Because these flows are in the same direction, the futures gain must be added to the actual cash purchase price to find the net price received. Alternatively, the net sale price shown at the bottom of Table 7.4A can be calculated by combining the expected cash price and the basis change:

$3.50 expected cash sale price + $0.10 basis gain = $3.60 net sale price

Notice that the basis gain ($0.10) is added to the expected cash sale price ($3.50), which increases the net sale price to $3.60. The expected cash sale price represents an inflow of funds; the basis gain also represents an inflow of funds. Because these flows are in the same direction, the basis gain must be added to the expected cash sale price to find the net price received. Regardless of the calculation method used, the increase in the basis from +$0.50 to +$0.60 results in a $0.10 increase in the net sale price. Consequently, a stronger (i.e., more positive or less negative) basis is helpful to a short hedger, all else the same. This is opposite the result we observed above for a long hedger, for which a stronger basis is harmful.

Falling Prices, Positive Initial Basis, and Basis Weakens

Next, we again use an initial basis of +$0.50, but in this case the basis weakens (rather than strengthens) by $0.10 over the life of the hedge (see Table 7.4B).

Table 7.4B Results for Short Hedge: Falling Prices, Basis Positive and Weakens

	Cash	—	Futures	=	Basis
Time 1:	[Long at $3.50]		Short at $3.00		+$0.50
Time 2:	Short at $3.00		Long at $2.60		+$0.40
Gain (Loss):	−$0.50		+$0.40		−$0.10
Net Price:	$3.00 actual cash sale price + $0.40 futures gain = $3.40 net sale price				

The gain on the futures position ($0.40) is added to the cash sale price ($3.00), which increases the net sale price to $3.40. Once again, the actual cash sale price represents an inflow of funds; likewise, the futures gain represents an inflow of funds. Because these flows are in the same direction, the futures gain must be added to the actual cash purchase price to find the net price received. Alternatively, the net sale price shown at the bottom of Table 7.4B can be calculated by combining the expected cash price and the basis change:

$3.50 expected cash sale price − $0.10 basis loss = $3.40 net sale price

Notice that the basis loss ($0.10) is subtracted from the expected sale price ($3.50), which reduces the net sale price to $3.40. The expected cash sale price represents an inflow of funds; the basis loss represents an outflow of funds. Because these flows are in opposite directions, the basis loss must be subtracted from the expected cash sale price to find the net price received. For either calculation method, the decrease in the basis from +$0.50 to +$0.40 results in a $0.10 decrease in the net sale price, so a weaker (i.e., less positive or more negative) basis is harmful to a short hedger, all else the same. This is opposite the result we observed above for a long hedger, for which a weaker basis is helpful.

From these two examples, it appears that a short hedger is helped by a stronger basis and harmed by a weaker basis, all else the same, when using a positive initial basis. Next, we will verify this finding with examples using a negative initial basis.

Falling Prices, Negative Initial Basis, and Basis Strengthens

We begin with an initial basis of −$0.50, which strengthens by $0.10 over the life of the hedge (see Table 7.4C).

Table 7.4C Results for Short Hedge: Falling Prices, Basis Negative and Strengthens

	Cash	−	Futures	=	Basis
Time 1:	[Long at $3.50]		Short at $4.00		−$0.50
Time 2:	Short at $3.00		Long at $3.40		−$0.40
Gain (Loss):	−$0.50		+$0.60		+$0.10
Net Price:	$3.00 actual cash sale price + $0.60 futures gain = $3.60 net sale price				

The gain on the futures position ($0.60) is added to the actual cash sale price ($3.00), which increases the net sale price to $3.60, same as in Table 7.4A. The actual cash sale price represents an inflow of funds; likewise, the futures gain represents an inflow of funds. Because these flows are in the same direction, the futures gain must be added to the actual cash purchase price to find the net price received. Alternatively, the net sale price shown at the bottom of Table 7.4C can be calculated by combining the expected cash price and the basis change:

$3.50 expected cash sale price + $0.10 basis gain = $3.60 net sale price

The basis gain ($0.10) is added to the expected cash sale price ($3.50), which increases the net sale price to $3.60, same as in Table 7.4A. The expected cash sale price represents an inflow of funds; the basis gain also represents an inflow of funds. Because these flows are in the same direction, the basis gain must be added to the expected cash sale price to find the net price received. Once again, we find that a stronger (i.e., more positive or less negative) basis is helpful to a short hedger, all else the same.

Falling Prices, Negative Initial Basis, and Basis Weakens

We also consider the results for a negative initial basis (−$0.50), which weakens (by $0.10) over the life of the hedge (see Table 7.4D).

Table 7.4D Results for Short Hedge: Falling Prices, Basis Negative and Weakens

	Cash	−	Futures	=	Basis
Time 1:)	[Long at $3.50]		Short at $4.00		−$0.50
Time 2:	Short at $3.00		Long at $3.60		−$0.60
Gain (Loss):	−$0.50		+$0.40		−$0.10
Net Price:	$3.00 actual cash sale price + $0.40 futures gain = $3.40 net sale price				

The gain on the futures position ($0.40) is added to the cash sale price ($3.00), which increases the net sale price to $3.40, identical to the result in Table 7.4B. The actual cash sale price represents an inflow of funds; likewise, the futures gain represents an inflow of funds. Because these flows are in the same direction, the futures gain must be added to the actual cash purchase price to find the net price received. Alternatively, the net sale price shown at the bottom of Table 7.4D can be calculated by combining the expected cash price and the basis change:

$3.50 expected cash sale price − $0.10 basis loss = $3.40 net sale price

The basis loss ($0.10) is subtracted from the expected cash sale price ($3.50), which reduces the net sale price to $3.40, and which once again is exactly the same result as in Table 7.4B. The expected cash sale price represents an inflow of funds; the basis loss represents an outflow of funds. Because these flows are in opposite directions, the basis loss must be subtracted from the expected cash sale price to find the net price received.

The results for Tables 7.4C and 7.4D agree with our results from Tables 7.4A and 7.4B, specifically that a short hedger is helped by a stronger basis and harmed by a weaker basis, all else the same. These findings are based only on examples using falling prices, so we will complete our review by examining hedging results with a stronger or weaker basis during periods of rising prices.

To determine the impact of basis changes on hedging results when prices are rising, we begin by adding a column for the basis values to Table 6.5 from Chapter 6, which will be designated as Table 7.5.

Table 7.5 Results for Short Hedge: Rising Prices, Basis Zero and Unchanged

	Cash	−	Futures	=	Basis
Time 1:	[Long at $3.50]		Short at $3.50		$0.00
Time 2:	Short at $4.00		Long at $4.00		$0.00
Gain (Loss):	+$0.50		−$0.50		$0.00
Net Price:	$4.00 actual cash sale price − $0.50 futures loss = $3.50 net sale price				

Rising Prices, Positive Initial Basis, and Basis Strengthens

We will further modify this example so there is an initial basis of +$0.50 (rather than zero), and the basis strengthens by $0.10 (rather than remains unchanged) over the life of the hedge (see Table 7.5A).

Table 7.5A Results for Short Hedge: Rising Prices, Basis Positive and Strengthens

	Cash	−	Futures	=	Basis
Time 1:	[Long at $3.50]		Short at $3.00		+$0.50
Time 2:	Short at $4.00		Long at $3.40		+$0.60
Gain (Loss):	+$0.50		−$0.40		+$0.10
Net Price:	$4.00 actual cash sale price − $0.40 futures loss = $3.60 net sale price				

Alternatively, the net sale price shown at the bottom of Table 7.5A can be calculated by combining the expected cash price and the basis change:

$3.50 expected cash sale price + $0.10 basis gain = $3.60 net sale price

As we observed earlier in Table 7.4A, the increase in the basis from +$0.50 to +$0.60 results in a $0.10 increase in the net sale price. Therefore, a stronger (i.e., more positive or less negative) basis is helpful to a short hedger, all else the same.

Rising Prices, Positive Initial Basis, and Basis Weakens

Next, we use an initial basis of +$0.50 (same as in Table 7.5A), but in this case the basis weakens (rather than strengthens) by $0.10 (see Table 7.5B).

Alternatively, the net sale price shown at the bottom of Table 7.5B can be calculated by combining the expected cash price and the basis change:

$3.50 expected cash sale price − $0.10 basis loss = $3.40 net sale price

Table 7.5B Results for Short Hedge: Rising Prices, Basis Positive and Weakens

	Cash	−	Futures	=	Basis
Time 1:	[Long at $3.50]		Short at $3.00		+$0.50
Time 2:	Short at $4.00		Long at $3.60		+$0.40
Gain (Loss):	+$0.50		−$0.60		−$0.10
Net Price:	$4.00 actual cash sale price − $0.60 futures loss = $3.40 net sale price				

Notice that the decrease in the basis from +$0.50 to +$0.40 results in a $0.10 decrease in the net sale price, same as in Table 7.4B. Therefore, a weaker (i.e., less positive or more negative) basis is harmful to a short hedger, all else the same.

Rising Prices, Negative Initial Basis, and Basis Strengthens

We also examine the results for a negative basis, using an initial basis of −$0.50, which strengthens by $0.10 over the life of the hedge (see Table 7.5C).

Table 7.5C Results for Short Hedge: Rising Prices, Basis Negative and Strengthens

	Cash	−	Futures	=	Basis
Time 1:	[Long at $3.50]		Short at $4.00		−$0.50
Time 2:	Short at $4.00		Long at $4.40		−$0.40
Gain (Loss):	+$0.50		−$0.40		+$0.10
Net Price:	$4.00 actual cash sale price − $0.40 futures loss = $3.60 net sale price				

Alternatively, the net sale price shown at the bottom of Table 7.5C can be calculated by combining the expected cash price and the basis change:

$3.50 expected cash sale price + $0.10 basis gain = $3.60 net sale price

The increase in the basis from −$0.50 to −$0.40 increases the net sale price by $0.10. This is the same result as in Table 7.4C, so a stronger (i.e., more positive or less negative) basis is helpful to a short hedger, all else the same.

Rising Prices, Negative Initial Basis, and Basis Weakens

Finally, we also consider the results for a negative initial basis (−$0.50), which weakens (by $0.10) over the life of the hedge (see Table 7.5D).

Alternatively, the net sale price shown at the bottom of Table 7.5D can be calculated by combining the expected cash price and the basis change:

$3.50 expected cash sale price − $0.10 basis loss = $3.40 net sale price

The decrease in the basis from −$0.50 to −$0.60 decreases the net sale price by $0.10, demonstrating once again that a weaker (i.e., less positive or more negative) basis is harmful to a short hedger, all else the same.

Basis Impact on Short Hedging Results

From these short hedging examples, we see that hedging results are better than expected – in other words, the net sale price is higher – if the basis strengthens (Tables 7.4A, 7.4C, 7.5A, and 7.5C), and worse than expected – in other words, the net sale price is lower – if the basis weakens (Tables 7.4B, 7.4D, 7.5B, and 7.5D). These are opposite the results for a long hedger, which was harmed by a stronger basis and helped by a weaker basis.

Table 7.5D Results for Short Hedge: Rising Prices, Basis Negative and Weakens

	Cash	−	Futures	=	Basis
Time 1:	[Long at $3.50]		Short at $4.00		−$0.50
Time 2:	Short at $4.00		Long at $4.60		−$0.60
Gain (Loss):	+$0.50		−$0.60		−$0.10
Net Price:	$4.00 actual cash sale price − $0.60 futures loss = $3.40 net sale price				

We can summarize these short hedging results as shown in Table 7.6. Notice how in each case the basis gain or loss directly affects the net sale price. However, the basis impact for short hedgers is opposite the impact for long hedgers. For short hedgers, a strengthening of the basis increases the net sale price by an identical amount and results in a better-than-expected outcome, while a weakening of the basis decreases the net sale price by the same amount and results in a worse-than-expected outcome.

Table 7.6 Summary of Short Hedge Results with Basis Impact on Seller

Table	Basis gain or loss	Expected sale price	Actual sale price	Change in net saleprice	Change in basis	Impact on seller
7.4	$0.00	$3.50	$3.50	$0.00	None	n/a
7.4A	+$0.10	$3.50	$3.60	+$0.10	Stronger	Better
7.4B	−$0.10	$3.50	$3.40	−$0.10	Weaker	Worse
7.4C	+$0.10	$3.50	$3.60	+$0.10	Stronger	Better
7.4D	−$0.10	$3.50	$3.40	−$0.10	Weaker	Worse
7.5	$0.00	$3.50	$3.50	$0.00	None	n/a
7.5A	+$0.10	$3.50	$3.60	+$0.10	Stronger	Better
7.5B	−$0.10	$3.50	$3.40	−$0.10	Weaker	Worse
7.5C	+$0.10	$3.50	$3.60	+$0.10	Stronger	Better
7.5D	−$0.10	$3.50	$3.40	−$0.10	Weaker	Worse

Although the basis is simply the residual or difference between the cash price and the futures prices, we can treat the basis as a tangible, tradable value that can be bought and sold like any other derivative. We will discuss basis trading in Chapter 10, after we cover advanced hedging methods in Chapters 8 and 9.

8 Hedging Enhancements

The hedging examples presented thus far have assumed that the hedger establishes a futures position to *place the hedge* and maintains it until the expected purchase/sale date, when the hedger liquidates the futures position to *lift the hedge*. In practice, hedging usually is not this straightforward, and the hedger's plans frequently change between the time the hedge is placed and the time it is lifted. These examples also assumed that the commodity being hedged always had a corresponding futures contract. In practice, there are only a few dozen actively-traded futures contracts for the many thousands of different commodities that might need to be a hedged. The first part of this chapter examines how a hedge can be modified when there is a change in plans, and the second part shows how a commodity with no corresponding futures contract can be hedged effectively with a futures contract for a different underlying commodity.

Types of Hedges

Anticipatory Hedge

Each of the hedging examples presented in Chapter 6 and Chapter 7 is an example of an *anticipatory hedge*, because a futures position is used now as a temporary substitute for a cash market position that will be taken later. For both the processor and the farmer in our examples, there were no actual dollars or actual commodities exchanged at Time 1, but a transaction was anticipated or expected at Time 2. In each example the Time 1 cash positions used brackets to denote an implicit position, and the Time 1 futures position served as a temporary substitute for a cash position taken at Time 2. Notice that it is always possible to buy or sell a futures position, even when it is difficult or even impossible to buy or sell a cash commodity. Recall that the processor didn't have either the funds or the storage space to buy the cash corn, and the farmer wasn't able to sell the cash corn because the crop had not yet been harvested.

Inventory Hedge

Alternatively the hedger might begin with an actual, tangible cash position at Time 1, which it hedged with an offsetting futures position. This is commonly referred to as an *inventory hedge*, but is also known as a storage hedge (because the commodity has been stored), or production hedge (because the commodity has been produced), or transactional hedge (because the cash market transaction has already occurred). Regardless of the particular name used, an actual cash position already exists or has been established, so no brackets are used, and the futures position is used to offset any price change in the cash commodity. We can use the basic details of Example 6.1 and Table 7.1 to create an inventory hedge, which will be designated as Example 8.1.

Example 8.1: A processor buys and uses corn as part of its normal operations. Several months before Time 1, when prices were falling, it agreed to sell its surplus inventory of corn at whatever the market price happened to be at Time 1, expecting that it could buy back the corn later at a lower price. But when Time 1 arrives the processor has changed its mind and now expects corn prices to rise, so it buys corn futures at Time 1 to offset the sale agreement and lock in the price. At some later date it buys cash corn and simultaneously sells corn futures to liquidate its futures position. Assume the processor was right about the market direction, and when Time 2 arrives the cash price had increased from $3.50 per bushel to $4.50 per bushel (see Table 8.1).

Table 8.1 Results for Long Hedge: Rising Prices, Basis Zero and Unchanged

	Cash	−	Futures	=	Basis
Time 1:	Short at $3.5]		Long at $3.50		$0.00
Time 2:	Long at $4.50		Short at $4.50		$0.00
Gain (Loss):	−$1.00		+$1.00		$0.00
Net Price:	$4.50 actual cash purchase price − $1.00 futures gain =				
	$3.50 net purchase price				

Inventory hedges can be constructed to protect the hedger from the effects of a price increase, as in Example 8.1, by using a long futures position to offset the effects of a short cash position. In this situation a sale of the cash commodity has occurred – or an equivalent obligation such as a forward contract to sell the cash commodity has been created – and therefore a short cash position actually exists. The long futures position is used to offset the price change in the cash commodity between now and some later date when the cash position is liquidated.

We also can use the basic details of Example 6.4 and Table 7.4 to create an inventory hedge, which will be designated as Example 8.2.

Example 8.2: A farmer grows and sells corn as part of their normal operations. They have harvested corn which they have put into storage, and they believe prices might drop over the course of the next several months. However, they are unwilling to sell cash corn right now because of potential income tax issues. Instead, they sell corn futures at Time 1 to lock in the price. At some future date after the beginning of a new tax year, they sell cash corn and simultaneously buy corn futures to liquidate their futures position. Assume the farmer was right about the market direction, and when Time 2 arrives the cash price had decreased from $3.50 per bushel to $3.00 per bushel (see Table 8.2).

Table 8.2 Results for Short Hedge: Falling Prices, Basis Zero and Unchanged

	Cash	−	Futures	=	Basis
Time 1:	[Long at $3.50]		Short at $3.50		$0.00
Time 2:	Short at $3.00		Long at $3.00		$0.00
Gain (Loss):	−$0.50		+$0.50		$0.00
Net Price:	$3.00 actual cash sale price + $0.50 futures gain = $3.50 net sale price				

Inventory hedges can be constructed to protect the hedger from the effects of a price decrease, as in Example 8.2, by using a short futures position to offset the effects of a long cash position. In this situation a cash market purchase has occurred – or an equivalent obligation such as a forward contract to purchase the cash commodity has been created – and therefore a long cash position actually exists. The short futures position is used to offset the price change in the cash commodity between now and some later date when the cash position is liquidated.

For the purposes of this book we will not distinguish between anticipatory hedges and inventory hedges, beyond using square brackets to designate implicit cash positions. Anticipatory hedges and inventory hedges may receive different accounting treatment. However, the accounting treatment of hedges is a complex topic that is beyond the scope of this book.

Rolling a Hedge

Reasons for Rolling a Hedge

Sometimes a hedger's plans will change between the time the hedge is placed and when it is scheduled to be lifted. Because of this change in plans, the hedge may need to continue after the expected termination date, or it may need to end before the expected termination date. In either case, this often requires the hedger to *roll the hedge* to a different contract month. A hedge also may be rolled because the hedger observes a profitable basis trading opportunity – covered in Chapter 10 – and is willing to adjust the purchase or sale date for the cash commodity.

Rolling a hedge requires the simultaneous liquidation of the existing futures position and the creation of a new futures position in a different contract month. This is best accomplished with a *spread* order, in which one contract is purchased and the other is sold at the same time, typically at some specified price relationship or differential between the two contract months. Using a spread order guarantees that both *legs* or positions of the spread will be filled if the order is executed. Otherwise, there is a possibility that the existing futures position will be eliminated but the new futures position will not be created, leaving the hedger with an *unhedged* cash position. Alternatively, there is a possibility that the existing futures position is not eliminated and a new futures position is created, leaving the hedger *double hedged* with an additional futures position that has no corresponding cash position. Either situation can occur if the hedger attempts to roll the hedge using two separate orders – one order for the existing futures position and another order for the new futures position – and one of the orders is not executed.

Rolling Forward a Long Hedge

We will illustrate rolling a long hedge by beginning with Table 7.1B for our hypothetical processor.

Table 7.1B Results for Long Hedge: Rising Prices, Basis Positive and Weakens

	Cash	–	Futures	=	Basis
Time 1:	[Short at $3.50]		Long at $3.00		+$0.50
Time 2:	Long at $4.50		Short at $4.10		+$0.40
Gain (Loss):	–$1.00		+$1.10		+$0.10
Net Price:	$4.50 actual cash purchase price – $1.10 futures gain = $3.40 net purchase price				

We modify this example, which will be designated as Table 8.3, by adding the alternative calculation for the net purchase price using the basis gain/loss, by replacing Time 1 and Time 2 with calendar months, and by inserting specific futures contract months and corresponding calendar years, designated Y1 and Y2, when the hedge spans two different calendar years.

Table 8.3 Results for Long Hedge: Rising Prices, Basis Positive and Weakens

	Cash	–	Futures	=	Basis
Oct Y1	[Short at $3.50]		Long MarY2 at $3.00		+$0.50
Feb Y2:	Long at $4.50		Short MarY2 at $4.10		+$0.40
Gain (Loss):	–$1.00		+$1.10		+$0.10
Net Price:	$4.50 actual cash purchase price – $1.10 futures gain = $3.40 net purchase price				
or:	$3.50 expected cash purchase price – $0.10 basis gain = $3.40 net purchase price				

Notice that the hedger uses the March contract month to hedge its planned purchase in February. In the case of corn futures there is no February contract month; the available months are March, May, July, September, and December. Hedgers typically use the contract month which expires on or immediately following the date of the cash transaction. This is done so the market conditions reflected by the futures contract will most closely match those of the cash transaction, and consequently provide the best correlation between cash and futures. It also prevents the futures contract from expiring before the date of the cash transaction, which would leave the hedger unhedged.

Also notice that we will use the three-letter month abbreviations for the remainder of this book (see Table 8.4).

Table 8.4 Abbreviations for Calendar Months and Contract Months

Month	Abbreviation	Month	Abbreviation
January	Jan	July	Jul
February	Feb	August	Aug
March	Mar	September	Sep
April	Apr	October	Oct
May	May	November	Nov
June	Jun	December	Dec

Suppose that the processing plant placed the hedge in October of one calendar year, designated Y1, and planned to maintain the hedge until February of the following calendar year, designated Y2. However, in December the processing plant experiences a serious breakdown, and operations are suspended for 2 months while repairs are being made. The hedge was performing as expected, but now the corn that normally would have been used in February will not be needed until April. Rather than terminate the hedge and reinstate it after the plant is back in operation, the processor can *roll forward* the hedge by 2 months so the expiration date more closely matches the new April date when the cash corn should be purchased.

To roll forward this hedge, the hedger sells the March futures contract and simultaneously buys the May futures contract. On the December date when the hedge is rolled, the cash price is $4.30 and March futures are trading at $3.90, so the basis for the March futures contract has weakened to +$0.40 (= $4.30 − $3.90). At the same time, May futures are trading at $4.05, so the basis for the May futures contract is +$0.25 (= $4.30 − $4.05). Partial results through December, after the futures position has been rolled, are presented in Table 8.5–Partial.

Table 8.5 Results for Long Hedge: Rising Prices, Basis Positive and Weakens, Rolled Forward (Partial)

	Cash	−	Futures	=	Basis
OctY1:	[Short at $3.50]		Long MarY2 at $3.00		+$0.50
DecY1:	{$4.30}		Short MarY2 at $3.90		+$0.40
DecY1:	{$4.30}		Long MayY2 at $4.05		+$0.25

The processing plant resumes operation in February. In April the processor buys the cash corn that was originally scheduled to be purchased in February and simultaneously sells the May futures position to lift the hedge. On the April date when the cash corn is purchased and the futures position is liquidated, the cash price is $4.60 and May futures are trading at $4.55, so the basis is +$0.05. Final results through April are presented in Table 8.5.

Notice that the $4.30 cash price in December, shown in curved brackets, is used simply as a reference price for calculating the basis values; no cash transaction occurs until April

Table 8.5 Results for Long Hedge: Rising Prices, Basis Positive and Weakens, Rolled Forward

	Cash	−	Futures	=	Basis
OctY1:	[Short at $3.50]		Long MarY2 at $3.00		+$0.50
DecY1:	{$4.30}		Short MarY2 at $3.90		+$0.40
DecY1:	{$4.30}		Long MayY2 at $4.05		+$0.25
AprY2:	Long at $4.60		Short MayY2 at $4.55		+$0.05
Gain (Loss):	−$1.10		+$0.90 on MarY2 +		+$0.10 on MarY2 +
			+$0.50 on MayY2		+$0.20 on MayY2
Net Price:	$4.60 actual cash purchase price −				
	$0.90 futures gain on MarY2 (= $3.90 − $3.00) −				
	$0.50 futures gain on MayY2 (= $4.55 − $4.05) =				
	$3.20 net purchase price				
or:	$3.50 expected cash purchase price −				
	$0.10 basis gain on MarY2 (= +$0.50 − $0.40) −				
	$0.20 basis gain on MayY2 (= +$0.25 − $0.05) =				
	$3.20 net purchase price				

when the cash corn is purchased. Also notice that the gains or losses on the futures positions and on the basis positions are calculated separately for each futures contract. Finally, notice that in this particular example the processor captured a basis gain on both the March futures contract and the May futures contract. Consequently the $3.20 net purchase price was $0.30 less than the $3.50 expected purchase price, because of the combined $0.30 basis gain from the two different futures contract months. Depending on market conditions, the hedger may experience a basis gain on all parts of the hedge, a basis gain on some part(s) of the hedge and a basis loss on the other part(s), or a basis loss on all parts. The final outcome from rolling a hedge is directly related to basis behavior, and the difference between the expected purchase price and the actual (net) purchase price is equal to the basis gain or loss. We will not demonstrate how to roll forward a short hedge, but the principles behind rolling forward a short hedge are identical to those presented here for rolling forward a long hedge.

Rolling Back a Short Hedge

In the event that a cash transaction must be made sooner (rather than later) than originally expected, it is possible to *roll back* the hedge to an earlier date. We will illustrate rolling back a short hedge by beginning with Table 7.4C for our hypothetical farmer.

We modify this example, which will be designated as Table 8.6, by adding the alternative calculation for the net purchase price using the basis gain/loss, by replacing Time 1 and Time 2 with calendar months, and by inserting specific futures contract months and corresponding calendar years, designated Y1 and Y2, when the hedge spans two different calendar years.

Notice that the hedger uses the July contract month to hedge its planned sale in June. The July contract expires closest to and immediately following the scheduled date of the cash transaction, and therefore will provide the best correlation between cash and futures.

Table 7.4C Results for Short Hedge: Falling Prices, Basis Negative and Strengthens

	Cash	–	Futures	=	Basis
Time 1:	[Long at $3.50]		Short at $4.00		–$0.50
Time 2:	Short at $3.00		Long at $3.40		–$0.40
Gain (Loss):	–$0.50		+$0.60		+$0.10
Net Price:	$3.00 actual cash sale price + $0.60 futures gain = $3.60 net sale price				

Table 8.6 Results for Short Hedge: Falling Prices, Basis Negative and Strengthens

	Cash	–	Futures	=	Basis
AugY1:	[Long at $3.50]		Short JulY2 at $4.00		–$0.50
JunY2:	Short at $3.00		Long JulY2 at $3.40		–$0.40
Gain (Loss):	–$0.50		+$0.60		+$0.10
Net Price:	$3.00 actual cash sale price + $0.60 futures gain = $3.60 net sale price				
or:	$3.50 expected cash sale price + $0.10 basis gain = $3.60 net sale price				

Suppose that the farmer placed the hedge in August of one calendar year, designated Y1, and planned to maintain the hedge until June of the following calendar year, designated Y2. However, in November the farmer learns that a neighboring farm will be sold in February, and the farmer may need to sell the cash corn sooner than originally expected if they are the winning bidder. Rather than simply terminate the existing hedge early if it becomes necessary, the farmer can *roll back* the hedge by four months so the expiration date more closely matches the new February date when the cash corn may be sold.

To roll back this hedge, the hedger buys the July futures contract and simultaneously sells the March futures contract. On the November date when the hedge is rolled, the cash price is $3.30 and July futures are trading at $3.70, so the basis for the July futures contract has strengthened to –$0.40 (= $3.30 – $3.70). At the same time, March futures are trading at $3.55, so the basis for the March futures contract is –$0.25 (= $3.30 – $3.55). Partial results through November, after the futures position has been rolled, are presented in Table 8.7–Partial.

Table 8.7 Results for Short Hedge: Falling Prices, Basis Negative and Strengthens, Rolled Back (Partial)

	Cash	–	Futures	=	Basis
AugY1:	[Long at $3.50]		Short JulY2 at $4.00		–$0.50
NovY1	{$3.30}		Long JulY2 at $3.70		–$0.40
NovY1	{$3.30}		Short MarY2 at $3.55		–$0.25

In February, the farmer is the winning bidder at the auction for the neighboring farm, so they sell the cash corn that was originally scheduled to be sold in June and simultaneously buy the March futures position to lift the hedge. On the February date when the cash corn is sold and the futures position is liquidated, the cash price is $3.00 and March futures are trading at $3.15, so the basis is −$0.15. Final results through February are presented in Table 8.7.

Table 8.7 Results for Short Hedge: Falling Prices, Basis Negative and Strengthens, Rolled Back

	Cash	−	*Futures*	=	*Basis*
AugY1:	[Long at $3.50]		Short JulY2 at $4.00		−$0.50
NovY1	{$3.30}		Long JulY2 at $3.70		−$0.40
NovY1	{$3.30}		Short MarY2 at $3.55		−$0.25
FebY2:	Short at $3.00		Long MarY2 at $3.15		−$0.15
Gain (Loss):	−$0.50		+$0.60		+$0.10
Net Price:	$3.00 actual cash sale price + $0.30 futures gain on JulY2 (= $4.00 − $3.70) + $0.40 futures gain on MarY2 (= $3.55 − $3.15) = $3.70 net sale price				
or:	$3.50 expected cash sale price + $0.10 basis gain on JulY2 (= −$0.40 + $0.50) + $0.10 basis gain on MarY2 (= −$0.25 + $0.15) = $3.70 net sale price				

Notice that the $3.30 cash price in November, shown in curved brackets, is used simply as a reference price for calculating the basis values; no cash transaction occurs until February when the cash corn is sold. Also notice that the gains or losses on the futures positions and on the basis positions are calculated separately for each futures contract. Finally, notice that in this particular example the farmer captured a basis gain on both the July futures contract and the March futures contract. Consequently the $3.70 net sale price was $0.20 more than the $3.50 expected sale price, because of the combined $0.20 basis gain from the two different futures contract months. As in the previous example, the final outcome from rolling a hedge is directly related to basis behavior, and the difference between the expected sale price and the net sale price is equal to the basis gain or loss. Also as in the previous example, we will not demonstrate how to roll back a long hedge, but the principles behind rolling back a long hedge are identical to those presented here for rolling back a short hedge.

Limits on Rolling Forward or Rolling Back

Suppose that the farmer was not the winning bidder for the farmland and therefore did not need to sell cash corn in February. The farmer then could have rolled the hedge forward to the July futures contract and resumed their original strategy of waiting until June to sell cash corn, or they could have formulated an entirely new hedging strategy and rolled to any other futures contract month consistent with that strategy. There is no practical limit to the number of times a hedge may be rolled forward or rolled back. However, each time a hedge is rolled, the hedger will lose the bid-ask spread plus related transaction costs on both the old and new futures positions.

Cross-Hedging

Why Cross-Hedging is Necessary

In all of our hedging examples thus far we have assumed – or at least left the impression – that there is always a futures contract available that matches the underlying cash commodity being hedged. In fact, most cash commodities do not have corresponding futures contracts, and consequently cash commodities frequently are hedged using futures contracts for other commodities. Hedging one commodity using a futures contract for a different underlying commodity is known as *cross-hedging*.

There are far fewer liquid futures contracts on physical commodities than the many thousands of commodities that potentially need to be hedged. From a supply-of-futures-contracts standpoint, there is only a finite amount of liquidity available at any point in time, and therefore the futures markets can support only a limited number of liquid futures contracts. From a demand-for-futures-contracts standpoint, hedgers require a high degree of liquidity, and generally will accept a higher level of basis risk in return for a higher level of liquidity. Consequently, futures trading activity tends to be concentrated in a relatively small number of highly liquid contracts, which are used for a wide range of regular hedging and cross-hedging applications. Although cross-hedging typically involves a higher level of basis risk, all else the same, a hedger typically will be better off by cross-hedging than by not hedging at all. Often there will be a futures contract for a commodity with similar supply/demand characteristics and similar price behavior as the commodity being hedged, which helps keep basis risk to a manageable level.

For example, the underlying physical commodity for the corn futures contract is yellow corn, which is the predominant type raised in the US. There is no futures contract for white corn, which is used for corn chips and other food items. However, white corn prices are highly correlated with yellow corn prices, so the corn futures contract serves as an effective hedging tool, and may be used bushel-for-bushel to hedge white corn purchases or sales. Yellow corn thus serves as a benchmark or reference price for all corn traded in the US.

Cross-Hedging Grain Sorghum Using Corn Futures

Similarly, there is no futures contract for grain sorghum (also known as milo), which is used as a substitute for corn in livestock feed, often in areas with too little rainfall to raise corn. Since grain sorghum and corn are substitutes, and the price levels and price changes of the two commodities are highly correlated, grain sorghum can be hedged effectively using corn futures. A comparison of daily cash prices for grain sorghum and daily nearby corn futures prices for January 2001 through December 2016 is shown in Figure 8.1.

Often the commodity being hedged and the commodity underlying the futures contract have different units of measure (e.g., pounds vs. tons), and therefore different pricing conventions. For example, corn is priced in dollars per bushel, abbreviated "bu," where 1 bushel of corn equals 56 pounds, abbreviated "lbs," while grain sorghum is commonly priced in dollars per hundredweight, abbreviated "cwt," where 1 hundredweight equals 100 pounds.

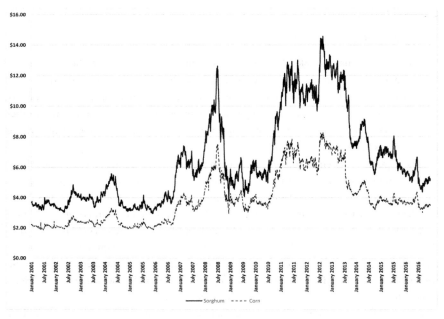

Figure 8.1 Grain Sorghum Cash Prices ($/cwt), Texas Triangle Region and Corn Futures Prices ($/bu), Nearby Contract, January 2001–December 2016

To hedge grain sorghum using corn futures, we need to know how many bushels of corn futures are needed to hedge 1 hundredweight of grain sorghum, which is known as the *hedge ratio*. Then, for a particular quantity of grain sorghum to be hedged, we can use the hedge ratio to determine how many corn futures contracts should be used. It also would be useful to know beforehand how effective the cross-hedge should be at managing the price risk for grain sorghum, which is known as *hedging effectiveness*.

The hedge ratio can be determined via linear regression using ordinary least squares (OLS) to regress the change in grain sorghum prices against the change in corn futures prices. The regression equation can be expressed as:

$$\text{Change in Grain Sorghum Price} = \alpha + \beta \times (\text{Change in Corn Futures Price}) + \varepsilon$$

where α = intercept of regression line on y-axis
        β = slope of regression line
        ε = residual term

Both Change in Grain Sorghum Price and Change in Corn Futures Price are calculated using the daily prices for sorghum and corn, respectively, shown in Figure 8.1. After adjusting for holidays and other missing values, there were 3,882 days with price change (i.e., return) observations for both variables over this 16-year period.

Regression Equation

The regression results are presented in Table 8.8, with the following coefficients:

- α = Intercept = −8.1638E-05
- β = Slope = 1.399539526

so the regression equation can be expressed as:

Change in Grain Sorghum Price = −8.1638E-05 + (1.399539526 × Change in Corn Futures Price)

Notice that the values for the intercept coefficient α and slope coefficient β represent average values based on the entire 2001–2016 period. Using different time periods likely would produce different values, so regression results are sensitive to the time period used. Also notice that the residual term ε is equal to zero, on average, but typically will not be equal to zero on any particular day.

Hedge Ratio

The regression equation indicates that each hundredweight of grain sorghum should be hedged with 1.399539526 bushels of corn futures. Therefore the slope coefficient β is the

Table 8.8 Results for Linear Regression of Change in Grain Sorghum Cash Prices on Change in Corn Futures Prices, Daily, January 2001–December 2006

SUMMARY OUTPUT

Regression Statistics	
Multiple R	0.825070284
R Square	0.680740974
Adjusted R Square	0.680658691
Standard Error	0.087471724
Observations	3882

ANOVA

	df	*SS*	*MS*	*F*	*Significance F*
Regression	1	63.30030495	63.3003	8273.141	0
Residual	3880	29.68705345	0.007651		
Total	3881	92.9873584			

	Coefficients	*Standard Error*	*t Stat*	*P-value*	*Lower 95%*	*Upper 95%*
Intercept	−8.1638E-05	0.001403921	−0.05815	0.953632	−0.002834131	0.00267086
Slope	1.399539526	0.015386858	90.95681	0	1.369372427	1.42970662

hedge ratio, also known as the *optimal hedge ratio* or *minimum variance hedge ratio*. Notice that it is not necessary to convert hundredweights of grain sorghum into bushels of corn, because the regression process automatically makes this adjustment. We know that a hedge typically involves opposite (i.e., long vs. short) positions in cash and futures, so although β is positive, a short (or long) position in corn futures would be required to hedge a long (or short) position in grain sorghum to obtain the desired offset of gains and losses between cash and futures. Notice that the value of the hedge ratio, in and of itself, tells us nothing about the performance of a cross-hedge. Although the hedge ratio will be close to 1.0 when the commodity being hedged and the commodity underlying the futures contract are the same, a value of 1.0 is unlikely to occur when the units of measurement for the two commodities are different, as they are in this example.

The t-statistic for the slope coefficient is 90.95681, which is highly statistically significant, and the F-statistic for the entire regression equation is 8273.141, which also is highly statistically significant. Therefore we can be confident that using approximately 1.4 bushels of corn futures to hedge each hundredweight of grain sorghum will be useful as a risk-reduction strategy, assuming that the price relationship between grain sorghum and corn remains the same as it was during the 2001–2016 period.

Converting the Hedge Ratio into Futures Contracts

Recall from Chapter 5 that futures contracts represent commercial quantities of the underlying commodity, and these quantities vary from one commodity to another. For corn, each futures contract contains 5,000 bushels, and there are no fractional futures contracts, so each hedge must be constructed in whole-number multiples of 5,000-bushel contracts. Suppose that we need to hedge 10,000 hundredweights of grain sorghum. From the regression results above, we know that hedging each hundredweight of grain sorghum requires approximately 1.4 bushels of corn futures, so we need to use:

10,000 cwt of grain sorghum × 1.4 bu of corn futures per cwt of grain sorghum = 14,000 bu of corn futures

which is equivalent to:

14,000 bu of corn futures ÷ 5,000 bu of corn futures per futures contract = 2.8 futures contracts

However, there are no fractional futures contracts, so we must round this answer to the nearest whole futures contract:

14,000 bu of corn futures ÷ 5,000 bu of corn futures per futures contract ≈ 3 futures contracts

Using 3 futures contracts will cause us to be slightly *over-hedged*, by the equivalent of 0.2 futures contracts (i.e., 2.8 vs. 3 contracts). However, this is better than rounding down to 2 futures contracts, which would cause us to be *under-hedged* by the equivalent of 0.8 futures contracts (i.e., 2.8 vs. 2 contracts). This over-hedging/under-hedging problem is more important when hedging smaller quantities of cash commodities, all else the same, because the rounded amount (up or down) is a larger proportion of the total amount of cash commodity being hedged.

Hedging Effectiveness

The R Square value in Table 8.8 is 0.68070974. This statistic, which is also referred to as the R^2 or coefficient of determination, ranges from 0 to 1.0 and represents the percentage of variation explained by the regression equation. In hedging applications, R^2 represents the percentage of variation eliminated by the hedge, and is used as a measure of hedging effectiveness. When a hedge is totally effective, R^2 will be 1.0 and 100% of the price risk is eliminated; when a hedge is totally ineffective, R^2 will be 0 and 0% of the price risk is eliminated. In this particular case, approximately 68% of the price risk in grain sorghum is eliminated by hedging with corn futures. The remaining 32% represents basis risk and cannot be eliminated by hedging with corn futures.

The Multiple R value of 0.825070284 in Table 8.8 is equal to the square root of the R Square value, and is the absolute value of the correlation between the change in the daily grain sorghum cash price and the change in the daily corn futures price. The correlation coefficient can range between -1.0 and $+1.0$, so a correlation of $+0.825$ suggests a strong statistical relationship between grain sorghum price changes and corn futures price changes. As a rule of thumb, many practitioners use a correlation of $+0.80$ ($R^2 = .64$) as the minimum acceptable level for a cross-hedge. Notice that the results from our grain sorghum hedging example are comfortably above these levels.

Using Price Changes vs. Price Levels in Regressions

As a final comment, there are differing opinions among practitioners regarding the proper way to structure the regression equation for a cross-hedge. In our grain sorghum hedging example, we used price changes (i.e., returns) for the commodity being hedged (grain sorghum) and the hedging instrument (corn futures). In contrast, some practitioners advocate the use of prices rather than price changes, and still others promote the use of percentage price changes (i.e., rates of return), particularly for hedges involving investment products and other financial applications.

We prefer to use price changes (i.e., returns) for a number of reasons. First, the purpose of hedging is to stabilize the net price paid or received by using gains on one position to offset losses on the other. This suggests that a hedger should focus on price changes rather than price levels.

Second, from a statistical standpoint, commodity price data typically have high levels of autocorrelation which can distort the regression results. Using price changes, also known as *first differences*, is a common method to correct for autocorrelation and provides more statistically reliable results. Third, while it might seem at first glance that using price levels, price changes, and percentage price changes should produce similar results, this is not the case. In fact, the hedge ratio (β) and hedging effectiveness (R^2) values can be dramatically different, depending on which type of data are used. Price changes generally produce more conservative hedging effectiveness (R^2) values than price levels, all else the same, so there is less chance for disappointment when regression results are used in real-world applications.

9 Profit Margin Hedging and Inverse Hedging

All of the hedging examples we have examined thus far have dealt with "locking in" the price for a single commodity, which stabilizes the net price for a cash position. This chapter will examine how hedging can be used with multiple commodities to stabilize gross profit margins. It also will look at how futures contracts can be used to offset forward contracts and other obligations that cannot easily be cancelled or liquidated.

Profit Margin Hedging

The same principles used to hedge a single commodity can be applied to processing or input–output relationships in which one or more commodities are used to produce one or more other commodities. Any changes in the prices for any of these inputs or outputs will affect the overall profitability of the relationship. The total value of the outputs minus the total value of the inputs is commonly referred to as the *processing margin* or *gross profit margin* (notice that this "margin" is not the same as the margin or collateral used to guarantee financial performance, discussed in Chapter 4). Hedging the individual input prices and output prices can also stabilize the gross profit margin of the process, hence the name profit margin hedging. In the following examples we will look at applications of profit margin hedging to soybean processing, petroleum refining, and cattle feeding.

Soybean Crush Margin

Soybeans are processed or "crushed" into two primary co-products, soybean oil and soybean meal. A 60-pound bushel of soybeans produces approximately 11 pounds of soybean oil and approximately 48 pounds of soybean meal, plus 1 pound of hulls and other products. Notice that soybean oil and soybean meal occur in fixed proportions, so there is no way the processor can produce more of one product and less of the other in response to changing market conditions.

The futures contracts for these three commodities represent 5,000 bushels of soybeans, 60,000 pounds of soybean oil, and 100 tons of soybean meal, respectively. Solving for the lowest common denominator so that all three commodities can be fully hedged, we find that

10 contracts (i.e., 50,000 bushels) of soybeans will produce 9 contracts (i.e., 540,000 pounds) of soybean oil and 12 contracts (i.e., 2,400,000 pounds) of soybean meal. Consequently, buying 10 contracts of soybean futures (or 50,000 bushels of cash soybeans) at $10.00 per bushel, and simultaneously selling 9 contracts of soybean oil futures (or 540,000 pounds of cash soybean oil) at $0.30 per pound and selling 12 contracts of soybean meal futures (or 1,200 tons of cash soybean meal) at $300.00 per ton, will result in a gross processing margin or *crush margin* of +$0.44 per bushel of soybeans processed:

- Buy 10 contracts of soybean futures (or 50,000 bu of cash soybeans) at $10.00 per bu:
  = 10 contracts × 5,000 bu per contract × $10.00 per bu = $500,000
- Sell 9 contracts of soybean oil futures (or 540,000 lbs of cash soybean oil) at $0.30 per lb:
  = 9 contracts × 60,000 lbs per contract × $0.30 per lb = $162,000
- Sell 12 contracts of soybean meal futures (or 1,200 tons of cash soybean meal) at $300.00 per ton:
  = 12 contracts × 100 tons per contract × $300.00 per ton = $360,000
- Crush margin:
  = ($162,000 + $360,000) gross revenue − $500,000 gross expense
  = $522,000 − $500,000 = $22,000
- Crush margin per bushel:
  = $22,000.00 ÷ 50,000 bu = +$0.44 per bu

A soybean processor can establish the crush margin by buying cash soybeans and selling both cash soybean oil and cash soybean meal, or it can use a long hedge on the anticipated purchase of the cash soybeans, and short hedges on the anticipated sale of the soybean oil and the anticipated sale of the soybean meal. These hedges can be placed weeks or months before the cash soybeans are purchased and/or before the cash soybean oil and cash soybean meal are produced, giving the processor considerable flexibility in both pricing and timing. Locking in the prices of the major input and both major outputs assures the processor that it will receive the crush margin of $0.44 per bushel, plus or minus any variation in the three basis values and minus transaction costs. For simplicity we will assume zero basis and zero transaction costs in all examples in this chapter.

Suppose that the processor placed hedges on all three commodities as described above. Also suppose that when the processor makes its cash market transactions, the prices of all three commodities have changed unfavorably by 5%: cash soybeans are now $10.50 per bushel (vs. $10.00), cash soybean oil is now $0.2850 per pound (vs. $0.30), and cash soybean meal is now $285.00 per ton (vs. $300.00). Using the same quantities as above, the crush margin without hedging is now −$0.5820 per bushel of soybeans processed:

- Buy 50,000 bu of cash soybeans at $10.50 per bu:
  = 50,000 bu of cash soybeans × $10.50 per bu = $525,000
- Sell 540,000 lbs of cash soybean oil at $0.2850 per lb:
  = 540,000 lbs of cash soybean oil × $0.2850 per lb = $153,900

- Sell 1,200 tons of cash soybean meal at $285.00 per ton:
  = 1,200 tons × $285.00 per ton = $342.000
- Crush margin:
  = ($153,900 + $342,000) gross revenue − $525,000 gross expense
  = $495,900 − $525,000 = −$29,100
- Crush margin per bushel:
  = −$29,100 ÷ 50,000 bu = −$0.5820 per bu

However, because the processor hedged each of the three commodities, the net purchase price it pays and the net sale prices it receives will be the same as those that resulted in the +$0.44 per bushel crush margin that we calculated at the beginning of this example. We can present these hedging results in a series of standard hedging tables (Tables 9.1, 9.2, and 9.3) for each commodity, in which the net price is the same as the Time 1 cash price.

Notice that by hedging, the processor had a net purchase price of $10.00 per bushel for soybeans, and net sale prices of $0.30 per pound for soybean oil and $300.00 per ton for soybean meal. These are the prices that resulted in the original crush margin of +$0.44 per bushel, and confirms that we can hedge the profit margin by hedging the inputs and outputs.

Table 9.1 Results for Long Hedge on Soybeans, Crush Margin Example

	Cash	−	Futures	=	Basis
Time 1:	[Short at $10.00]		Long at $10.00		$0.00
Time 2:	Long at $10.50		Short at $10.50		$0.00
Gain (Loss):	−$0.50		+$0.50		$0.00
Net Price:	$10.50 actual cash purchase price − $0.50 futures gain = $10.00 net purchase price				

Table 9.2 Results for Short Hedge on Soybean Oil, Crush Margin Example

	Cash	−	Futures	=	Basis
Time 1:	[Long at $0.30]		Short at $0.30		$0.00
Time 2:	Short at $0.2850		Long at $0.2850		$0.00
Gain (Loss):	−$0.0150		+$0.0150		$0.00
Net Price:	$0.2850 actual cash sale price + $0.0150 futures gain = $0.30 net sale price				

Table 9.3 Results for Short Hedge on Soybean Meal, Crush Margin Example

	Cash	−	Futures	=	Basis
Time 1:	[Long at $300.00]		Short at $300.00		$0.00
Time 2:	Short at $285.00		Long at $285.00		$0.00
Gain (Loss):	−$15.00		+$15.00		$0.00
Net Price:	$285.00 actual cash sale price + $15.00 futures gain = $300.00 net sale price				

Crude Oil Refining Margin

Crude oil is refined or "cracked" into two primary co-products, gasoline and heating oil (or, equivalently, diesel fuel). A 42-gallon barrel of crude oil produces approximately ⅔ gasoline and ⅓ heating oil. Notice that these proportions can be modified somewhat, but a refiner cannot produce all gasoline or all heating oil. Also notice that crude oil is priced in dollars per barrel, abbreviated "bbl," while gasoline and heating oil are priced in dollars per gallon, abbreviated "gal."

The futures contracts for these three commodities represent 1,000 barrels of crude oil, 42,000 gallons of gasoline, and 42,000 gallons of heating oil, respectively. Solving for the lowest common denominator so that all three commodities can be fully hedged, we find that 3 contracts (i.e., 3,000 barrels) of crude oil produces 2 contracts (i.e., 84,000 gallons) of gasoline and 1 contract (i.e., 42,000 gallons) of heating oil. Consequently, buying 3 contracts of crude oil futures (or 3,000 barrels of cash crude oil) at $45.00 per barrel, and simultaneously selling 2 contracts of gasoline futures (or 84,000 gallons of cash gasoline) at $1.20 per gallon and 1 contract of heating oil futures (or 42,000 gallons of cash heating oil) at $1.00 per gallon, will result in a gross processing margin or *refining margin* – also referred to as the *crack spread* – of +$2.60 per barrel of crude oil refined:

- Buy 3 contracts of crude oil futures (or 3,000 bbl of cash crude oil) at $45.00 per bbl:
  = 3 contracts × 1,000 bbl per contract × $45.00 per bbl = $135,000
- Sell 2 contracts of gasoline futures (or 84,000 gal of cash gasoline) at $1.20 per gal:
  = 2 contracts × 42,000 gal per contract × $1.20 per gal = $100,800
- Sell 1 contract of heating oil futures (or 42,000 gal of cash heating oil) at $1.00 per gal:
  = 1 contract × 42,000 gal per contract × $1.00 per gal = $42,000
- Refining margin:
  = ($100,800 + $42,000) gross revenue − $135,000 gross expense
  = $142,800 − $135,000 = $7,800
- Refining margin per barrel:
  = $7,800 ÷ 3,000 bbl = +$2.60 per bbl

All three commodities can be hedged to lock in the refining margin, in the same manner as shown above for the soybean crush margin.

Cattle Feeding Margin

The previous two processing margin examples used a single input and two outputs. In contrast, the *cattle feeding spread*, also referred to as the *cattle crush*, has only a single output – live cattle – but two primary inputs – feeder cattle and corn. Feeder cattle are younger, lighter-weight animals which each consume approximately 38 bushels of corn to become live cattle, or mature, market-weight animals. Notice that feeder cattle and corn are joint inputs, and while the amount of corn consumed by each animal can be adjusted somewhat, live cattle cannot be produced using only feeder cattle or only corn.

The futures contracts for these three commodities represent approximately 33 head of live cattle, 66 head of feeder cattle, and 5,000 bushels of corn, respectively. Solving for the lowest common denominator so that all three commodities can be fully hedged, we find that 4 contracts (i.e., 160,000 pounds) of live cattle can be produced from 2 contracts (i.e., 100,000 pounds) of feeder cattle and 1 contract (i.e., 5,000 bushels) of corn. Consequently, selling 4 contracts of live cattle futures (or 160,000 pounds of cash live cattle) at $1.05 per pound and simultaneously buying 2 contracts of feeder cattle futures (or 100,000 pounds of cash feeder cattle) at $1.15 per pound and 1 contract of corn futures (or 5,000 bushels of cash corn) at $3.40 per bushel results in a gross processing margin or *feeding margin* of +$0.1438 per pound of live cattle produced:

- Buy 2 contracts of feeder cattle futures (or 100,000 lbs of cash feeder cattle) at $1.20 per lb:
    = 2 contracts × 50,000 lbs per contract × $1.20 per lb = $120,000
- Buy 1 contract of corn futures (or 5,000 bu of cash corn) at $3.40 per bu:
    = 1 contract × 5,000 bu per contract × $3.40 per bu = $17,000
- Sell 4 contracts of live cattle futures (or 160,000 lbs of cash live cattle) at $1.00 per lb:
    = 4 contracts × 40,000 lbs per contract × $1.00 per lb = $160,000
- Feeding margin:
    = $160,000 revenue − ($120,000 + $17,000) expense
    = $160,000 − $137,000 = +$23,000
- Feeding margin per pound:
    = $23,000 ÷ 160,000 lbs = +$0.1438 per lb

A cattle feeder can establish the feeding margin by buying both feeder cattle and corn and selling live cattle, or it can use long hedges on the anticipated purchases of feeder cattle and corn, and a short hedge on the anticipated sale of the live cattle. These hedges can be placed weeks or months before the cash feeder cattle and cash corn are purchased and/or before the cash live cattle are produced, giving the cattle feeder considerable flexibility in both pricing and timing. Locking in the prices of both major inputs and the major output assures the cattle feeder that it will receive the feeding margin of +$0.1438.

Suppose that the cattle feeder placed hedges on all three commodities as described above. Also suppose that when the cattle feeder makes its cash market transactions, the prices of all three commodities have changed unfavorably by 10%: cash feeder cattle are now $1.32 per pound (vs. $1.20), cash corn is now $3.74 per bushel (vs. $3.40), and cash live cattle are now $0.90 per pound (vs. $1.00). Using the same quantities as above, the feeding margin without hedging is now −$0.0419 per pound of cattle produced:

- Buy 2 contracts of feeder cattle futures (or 100,000 lbs of cash feeder cattle) at $1.32 per lb:
    = 2 contracts × 50,000 lbs per contract × $1.32 per lb = $132,000

- Buy 1 contract of corn futures (or 5,000 bu of cash corn) at $3.74 per bu:
  = 1 contract × 5,000 bu per contract × $3.74 per bu = $18,700
- Sell 4 contracts of live cattle futures (or 160,000 lbs of cash live cattle) at $0.90 per lb:
  = 4 contracts × 40,000 lbs per contract × $0.90 per lb = $144,000
- Feeding margin:
  = $144,000 revenue − ($132,000 + $18,700) expense
  = $144,000 − $150,700 = −$6,700
- Feeding margin per pound:
  = −$6,700 ÷ 160,000 lbs = −$0.0419 per lb

However, because the cattle feeder hedged each of the three commodities, the net purchase prices it pays and the net sale price it receives will be the same as those that resulted in the +$0.1438 per pound feeding margin that we calculated at the beginning of this example. We can present these hedging results in a series of standard hedging (Tables 9.4, 9.5, and 9.6) tables for each commodity, in which the net price is the same as the Time 1 cash price.

Table 9.4 Results for Long Hedge on Feeder Cattle, Feeding Margin Example

	Cash	−	Futures	=	Basis
Time 1:	[Short at $1.20]		Long at $1.20		$0.00
Time 2:	Long at $1.32		Short at $1.32		$0.00
Gain (Loss):	−$0.12		+$0.12		$0.00
Net Price:	$1.32 actual cash purchase price − $0.12 futures gain = $1.20 net purchase price				

Table 9.5 Results for Long Hedge on Corn, Feeding Margin Example

	Cash	−	Futures	=	Basis
Time 1:	[Short at $3.40]		Long at $3.40		$0.00
Time 2:	Long at $3.74		Short at $3.74		$0.00
Gain (Loss):	−$0.34		+$0.34		$0.00
Net Price:	$3.74 actual cash purchase price − $0.34 futures gain = $3.40 net purchase price				

Table 9.6 Results for Short Hedge on Live Cattle, Feeding Margin Example

	Cash	−	Futures	=	Basis
Time 1:z	[Long at $1.00]		Short at $1.00		$0.00
Time 2:	Short at $0.90		Long at $0.90		$0.00
Gain (Loss):	−$0.10		+$0.10		$0.00
Net Price:	$0.90 actual cash sale price + $0.10 futures gain = $1.00 net sale price				

Notice that by hedging, the cattle feeder had net purchase prices of $1.20 per pound for feeder cattle and $3.40 per bushel for corn, and a net sale price of $1.00 per pound for live cattle. These are the prices that resulted in the original feeding margin of +$0.1438 per pound, and confirms that we can hedge the profit margin by hedging the inputs and outputs.

Other Processing Spreads

Recall that most cash commodities do not have corresponding futures contracts, so they must be cross-hedged using futures contracts on other commodities. However, the process for hedging the processing margin is the same for any commodity, regardless of whether or not it involves a cross-hedge. We can demonstrate a profit margin hedge that involves a cross-hedge by modifying the cattle feeding example above, replacing cash corn with grain sorghum which is cross-hedged using corn futures as shown in Chapter 8.

From the cattle feeding example above, 4 contracts (i.e., 160,000 pounds) of live cattle can be produced from 2 contracts (i.e., 100,000 pounds) of feeder cattle and 1 contract (i.e., 5,000 bushels) of corn. Each bushel of corn weighs 56 pounds, so 1 contract (i.e., 5,000 bushels) of corn weighs 280,000 pounds (= 5,000 bushels × 56 pounds per bushel). Using a common rule of thumb, grain sorghum has 85% of the feeding value of corn, so we need to use approximately 330,000 pounds (≈ 280,000 pounds ÷ 0.85) or 3,300 hundredweight of grain sorghum to replace 5,000 bushels of corn. Using the hedge ratio of 1.4 bushels of corn futures per hundredweight of grain sorghum from Chapter 8, we need to use:

3,300 cwt of grain sorghum × 1.4 bu of corn futures per cwt of grain sorghum = 4,620 bu of corn futures

which is slightly less than one 5,000-bushel corn futures contract, so we will be slightly over-hedged.

Suppose that we replace 5,000 bushels of cash corn at $3.40 per bushel with 3,300 hundredweight of grain sorghum at $5.15 per hundredweight, and leave the feeder cattle and live cattle components unchanged. The gross feeding margin for this revised version, calculated in terms of the cash commodities, would be +$0.1438 per pound of live cattle produced:

- Buy 100,000 lbs of cash feeder cattle at $1.20 per lb:
  = 100,000 lbs × $1.20 per lb = $120,000 (unchanged)
- Buy 3,300 cwt of cash grain sorghum at $5.15 per cwt:
  = 3,300 cwt × $5.15 per cwt = $16,995 (≈ $17,000 cost of cash corn in original)
- Sell 160,000 lbs of cash live cattle at $1.00 per lb:
  = 160,000 lbs × $1.00 per lb = $160,000 (unchanged)

- Feeding margin:
    = $160,000 revenue − ($120,000 + $16,995) expense
    = $160,000 − $136,995 = +$23,005
- Feeding margin per pound:
    = $23,005 ÷ 160,000 lbs = +$0.1438 per lb

Notice that the cost of the grain sorghum in this revised version is virtually identical to the cost of the cash corn in our original example, and consequently the beginning value for the feeding margin is effectively unchanged.

Next, suppose that when the cattle feeder makes their cash transactions, the prices of all four commodities have changed unfavorably by 10%: both cash and futures feeder cattle are now $1.32 per pound (vs. $1.20), cash grain sorghum is now $5.6650 (vs. $5.15); corn futures are now $3.74 per bushel (vs. $3.40); and both cash and futures live cattle are now $0.90 per pound (vs. $1.00). The gross feeding margin for this revised version, calculated in terms of the cash commodities, would be −$0.0418 per pound of live cattle produced:

- Buy 100,000 lbs of cash feeder cattle at $1.32 per lb:
    = 100,000 lbs × $1.32 per lb = $132,000
- Buy 3,300 cwt of cash grain sorghum at $5.6650 per cwt:
    = 3,300 cwt × $5.6650 per cwt = $18,694.50
- Sell 160,000 lbs of cash live cattle at $0.90 per lb:
    = 160,000 lbs × $0.90 per lb = $144,000
- Feeding margin:
    = $144,000 revenue − ($132,000 + $18,694.50) expense
    = $144,000 − $150,694.50 = −$6,694.50
- Feeding margin per pound:
    = −$6,694.50 ÷ 160,000 lbs = −$0.0418 per lb

However, recall from Table 9.4 that feeder cattle futures exactly offset the 10% price increase in cash feeder cattle. Also recall from Table 9.6 that live cattle futures exactly offset the 10% price decrease in cash live cattle, so the price changes for these two commodities had no net impact on the feeding margin. Consequently, our only question is how well the long corn futures position offset the effects of the short cash grain sorghum position, and the resulting impact on the feeding margin.

To answer this question, the reader might be tempted to construct a modified version of Table 9.5 using the cash price for grain sorghum and the futures price for corn to determine the effectiveness of the cross-hedge. Table 9.7 shows why this approach is incorrect, because it does not take into consideration the different quantities of grain sorghum (i.e., 3,300 hundredweight) and corn (5,000 bushels). When using a cross-hedge, the total value (i.e., price multiplied by the respective quantity) must be calculated for the cash commodity and for the futures contract, at Time 1 and at Time 2. The relative changes in the total values for cash and futures determine the effectiveness of the cross-hedge. Only when the cash and futures

Table 9.7 Incorrect Approach to Calculation of Results for Long Hedge on Grain Sorghum Using Corn Futures, Feeding Margin Example

	Cash	−	Futures	=	Basis
Time 1:	[Short at $5.15]		Long at $3.40		
Time 2:	Long at $5.6650		Short at $3.74		
Gain (Loss):	−$0.5150		+$0.34		
Net Price:					

quantities are identical is it appropriate to simplify matters and compare only the cash and futures prices.

When we compare the changes in the total values for cash grain sorghum and corn futures, we find that:

- The corn futures price increased from $3.40 to $3.74, so the impact on a 1-contract long futures position would be:
  ($3.74 − $3.40) per bu × 5,000 bu = $0.34 per bu × 5,000 bu = +$1,700
- The cash grain sorghum price increased from $5.15 to $5.6650 per cwt, so the impact on a 3,300-cwt short cash position would be:
  ($5.15 − $5.6650) per cwt × 3,300 cwt = −$0.5150 × 3,300 cwt = −$1,699.50
- The net impact on the feeding margin from cash grain sorghum hedged with corn futures:
  = $1,700 revenue − $1,699.50 expense
  = $1,700 − $1,699.50 = +$0.50
- The net impact on the feeding margin per pound:
  = +$0.50 ÷ 160,000 lbs ≈ $0 per lb

This cross-hedge using corn futures was highly effective in offsetting the change in grain sorghum prices. Despite large differences in price levels, price changes, and quantities of the respective commodities, the long corn futures position almost exactly offset the 10% price increase in cash grain sorghum, demonstrating the usefulness of cross-hedging in stabilizing gross margins in profit margin hedges.

Inverse Hedging

Hedging with futures is not the only way to manage price risk. Most commodities have various forward contracts available off-exchange that can be used to establish a buying or selling price for some later date. The only requirement to create a forward contract is a commitment between a buyer and a seller to exchange an agreed-upon sum of money for some agreed-upon quality and quantity of a commodity, at some agreed-upon time and place. Recall that futures contracts are a highly-standardized type of forward contract in which all of the terms have been established beforehand except the price. This high degree of standardization allows futures contracts to be traded on exchanges.

When a buyer or seller enters into a forward contract, there is usually no need to hedge with a futures contract because the price already has been established, and consequently there is no price risk (i.e., price variation) for either party. However, the absence of price risk does not imply that both parties will be satisfied with the agreed-upon price at the completion of the transaction. The price of the commodity almost always will change between the date when the agreement is made and the date when it is fulfilled. This situation is commonly referred to as *seller's remorse* if the price rises, or *buyer's remorse* if the price falls, after the agreement is made. Often a better outcome would have resulted by doing something else, or doing nothing at all and avoiding the agreement altogether.

The losing party in the transaction might wish to cancel or renegotiate the contract to avoid further losses, but it is unlikely that the winning party would agree to such a step. Alternatively, the losing party could take an offsetting futures position and create an *inverse hedge* or *reverse hedge* which would have the same financial effect as cancelling the forward contract. Losses caused by unfavorable price changes up to that point cannot be recovered, but further losses from continued unfavorable price changes can be avoided. Strictly speaking, some practitioners do not consider this to be a true hedge because it does not reduce risk, and for this reason it is sometimes referred to as quasi-hedging. Nevertheless, we include inverse hedging here it because it can be a useful tool for adjusting positions involving forward contracts or other instruments that are illiquid or difficult to cancel.

Long Inverse Hedge with a Short Forward Contract

Hedging with a Short Forward Contract

We can illustrate an inverse hedge with the following example using our hypothetical corn farmer.

Example 9.1: A farmer grows and sells corn as part of their normal operations. They believe that corn prices might drop over the course of the growing season, but they are unable to sell cash corn right now because the crop has not yet been harvested. Instead, they enter into a forward contract at Time 1 to sell cash corn for $3.50 at Time 2, following harvest. Assume the farmer was wrong about the market direction, and the cash price increased from $3.50 per bushel to $3.60 per bushel, and ultimately to $4.00 per bushel. Results for the cash position only are shown in Table 9.8–Partial.

Table 9.8 Results for Short Forward Contract Offset with Long Futures and Price Increases (Partial)

	Cash	−	Futures	=	Basis
Time 1:	Short at $3.50				
Time 2:	{3.60}				
Time 3:	[Long at $4.00]				
Gain (Loss):	−$0.50				
Net Price:					

Notice that by entering into the forward contract to sell at $3.50, the farmer effectively has a short cash position at Time 1 in which higher prices are harmful, at least in terms of missed opportunity. Also notice that because there was an actual – not implicit – cash transaction at Time 1 when the processor sold cash corn via the forward contract, the Time 1 cash position and price are shown without brackets. In contrast, there was not (yet) an actual cash transaction at Time 2 or Time 3, so the information is shown in brackets.

Using Long Futures to Offset a Short Forward

Suppose that as the price increases from $3.50, the farmer begins to regret entering into the forward contract. When the futures price reaches $3.60 – designated as Time 2 – the farmer decides to offset the short forward contract with a long futures position. Then at Time 3 the farmer delivers the cash corn to satisfy the forward contract and simultaneously sells corn futures to liquidate their futures position. The complete results are presented in Table 9.8.

Table 9.8 Results for Short Forward Contract Offset with Long Futures and Price Increases

	Cash	–	Futures	=	Basis
Time 1:	Short at $3.50				
Time 2:	{3.60}		Long at $3.60		
Time 3:	[Long at $4.00]		Short at $4.00		
Gain (Loss):	−$0.50		+0.40		
Net Price:	$3.50 actual cash sale price + $0.40 futures gain = $3.90 net sale price				

For simplicity we have set all basis values to zero, but it should be emphasized that basis behavior affects the performance of an inverse hedge in the same way that it affects the performance of a regular hedge. Notice that the farmer was unable to recover the initial $0.10 that was lost – or missed – as prices moved from $3.50 at Time 1 to $3.60 at Time 2, when the futures position was established. However, they were able to avoid missing the remaining $0.40 of the $0.50 price increase by using the long futures position to offset the short forward contract. Also notice that the actual cash price in this example is the Time 1 price, not the Time 2 or Time 3 price. Recall that the farmer agreed to sell cash corn at Time 1 at $3.50 per bushel, and if they had done nothing else the net sale price would have been $3.50 per bushel.

Drawbacks of a Long Inverse Hedge

Prices rarely move in one direction for extended periods of time, and frequently change course suddenly and unexpectedly. A long inverse hedge exposes the hedger to more price risk, not less, by offsetting the forward contract and leaving the hedger effectively unhedged. The potential danger is illustrated in Example 9.2.

Example 9.2: A farmer grows and sells corn as part of their normal operations. They believe that corn prices might drop over the course of the growing season, but they are unable to sell cash corn right now because the crop has not yet been harvested. Instead, they enter into a forward contract at Time 1 to sell cash corn for $3.50 at Time 3, following harvest. However, as the cash price increases from $3.50, the farmer begins to regret entering into the forward contract. When the cash price reaches $3.60 – designated as Time 2 – the farmer decides to offset the short forward contract with a long futures position at $3.60. Both prices then reverse direction and drop to $3.00 at Time 3. At Time 3 the farmer delivers the cash corn to satisfy the forward contract and simultaneously sells corn futures to liquidate their futures position. The results are presented in Table 9.9.

Table 9.9 Results for Short Forward Contract Offset with Long Futures and Price Decreases

	Cash	–	Futures	=	Basis
Time 1:	Short at $3.50				
Time 2:	{3.60}		Long at $3.60		
Time 3:	[Long at $3.00]		Short at $3.00		
Gain (Loss):	+$0.50		−0.60		
Net Price:	$3.50 actual cash sale price − $0.60 futures loss = $2.90 net sale price				

In this example, the loss on the futures position exceeds the gain on the cash position by $0.10. Stated differently, the farmer is worse off (by $0.10) than if they had not used either the forward contract or the futures position and simply sold cash corn for $3.00 at Time 3. Furthermore, the farmer is much worse off (by $0.60) than if they had not added the futures position and simply maintained the forward contract to sell cash corn for $3.50. Thus, using an inverse hedge exposed the farmer to greater price risk than if they had done nothing.

Short Inverse Hedge with a Long Forward Contract

Hedging with a Long Forward Contract

We also can illustrate an inverse hedge for our hypothetical processor with Example 9.3.

Example 9.3: A processor buys and uses corn as part of its normal operations. It expects corn prices to rise over the next several months, but it doesn't have either the funds or the storage space to buy cash corn now and store it for several months. Instead, it enters into a

Table 9.10 Results for Long Forward Contract Offset with Short Futures and Price Decreases (Partial)

	Cash	–	Futures	=	Basis
Time 1:	Long at $3.50				
Time 2:	{3.25}				
Time 3:	[Short at $2.50]				
Gain (Loss):	−$1.00				
Net Price:					

forward contract at Time 1 to buy cash corn for $3.50 at Time 2. Assume the processor was wrong about the market direction, and the cash price decreased from $3.50 per bushel to $2.50 per bushel. Results for the cash position only are shown in Table 9.10–Partial.

Notice that by entering into the forward contract to buy at $3.50, the processor effectively has a long cash position at Time 1, at least in terms of missed opportunity. Also notice that because there was an actual – not implicit – cash transaction at Time 1 when the processor bought cash corn via the forward contract, the Time 1 cash position and price are shown without brackets. In contrast, there was not (yet) an actual cash transaction at Time 2 or Time 3, so the information is shown in brackets.

Using Short Futures to Offset a Long Forward

Suppose that as the price decreases from $3.50, the processor begins to regret entering into the forward contract. When the price reaches $3.25 – designated as Time 2 – the processor decides to offset the long forward contract with a short futures position. Then at Time 3 the processor receives the cash corn to satisfy the forward contract and simultaneously buys corn futures to liquidate its futures position. The complete results are presented in Table 9.10.

Table 9.10 Results for Long Forward Contract Offset with Short Futures and Price Decreases

	Cash	–	Futures	=	Basis
Time 1:	Long at $3.50				
Time 2:	{3.25}		Short at $3.25		
Time 3:	[Short at $2.50]		Long at $2.50		
Gain (Loss):	−$1.00		+0.75		
Net Price:	$3.50 actual cash purchase price − $0.75 futures gain = $2.75 net purchase price				

For simplicity, we have set all basis values to zero. Notice that the processor was unable to recover the $0.25 that was lost (or missed) as prices moved from $3.50 at Time 1 to $3.25 at Time 2. However, it was able to capture the remaining $0.75 of the $1.00 price decrease by using the short futures contract to offset the long forward contract. As in the previous inverse hedging examples, the actual cash price in this example is the Time 1 price, not the Time 2 or Time 3 price. Recall that the processor agreed to buy cash corn at Time 1 at $3.50 per bushel, and if it had done nothing else the net purchase price would have been $3.50 per bushel.

Drawbacks of a Short Inverse Hedge

A short inverse hedge exposes the hedger to more price risk, not less, by offsetting the forward contract and leaving the hedger effectively unhedged. The potential danger to the hedger is illustrated in Example 9.4.

Example 9.4: A processor buys and uses corn as part of its normal operations. It expects corn prices to rise over the next several months, but it doesn't have either the funds or the storage space to buy cash corn now and store it for several months. Instead, it enters into a forward contract at Time 1 to buy cash corn for $3.50 at Time 3. However, as the price decreases from $3.50, the processor begins to regret entering into the forward contract. When the price reaches $3.25 – designated as Time 2 – the processor decides to offset the long forward contract with a short futures position at $3.25. Then at some point after Time 2 the market reverses direction, and by Time 3 the price has jumped to $4.50. At Time 3 the processor receives the cash corn to satisfy the forward contract and simultaneously buys corn futures to liquidate its futures position (see Table 9.11).

Table 9.11 Results for Long Forward Contract Offset with Short Futures and Price Increases

	Cash	–	Futures	=	Basis
Time 1:	Long at $3.50				
Time 2:	{3.25}		Short at $3.25		
Time 3:	[Short at $4.50]		Long at $4.50		
Gain (Loss):	+$1.00		–$1.25		
Net Price:	$3.50 actual cash purchase price + $1.25 futures loss = $4.75 net purchase price				

In this example, the loss on the futures position exceeds the gain on the cash position by $0.25. Stated differently, the processor is worse off (by $0.25) than if it had not used either the forward contract or the futures position and simply bought cash corn for $4.50 at Time 3. Furthermore, the processor is much worse off (by $1.25) than if it had not added the futures position and simply maintained the forward contract to buy cash corn for $3.50. Thus, using an inverse hedge exposed the processor to greater price risk than if it had done nothing.

10 Hedging and Basis Trading

Chapters 6 and 7 introduced the concept of the basis and examined the relationship between basis behavior and hedging performance. The basis was defined as the difference between the cash price and the futures price. A weaker (i.e., more negative or less positive) basis was shown to decrease the net purchase price for a long hedger, and a stronger (i.e., more positive or less negative) basis was shown to increase the net sale price for a short hedger. Stated differently, a weaker basis benefits a long hedger, while a stronger basis benefits a short hedger. In this chapter we will examine what happens when we treat the basis as a tangible value, rather than simply a residual, and how this view of the basis expands our hedging abilities.

Redefining the Basis and the Cash Price

Basis as a Tangible Value

Recall that in Chapter 6 we defined the basis as:

$$\text{Basis} = \text{Cash} - \text{Futures} \qquad \text{(Equation 6.1)}$$

in which the basis is the difference between the cash price and the futures price. We can rearrange Equation 6.1 so it expresses this relationship in terms of the cash price:

$$\text{Cash} = \text{Futures} + \text{Basis} \qquad \text{(Equation 10.1)}$$

When presented in this manner, the cash price is the sum of the futures price and the basis. The futures price functions as the price discovery mechanism to establish the general price level, while the basis functions as the adjustment mechanism to reflect local supply/demand conditions, including pricing variations due to time, space, and form which were discussed in Chapter 3. Notice that this approach treats the basis as a tangible value produced by the forces of supply and demand, rather than simply the difference between two prices. When we treat the basis as an observable value, and when we treat the cash price as the result from combining the futures price and the basis, then we can construct hedging tables consistent

Table 7.1B Results for Long Hedge: Rising Prices, Basis Positive and Weakens

	Cash	−	Futures	=	Basis
Time 1:	[Short at $3.50]		Long at $3.00		+$0.50
Time 2:	Long at $4.50		Short at $4.10		+$0.40
Gain (Loss):	−$1.00		+$1.10		+$0.10
Net Price:	$4.50 actual cash purchase price − $1.10 futures gain = $3.40 net purchase price				

Table 10.1 Results for Long Hedge: Rising Prices, Basis Positive and Weakens, Basis Trading Format, Generic Dates

	Futures	+	Basis	=	Cash
Time 1:	Long at $3.00		Short at +$0.50		[Short at $3.50]
Time 2:	Short at $4.10		Long at +$0.40		Long at $4.50
Gain (Loss):	+$1.10		+$0.10		−$1.00
Net Price:	$4.50 actual cash purchase price − $1.10 futures gain = $3.40 net purchase price				
or:	$3.50 expected cash purchase price − $0.10 basis gain = $3.40 net purchase price				
or:	*$3.00 futures price at Time 1 + $0.40 basis at Time 2 = $3.40 net purchase price*				

with this new view of the basis. For example, Table 7.1B from Chapter 7 can be rearranged into what we will call "basis trading format" and presented as Table 10.1.

Notice that the basis positions in Table 10.1 have been designated as long or short. A hedger is said to be *long the basis* when they benefit from an increase in the basis, and *short the basis* when they benefit from a decrease in the basis. In both Table 7.1B and Table 10.1 the long hedger benefits from a weaker (i.e., more negative or less positive) basis, and consequently long hedgers are short the basis. In this example the basis weakened from +$0.50 to +$0.40, which reduced the net purchase price from $3.50 to $3.40.

Also notice that basis trading format gives us a third way to calculate the net purchase price, shown in italics at the bottom of Table 10.1, as the sum of the beginning futures price and the ending basis value. The beginning futures price establishes the general price level, while the ending basis value reflects local supply/demand conditions at the time the transaction is completed. This is consistent with the definition of the cash price as the sum of the futures price and the basis, introduced earlier in this section.

From our original definition of the basis:

Basis = Cash − Futures   (Equation 6.1)

notice that we can designate each component of this equation as being short:

Short Basis = Short Cash − Short Futures   (Equation 10.2)

A long position is the opposite of a short position, so reversing the sign (i.e., + or −) on any expression in this formula effectively reverses the position from long to short or vice versa. But if we reverse the sign on the futures term from negative (−) to positive (+), and also reverse the position of the futures term from short to long, then the effects of the two reversals cancel and our equation becomes:

Short Basis = Short Cash + Long Futures   (Equation 10.3)

Recall that a short cash position plus a long futures position is a long hedge, so Equation 10.3 demonstrates why a long hedge is equivalent to being short the basis.

Similarly, we can rearrange Table 7.4C (Chapter 7) into basis trading format (see Table 10.2).

Table 7.4C Results for Short Hedge: Falling Prices, Basis Negative and Strengthens

	Cash	−	Futures	=	Basis
Time 1:	[Long at $3.50]		Short at $4.00		−$0.50
Time 2:	Short at $3.00		Long at $3.40		−$0.40
Gain (Loss):	−$0.50		+$0.60		+$0.10
Net Price:	$3.00 actual cash sale price + $0.60 futures gain = $3.60 net sale price				

Table 10.2 Results for Short Hedge: Falling Prices, Basis Negative and Strengthens, Basis Trading Format, Generic Dates

	Futures	+	Basis	=	Cash
Time 1:	Short at $4.00		Long at −$0.50		[Long at $3.50]
Time 2:	Long at $3.40		Short at −$0.40		Short at $3.00
Gain (Loss):	+$0.60		+$0.10		−$0.50
Net Price:	$3.00 actual cash sale price + $0.60 futures gain = $3.60 net sale price				
or:	$3.50 expected cash sale price + $0.10 basis gain = $3.60 net sale price				
or:	*$4.00 futures price at Time 1 + (−$0.40) basis at Time 2 = $3.60 net sale price*				

Notice that the basis positions in Table 10.2 have once again been designated as long or short. As in Table 10.1, a hedger is said to be long the basis when they benefit from an increase in the basis, and short the basis when they benefit from a decrease in the basis. In both Table 7.4C and Table 10.2 the short hedger benefits from a stronger (i.e., more positive or less negative) basis, and consequently short hedgers are long the basis. In this example the basis strengthened from −$0.50 to −$0.40, which increased the net sale price from $3.50 to $3.60.

We also have a third way to calculate the net purchase price, shown in italics at the bottom of Table 10.2, as the sum of the beginning futures price and the ending basis value. The beginning futures price establishes the general price level, while the ending basis value reflects local supply/demand conditions at the time the transaction is completed.

Referring once again to our original definition of the basis:

$$\text{Basis} = \text{Cash} - \text{Futures} \qquad \text{(Equation 6.1)}$$

we can designate each component of this formula as being long:

$$\text{Long Basis} = \text{Long Cash} - \text{Long Futures} \qquad \text{(Equation 10.4)}$$

If we reverse the sign on the futures term from negative ($-$) to positive ($+$), and also reverse the position of the futures term from long to short, then the effects of the two reversals cancel and our equation becomes:

$$\text{Long Basis} = \text{Long Cash} + \text{Short Futures} \qquad \text{(Equation 10.5)}$$

Recall that a long cash position plus a short futures position is a short hedge, so Equation 10.5 demonstrates why a short hedge is equivalent to being long the basis.

Defining the Impact of Basis Changes

We can further modify our new definition of the cash price:

$$\text{Cash} = \text{Futures} + \text{Basis} \qquad \text{(Equation 10.1)}$$

by creating one version that defines the actual cash price:

$$\text{Actual Cash} = \text{Futures} + \text{Actual Basis} \qquad \text{(Equation 10.6)}$$

and another version that defines the expected cash price:

$$\text{Expected Cash} = \text{Futures} + \text{Expected Basis} \qquad \text{(Equation 10.7)}$$

Recall that there are both actual and expected cash prices, and both actual and expected basis values, but there is only one futures price. Next, we can rearrange Equation 10.6 in terms of the futures price:

$$\text{Futures} = \text{Actual Cash} - \text{Actual Basis} \qquad \text{(Equation 10.8)}$$

and likewise rearrange Equation 10.7 in terms of the futures price:

$$\text{Futures} = \text{Expected Cash} - \text{Expected Basis} \qquad \text{(Equation 10.9)}$$

Both Equation 10.8 and Equation 10.9 are formulas for the futures price, so we can combine them into a single expression:

Actual Cash − Actual Basis = Expected Cash − Expected Basis   (Equation 10.10)

Finally, we can rearrange Equation 10.10 in terms of the actual cash price:

Actual Cash = Expected Cash − Expected Basis + Actual Basis
= Expected Cash + Actual Basis − Expected Basis
= Expected Cash + (Actual Basis − Expected Basis)   (Equation 10.11)

Equation 10.11 shows that if the actual basis is larger (i.e., stronger) than the expected basis, then the actual cash price will be larger (i.e., higher), all else the same. A stronger basis benefits a short hedger, because it results in a higher net sale price, all else the same. Conversely, if the actual basis is smaller (i.e., weaker) than the expected basis, then the actual cash price will be smaller (i.e., lower), all else the same. A weaker basis benefits a long hedger, because it results in a lower net purchase price, all else the same.

Alternatively, we can modify our original cash price equation to reflect changes in the individual components by converting Equation 10.1:

Cash = Futures + Basis   (Equation 10.1)

to:

Change in Cash = Change in Futures + Change in Basis   (Equation 10.12)

Notice in Equation 10.12 how a larger (i.e., stronger) basis results in a higher cash price, and how a smaller (i.e., weaker) basis results in a lower cash price. A stronger basis benefits a short hedger because it results in a higher net sale price, all else the same. Conversely, a weaker basis benefits a long hedger because it results in a lower net purchase price, all else the same. It then follows that a stronger basis harms a long hedger because it results in a lower net purchase price, and a weaker basis harms a short hedger because it results in a lower net sale price. Equation 10.12 and Equation 10.11 use different methods to arrive at the same conclusion, namely that basis changes have a direct impact on the cash price experienced by the hedger. Once again, we find that basis behavior determines hedging performance.

Commercial Hedging

The hedging examples presented in previous chapters assume that a hedger has a cash position and adds a futures position to lock in a purchase price or a sale price. This is often referred to as a *textbook hedge*, where the hedger expects any cash price change to be matched by a similarly-sized futures price change, and because one position is short and the other position is long, the two price changes will more or less cancel. To add some realism to these examples, let us define a *commercial hedger* as a firm that engages in buying and selling cash commodities, and routinely hedges those purchases and sales with futures positions. In contrast to a textbook hedger, a commercial hedger holds simultaneous positions in both cash and futures, and adjusts the sizes and *directions* (i.e., long or short) of those positions in response to changing market conditions. If the hedge is carefully structured and managed, it is possible for the hedger to capture a profit on the hedge from a favorable basis change. In fact, commercial hedgers routinely pursue these profitable basis opportunities via a process known as *basis trading*.

Simultaneously monitoring the price changes in two separate but related markets (i.e., cash and futures) can be extremely difficult, particularly when the interaction between those price changes – or, more specifically, the combined effects of the price changes in both cash and futures – determines whether there is a profit or loss. Stated differently, what matters in commercial hedging is not what happens to the cash price alone, or what happens to the futures price alone, but instead what happens to both prices, and the net amount (i.e., + or – and absolute size) of the combined changes.

We can illustrate this point by modifying our original basis equation to reflect changes in the individual components by converting Equation 6.1:

Basis = Cash – Futures   (Equation 6.1)

to:

Change in Basis = Change in Cash – Change in Futures   (Equation 10.13)

Notice how changes of differing amounts in the cash price and the futures price affect the basis. A larger increase (or smaller decrease) in the cash price relative to the futures price will cause the basis to strengthen; a larger increase (or smaller decrease) in the futures price relative to the cash price will cause the basis to weaken. Consequently, managing a basis position can be a complex process. However, it can be greatly simplified if the hedger ignores the separate changes to the cash and futures prices, and instead focuses on the combined result which is the basis change. This is why commercial hedgers routinely approach hedging in terms of the basis, and why they often describe their hedging activities as *buying the basis* (i.e., placing a short hedge or lifting a long hedge) and *selling the basis* (i.e., placing a long hedge or lifting a short hedge). Notice that trading the basis requires positions to be held in both cash and futures, because without positions in both markets there can be no basis, and therefore no change in the basis.

In addition to a cash position and an opposite futures position, a basis trader also needs to understand historical basis behavior. Historical basis data can be used to determine normal or typical basis levels and seasonal basis patterns throughout the year. With this knowledge, basis traders can identify abnormal or atypical basis levels – either unusually high or unusually low – and take appropriate positions when these opportunities present themselves. Most of all, a basis trader needs time for basis trades to play out. Basis values may take days, weeks, or even months to adjust, and may move farther away from normal before they revert to more economic levels.

Short Hedging – Buying the Basis

We can demonstrate basis trading by a short hedger with an example based on Table 10.2, but with wider price swings at Time 2 that could distract the hedger unless they focus exclusively on the basis.

Example 10.1: In a year with a large crop, suppose that Time 1 is at harvest (October), when cash prices are at their seasonal lows and the basis is typically weakest. The hedger owns cash corn in October, which they need to sell sometime before the next harvest. Time 2 is in the spring (April) when cash prices and the basis are typically stronger. Notice that October is in one calendar year, designated Y1, and April is in the next calendar year, designated Y2. The hedger believes that the basis in October, using the May futures contract, is unusually weak at −$0.50. The hedger knows that in years with a large crop the historical average basis in April, using the May futures contract, is −$0.10. This suggests a potential gain from buying the basis of $0.40 (= −$0.10 − (−$0.50)). The hedger buys the basis in October by placing a short hedge in the May contract (recall that a short hedge is long the basis).

Suppose that the basis strengthens to −$0.10 as expected, but cash prices decline to $3.00 from October to April (see Table 10.3). We can convert this table into basis trading format (see Table 10.4).

Table 10.3 Results for Short Hedge: Falling Prices, Basis Negative and Strengthens, Detailed Dates

	Cash	−	Futures	=	Basis
OctY1:	[Long at $3.50]		Short MayY2 at $4.00		−$0.50
AprY2:	Short at $3.00		Long MayY2 at $3.10		−$0.10
Gain (Loss):	−$0.50		+$0.90		+$0.40
Net Price:	$3.00 actual cash sale price + $0.90 futures gain = $3.90 net sale price				
or:	$3.50 expected cash sale price + $0.40 basis gain = $3.90 net sale price				

Table 10.4 Results for Short Hedge: Falling Prices, Basis Negative and Strengthens, Basis Trading Format, Detailed Dates

	Futures	+	Basis	=	Cash
OctY1:	Short MayY2 at $4.00		Long at −$0.50		[Long at $3.50]
AprY2:	Long MayY2 at $3.10		Short at −$0.10		Short at $3.00
Gain (Loss):	+$0.90		+$0.40		−$0.50
Net Price:	$3.00 actual cash sale price + $0.90 futures gain = $3.90 net sale price				
or:	$3.50 expected cash sale price + $0.40 basis gain = $3.90 net sale price				
or:	$4.00 futures price in OctY1 + (−$0.10) basis in AprY2 = $3.90 net sale price				

Notice how buying the basis resulted in a basis gain of $0.40, which increased the net sale price by $0.40. Monitoring the basis change, and incorporating this change into the net sale price, is much simpler for the hedger than simultaneously balancing futures market gains and cash market losses.

Suppose instead that the basis strengthens to −$0.10 as expected, but cash prices rise to $4.00 from October to April (see Table 10.5). We can convert this table into basis trading format (see Table 10.6).

Table 10.5 Results for Short Hedge: Rising Prices, Basis Negative and Strengthens, Detailed Dates

	Cash	−	Futures	=	Basis
OctY1:	[Long at $3.50]		Short MayY2 at $4.00		−$0.50
AprY2:	Short at $4.00		Long MayY2 at $4.10		−$0.10
Gain (Loss):	+$0.50		−$0.10		+$0.40
Net Price:	$4.00 actual cash sale price + $0.10 futures gain = $3.90 net sale price				
or:	$3.50 expected cash sale price + $0.40 basis gain = $3.90 net sale price				

Table 10.6 Results for Short Hedge: Rising Prices, Basis Negative and Strengthens, Basis Trading Format, Detailed Dates

	Futures	+	Basis	=	Cash
OctY1:	Short MayY2 at $4.00		Long at −$0.50		[Long at $3.50]
AprY2:	Long MayY2 at $4.10		Short at −$0.10		Short at $4.00
Gain (Loss):	−$0.10		+$0.40		+$0.50
Net Price:	$4.00 actual cash sale price + $0.10 futures gain = $3.90 net sale price				
or:	$3.50 expected cash sale price + $0.40 basis gain = $3.90 net sale price				
or:	$4.00 futures price in OctY1 + (−$0.10) basis in AprY2 = $3.90 net sale price				

Once again, notice how buying the basis resulted in a basis gain of $0.40, which increased the net sale price by $0.40. Monitoring the basis change, and incorporating this change into the net sale price, is much simpler for the hedger than simultaneously reconciling futures market losses and cash market gains. Also notice that for both scenarios, regardless of the market direction, buying the basis resulted in a basis gain of $0.40 and a net sale price of $3.90. Similar scenarios could be developed for each of the possible combinations of cash price change/futures price change and change/basis level/basis change (+ or −) for a short hedger, but all would show that focusing on the basis, instead of the separate cash and futures prices, can greatly simplify the hedging process.

Long Hedging – Selling the Basis

We also can demonstrate basis trading by a long hedger with an example based on Table 10.1, but with wider price swings at Time 2 that require the hedger to focus on the basis.

Example 10.2: In a year with weather problems during the growing season, suppose that Time 1 is during the summer (July) when supplies are tight. The hedger needs to buy cash corn sometime before spring. Time 2 is in the winter (January), after the size of the crop is known and the basis has had a chance to adjust to more normal levels. Notice that July is in one calendar year, designated Y1, and January is in the next calendar year, designated Y2. The hedger believes that the basis in July, using the March futures contract, is exceptionally strong at +$0.50. The hedger knows that in years with a short crop the historical average basis in January, using the March futures contract, is +$0.10. This suggests a potential gain from selling the basis of $0.40 (= +$0.50 − +$0.10). The hedger sells the basis in July by placing a long hedge in the March contract; recall that a long hedge is short the basis.

Suppose that the basis weakens to +$0.10 as expected, but cash prices increase to $4.50 from July to January (see Table 10.7). We can convert this table into basis trading format (see Table 10.8).

Table 10.7 Results for Long Hedge: Rising Prices, Basis Positive and Weakens, Detailed Dates

	Cash	−	Futures	=	Basis
JulY1:	[Short at $3.50]		Long MarY2 at $3.00		+$0.50
JanY2:	Long at $4.50		Short MarY2 at $4.40		+$0.10
Gain (Loss):	−$1.00		+$1.40		+$0.40
Net Price:	$4.50 actual cash purchase price − $1.40 futures gain =				
	$3.10 net purchase price				
or:	$3.50 expected cash purchase price − $0.40 basis gain =				
	$3.10 net purchase price				

Table 10.8 Results for Long Hedge: Rising Prices, Basis Positive and Weakens, Basis Trading Format, Detailed Dates

	Futures	+	Basis	=	Cash
JulY1:	Long MarY2 at $3.00		Short at +$0.50		[Short at $3.50]
JanY2:	Short MarY2 at $4.40		Long at +$0.10		Long at $4.50
Gain (Loss):	+$1.40		+$0.40		−$1.00
Net Price:	$4.50 actual cash purchase price − $1.40 futures gain =				
	$3.10 net purchase price				
or:	$3.50 expected cash purchase price − $0.40 basis gain =				
	$3.10 net purchase price				
or:	$3.00 futures price in JulY2 + $0.10 basis in JanY2 =				
	$3.10 net purchase price				

Notice how selling the basis resulted in a basis gain of $0.40, which reduced the net purchase price by $0.40. Monitoring the basis change, and incorporating this change into the net purchase price, is much simpler for the hedger than simultaneously balancing futures market gains and cash market losses.

Suppose instead that the basis weakens to +$0.10 as expected, but cash prices decrease to $2.50 from July to January (see Table 10.9). We can convert this table into basis trading format (see Table 10.10).

Once again, notice how selling the basis resulted in a basis gain of $0.40, which reduced the net purchase price by $0.40. Monitoring the basis change, and incorporating this change into the net purchase price, is much simpler for the hedger than simultaneously reconciling futures market losses and cash market gains. Also notice for both scenarios that, regardless of the market direction, selling the basis resulted in a basis gain of $0.40 and a net purchase price of $3.10. Similar scenarios could be developed for each of the possible combinations of cash price change/futures price change and change/basis level/basis change (+ or −) for a long hedger. However, all would show that focusing on the basis, instead of the separate cash and futures prices, can greatly simplify the hedging process.

Treating the basis as an observable measurement, rather than simply as the residual between two prices, paves the way for using the basis as a tradable value which can be bought and sold like any other instrument. Basis trading allows commercial hedgers to protect themselves from changes in the general price level. In the next chapter we will see how basis trading can allow commercial hedgers to speculate on basis changes as a way to enhance profits.

Table 10.9 Results for Long Hedge: Falling Prices, Basis Positive and Weakens, Detailed Dates

	Cash	−	Futures	=	Basis
JulY1:	[Short at $3.50]		Long MarY2 at $3.00		+$0.50
JanY2:	Long at $2.50		Short MarY2 at $2.40		+$0.10
Gain (Loss):	+$1.00		−$0.60		+$0.40
Net Price:	$2.50 actual cash purchase price + $0.60 futures loss = $3.10 net purchase price				
or:	$3.50 expected cash purchase price − $0.40 basis gain = $3.10 net purchase price				

Table 10.10 Results for Long Hedge: Falling Prices, Basis Positive and Weakens, Basis Trading Format, Detailed Dates

	Futures	+	Basis	=	Cash
JulY1:	Long MarY2 at $3.00		Short at +$0.50		[Short at $3.50]
JanY2:	Short MarY2 at $2.40		Long at +$0.10		Long at $2.50
Gain (Loss):	−$0.60		+$0.40		+$1.00
Net Price:	$2.50 actual cash purchase price + $0.60 futures loss = $3.10 net purchase price				
or:	$3.50 expected cash purchase price − $0.40 basis gain = $3.10 net purchase price				
or:	$3.00 futures price in JulY1 + $0.10 basis in JanY2 = $3.10 net purchase price				

11 Basis Trading and Rolling a Hedge

Basis traders often use historical values to select the contract month that provides the greatest profit opportunity from a favorable basis change. In Chapter 8, we introduced the concept of rolling futures positions, either forward in time to a later-to-expire contract month or back in time to a sooner-to-expire contract month. In this chapter, we will show how futures positions can be rolled forward or rolled back to capture favorable basis opportunities. As in previous chapters, we will ignore commissions and other transaction costs.

Rolling a Hedge to Capture a Favorable Basis

Rolling Forward a Long Hedge

At any given time there will be a number of futures contract months eligible for trading, and a number of different basis values that can be calculated. For example, if the cash price today is $3.00 and the futures prices today are $3.10 for the December contract, $3.20 for the March contract and $3.30 for the May contract, the basis values are −$0.10 (= $3.00 − $3.10) for the December contract, −$0.20 for the March contract, and −$0.30 for the May contract. Consequently there is not "the" basis but instead several different basis values, as shown in Figure 11.1, each with its own historical values that can be used to determine the normal levels and seasonal patterns throughout the year.

In Example 8.1 from Chapter 8, a processor buys March corn futures in October to lock in the price until February. However, in December it rolls forward the hedge by two months, simultaneously selling March futures and buying May futures to lock in the price. In April, it buys cash corn and simultaneously sells the May futures position to lift the hedge. Recall that October and December are in one calendar year, designated Y1, and April is in the next calendar year, designated Y2. The final results are shown in Table 8.5.

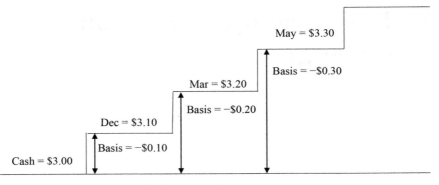

Figure 11.1 Basis Values for Multiple Futures Contracts

Table 8.5 Results for Long Hedge: Rising Prices, Basis Positive and Weakens, Rolled Forward

	Cash −	Futures =	Basis
OctY1:	[Short at $3.50]	Long MarY2 at $3.00	+$0.50
DecY1:	{$4.30}	Short MarY2 at $3.90	+$0.40
DecY1:	{$4.30}	Long MayY2 at $4.05	+$0.25
AprY2:	Long at $4.60	Short MayY2 at $4.55	+$0.05
Gain (Loss):	−$1.10	+$0.90 on MarY2 +	+$0.10 on MarY2 +
		+$0.50 on MayY2	+$0.20 on MayY2
Net Price:	$4.60 actual cash purchase price −		
	$0.90 futures gain on MarY2 (= $3.90 − $3.00) −		
	$0.50 futures gain on MayY2 (= $4.55 − $4.05) =		
	$3.20 net purchase price		
or:	$3.50 expected cash purchase price −		
	$0.10 basis gain on MarY2 (= +$0.50 − $0.40) −		
	$0.20 basis gain on MayY2 (= +$0.25 − $0.05) =		
	$3.20 net purchase price		

Recall that the $4.30 cash price in December, shown in curved brackets, is used simply as a reference price for calculating the basis values; no cash transaction occurs until April when the cash corn is purchased. Also recall that the gains or losses on the futures positions and on the basis positions must be calculated separately for each futures contract. Finally, recall that in this example the processor captured a basis gain on both the March futures contract and the May futures contract. In the scenario for Example 8.1, the processor rolled the hedge due to a change in plans, but it also could have rolled the hedge to take advantage of basis trading opportunities.

Example 11.1: A processor buys and uses corn as part of its normal operations. It plans to buy cash corn in the spring, so in October it hedges using a long position in the March futures contract at $3.00 with the basis at +$0.50. In December the basis using the March futures contract has weakened by $0.10, and the processor now believes that the basis using the May futures contract is unusually strong at +$0.25. It knows that the historical average basis in April, using the May futures contract, is +$0.05, which suggests a potential gain from selling the basis of $0.20 (= +$0.25 − $0.05). Therefore, in December the processor rolls the futures position from the March contract at $3.90 to the May contract at $4.05. It lifts the hedge in April when the basis reaches +$0.05 and May futures are at $4.55. Notice that these are the same basic facts used in Example 8.1 and presented in Table 8.5. Also notice that October and December are in one calendar year, designated Y1, and April is in the next calendar year, designated Y2. We can convert this example into basis trading format (see Table 11.1).

Table 11.1 Results for Long Hedge: Rising Prices, Basis Positive and Weakens, Rolled Forward

	Futures +	Basis =	Cash
OctY1:	Long MarY2 at $3.00	Short at +$0.50	[Short at $3.50]
DecY1:	Short MarY2 at $3.90	Long at +$0.40	{$4.30}
DecY1:	Long MayY2 at $4.05	Short at +$0.25	{$4.30}
AprY2:	Short MayY2 at $4.55	Long at +$0.05	Long at $4.60
Gain (Loss):	+$0.90 on MarY2 +	+$0.10 on MarY2 +	−$1.10
	+$0.50 on MayY2	+$0.20 on MayY2	
Net Price:	$4.60 actual cash purchase price −		
	$0.90 futures gain on MarY2 (= $3.90 − $3.00) −		
	$0.50 futures gain on MayY2 (= $4.55 − $4.05) =		
	$3.20 net purchase price		
or:	$3.50 expected cash purchase price −		
	$0.10 basis gain on MarY2 (= +$0.50 − $0.40) −		
	$0.20 basis gain on MayY2 (= +$0.25 − $0.05) =		
	$3.20 net purchase price		

Notice that we cannot simply express the net purchase price in terms of the beginning futures price and the ending basis value, as we did in the previous examples, because we have two different futures contracts and two different basis values, each based on a different futures contract. However, we can standardize the futures prices and the basis values to the same futures contract via the *spread* or difference between the two futures contracts at the time the positions were rolled. In December, the March futures price was $3.90 and the May futures price was $4.05, so the spread was $0.15. This spread can be expressed as the premium of May futures relative to March futures (i.e., spread = +$0.15, so May futures = March futures + $0.15), or equivalently as the discount of March futures relative to May futures (i.e., spread = −$0.15, so March futures = May futures − $0.15). Standardizing futures and basis values to a common futures contract allows us to express all futures changes with a single number, and all basis changes with a single number.

Spread-Adjusted Futures Prices

If we standardize all futures prices to the March futures, then the $0.15 spread should be subtracted from the $4.55 price of the May futures in April, resulting in a $4.40 (= $4.55 − $0.15) spread-adjusted price for the March futures in April. This conversion implies that the March futures contract still exists in April, despite the fact that the March futures contract expired in March. When the long $3.00 March futures price in October is subtracted from this spread-adjusted short $4.40 March futures price in April, the result is a spread-adjusted futures gain of $1.40 (= $4.40 − $3.00). Notice that this spread-adjusted $1.40 gain is equal to the $0.90 gain on March futures (= $3.90 − $3.00) plus the $0.50 gain on May futures (= $4.55 − $4.05) from Table 11.1.

Conversely, if we standardize to the May futures, then the $0.15 spread should be added to the $3.00 price of the March futures in October, resulting in a $3.15 (= $3.00 + $0.15) spread-adjusted futures price for the May futures in October. When the long $3.15 spread-adjusted May futures price in October is subtracted from the short $4.55 May futures price in April, the result is a spread-adjusted futures gain of $1.40 (= $4.55 − $3.15). Notice that the futures gains are the same, regardless of whether prices are standardized to the March futures contract or the May futures contract.

Spread-Adjusted Basis Values

This same standardization process must be performed on the basis values, using the same $0.15 spread. If we standardize all basis values to the March futures, then the $0.15 spread should be added to the long +$0.05 basis for the May futures contract in April, resulting in a long +$0.20 (= $+0.05 + $0.15) spread-adjusted basis. When this long +$0.20 spread-adjusted basis is subtracted from the short +$0.50 basis for the March futures price in October, the result is a spread-adjusted basis gain of $0.30. Notice that this $0.30 spread-adjusted gain is equal to the $0.10 basis gain for the March futures (= +$0.50 − $0.40) plus the $0.20 basis gain for the May futures (= +$0.25 − $0.05) from Table 11.1.

Conversely, if we standardize the basis values to the May futures, then the $0.15 spread should be subtracted from the short +$0.50 basis for the March futures contract in October, resulting in a short +$0.35 (= +$0.50 − $0.15) spread-adjusted basis for the May futures in October. When the long +0.05 basis for the May futures contract in April is subtracted from

Table 11.1A Results for Long Hedge: Rising Prices, Basis Positive and Weakens, Rolled Forward Using Spread-Adjusted Futures Prices and Basis Values

	Futures	+	Basis	=	Cash
OctY1:	Long MarY2 at $3.00		Short at +$0.50		[Short at $3.50]
DecY1:	Short MarY2 at $3.90		Long at +$0.40		{$4.30}
DecY1:	Long MayY2 at $4.05		Short at +$0.25		{$4.30}
AprY2:	Short MayY2 at $4.55		Long at +$0.05		Long at $4.60
Gain (Loss):	+$0.90 on MarY2 +		+$0.10 on MarY2 +		−$1.10
	+$0.50 on MayY2		+$0.20 on MayY2		
Net Price:	$4.60 actual cash purchase price −				
	$0.90 futures gain on MarY2 (= $3.90 − $3.00) −				
	$0.50 futures gain on MayY2 (= $4.55 − $4.05) =				
	$3.20 net purchase price				
or:	$3.50 expected cash purchase price −				
	$0.10 basis gain on MarY2 (= +$0.50 − $0.40) −				
	$0.20 basis gain on MayY2 (= +$0.25 − $0.05) =				
	$3.20 net purchase price				
or:	*$3.00 MarY2 futures price in OctY1 +*				
	$0.20 spread-adjusted basis using MarY2 futures in AprY2 (= +$0.05 + $0.15) =				
	$3.20 net purchase price				
or:	*$3.15 spread-adjusted MayY2 futures price in OctY1 (= $3.00 + $0.15) +*				
	$0.05 basis using MayY2 futures in AprY2 =				
	$3.20 net purchase price				

this short +$0.35 spread-adjusted basis, the result is a basis gain of $0.30 (= +$0.35 − $0.05). Notice that the spread-adjusted basis gains are the same, regardless of whether basis values are standardized to the March futures contract or the May futures contract.

With these standardized futures and basis values, we now can express the net purchase price in terms of the beginning futures price and the ending basis value, shown in italics at the bottom of Table 11.1A.

Rolling Back a Short Hedge

The same principles can be applied to rolling a short hedge, and to rolling back the hedge to an earlier time. In Example 8.2 from Chapter 8, a farmer in August locks in the price for the following June by selling July corn futures. However, in November the farmer rolls back the hedge by four months to March, simultaneously buying July futures and selling March futures to lock in the price. In February they sell cash corn and simultaneously buy the March futures to lift the hedge. Recall that August and November are in one calendar year, designated Y1, and February is in the next calendar year, designated Y2. The final results are shown in Table 8.7.

Table 8.7 Results for Short Hedge: Falling Prices, Basis Negative and Strengthens, Rolled Back

	Cash −	Futures =	Basis
AugY1:	[Long at $3.50]	Short JulY2 at $4.00	−$0.50
NovY1	{$3.30}	Long JulY2 at $3.70	−$0.40
NovY1	{$3.30}	Short MarY2 at $3.55	−$0.25
FebY2:	Short at $3.00	Long MarY2 at $3.15	−$0.15
Gain (Loss):	−$0.50	+$0.60	+$0.10
Net Price:	$3.00 actual cash sale price +		
	$0.30 futures gain on JulY2 (= $4.00 − $3.70) +		
	$0.40 futures gain on MarY2 (= $3.55 − $3.15) =		
	$3.70 net sale price		
or:	$3.50 expected cash sale price +		
	$0.10 basis gain on JulY2 (= −$0.40 + $0.50) +		
	$0.10 basis gain on MarY2 (= −$0.25 + $0.15) =		
	$3.70 net sale price		

Recall that the $3.30 cash price in November, shown in curved brackets, is used simply as a reference price for calculating the basis values; no cash transaction occurs until February when the cash corn is sold. Also recall that the gains or losses on the futures positions and on the basis positions must be calculated separately for each futures contract. Finally, recall that in this example the farmer captured a basis gain on both the July futures contract and the March futures contract. In the scenario for Example 8.2 the farmer rolled the hedge due to a change in plans, but they also could have rolled the hedge to take advantage of basis trading opportunities.

Example 11.2: A farmer grows and sells corn as part of their normal operations. They plan to sell cash corn in the following calendar year when the basis is stronger, so in August they hedge using a short position in the July futures contract at $4.00 with the basis at −$0.50. In November the basis using the July futures contract has strengthened by $0.10, and the farmer now believes that the basis using the March futures contract is unusually weak at −$0.25. They know that the historical average basis in February, using the March futures contract, is −$0.15, which suggests a potential gain from buying the basis of $0.10 (= −$0.15 −(−$0.25)). Therefore, in November the farmer rolls the futures position from the July contract at $3.70 to the March contract at $3.55. They lift the hedge in February when the basis reaches −$0.15 and March futures are at $3.15. Notice that these details are consistent with those in Example 8.2 and presented in Table 8.7. Also notice that August and November are in one calendar year, designated Y1, and February is in the next calendar year, designated Y2. We can convert this example into basis trading format (see Table 11.2).

Table 11.2 Results for Short Hedge: Falling Prices, Basis Negative and Strengthens, Rolled Back

	Futures +	Basis =	Cash
AugY1:	Short JulY2 at $4.00	Long at −$0.50	[Long at $3.50]
NovY1	Long JulY2 at $3.70	Short at −$0.40	{$3.30}
NovY1	Short MarY2 at $3.55	Long at −$0.25	{$3.30}
FebY2:	Long MarY2 at $3.15	Short at −$0.15	Short at $3.00
Gain (Loss):	+$0.60	+$0.10	−$0.50
Net Price:	$3.00 actual cash sale price + $0.30 futures gain on JulY2 (= $4.00 − $3.70) + $0.40 futures gain on MarY2 (= $3.55 − $3.15) = $3.70 net sale price		
or:	$3.50 expected cash sale price + $0.10 basis gain on JulY2 (= −$0.40 + $0.50) + $0.10 basis gain on MarY2 (= −$0.25 + $0.15) = $3.70 net sale price		

Notice that we cannot simply express the net sale price in terms of the beginning futures price and the ending basis value, because we have two different futures contracts and two different basis values, each based on a different futures contract. However, we can standardize the futures prices and the basis values to the same futures contract, using the spread between the two futures contracts at the time the positions were rolled. In November, the July futures price was $3.70 and the March futures price was $3.55, so the spread was $0.15. This spread can be expressed as the premium of July futures relative to March futures (i.e., spread = +$0.15, so July futures = March futures + $0.15), or equivalently as the discount of March futures relative to July futures (i.e., spread = −$0.15, so March futures = July futures − $0.15).

Spread-Adjusted Futures Prices

If we standardize all futures prices to the March futures, then the $0.15 spread should be subtracted from the $4.00 price of the July futures in August, resulting in a $3.85 (= $4.00 − $0.15) spread-adjusted price for the March futures in August. When the long $3.15 March futures price in February is subtracted from this spread-adjusted short $3.85 March futures price in August, the result is a spread-adjusted futures gain of $0.70 (= $3.85 − $3.15). Notice that this spread-adjusted $0.70 gain is equal to the $0.30 gain on July futures (= $4.00 − $3.70) plus the $0.40 gain on March futures (= $3.55 − $3.15) from Table 11.2.

Conversely, if we standardize to the July futures, then the $0.15 spread should be added to the $3.15 price of the March futures in February, resulting in a $3.30 (= $3.15 + $0.15) spread-adjusted futures price for the July futures in February. When the long $3.30 spread-adjusted July futures price in February is subtracted from the short $4.00 July futures price in August, the result is a spread-adjusted futures gain of $0.70 (= $4.00 − $3.30). Notice that the futures gains are the same, regardless of whether prices are standardized to the March futures contract or the July futures contract.

Spread-Adjusted Basis Values

This same standardization process must be performed on the basis values, using this same $0.15 spread. If we standardize all basis values to the March futures, then the $0.15 spread should be added to the long −$0.50 basis using the July futures in August, resulting in a long −$0.35 (= −$0.50 + $0.15) spread-adjusted basis for the March futures in August. When this long −$0.35 spread-adjusted basis is subtracted from the short −$0.15 basis for the March futures in February, the result is a spread-adjusted basis gain of $0.20. Notice that this $0.20 spread-adjusted gain is equal to the $0.10 basis gain for the July futures (= −$0.40 + $0.50) plus the $0.10 basis gain for the March futures (= −$0.15 + $0.25) from Table 11.2.

Conversely, if we standardize the basis values to the July futures, then the $0.15 spread should be subtracted from the short −$0.15 basis for the March futures in February, resulting in a short −$0.30 spread-adjusted basis for the July futures in February. When the long −0.50 basis for the July futures in August is subtracted from this short −$0.30 spread-adjusted basis, the result is a basis gain of $0.20. Notice that the spread-adjusted basis gains are the same, regardless of whether basis values are standardized to the March futures contract or the July futures contract.

With these standardized futures and basis values, we now can express the net sale price in terms of the beginning futures price and the ending basis value, shown in italics at the bottom of Table 11.2A.

Spreads, the Forward Curve, and Basis Behavior

In both Example 11.1 and Example 11.2, the hedger rolled the futures position one time, and in each case the position was rolled in a particular direction. In practice, there is no limit to the number of times a futures position may be rolled, and a futures position may be rolled forward or rolled back to any available futures contract. Regardless of the number of times a hedge is rolled, the number of different futures contracts used, or the direction of the roll

Table 11.2A Results for Short Hedge: Falling Prices, Basis Negative and Strengthens, Rolled Back Using Spread-Adjusted Futures Prices and Basis Values

	Futures	+	Basis	=	Cash
AugY1:	Short JulY2 at $4.00		Long at −$0.50		[Long at $3.50]
NovY1	Long JulY2 at $3.70		Short at −$0.40		{$3.30}
NovY1	Short MarY2 at $3.55		Long at −$0.25		{$3.30}
FebY2:	Long MarY2 at $3.15		Short at −$0.15		Short at $3.00
Gain (Loss):	+$0.60		+$0.10		−$0.50
Net Price:	$3.00 actual cash sale price +				
	$0.30 futures gain on JulY2 (= $4.00 − $3.70) +				
	$0.40 futures gain on MarY2 (= $3.55 − $3.15) =				
	$3.70 net sale price				
or:	$3.50 expected cash sale price +				
	$0.10 basis gain on JulY2 (= −$0.40 + $0.50) +				
	$0.10 basis gain on MarY2 (= −$0.25 + $0.15) =				
	$3.70 net sale price				
or:	*$4.00 JulY2 futures price in AugY1 −*				
	$0.30 spread-adjusted basis using JulY2 futures in FebY2 (= −$0.15 − $0.15) =				
	$3.70 net purchase price				
or:	*$3.85 spread-adjusted MarY2 futures price in AugY1 (= $4.00 − $0.15) −*				
	$0.15 basis using MarY2 futures in FebY2 =				
	$3.70 net purchase price				

(i.e., forward or back), the methods presented above can be used to determine the spread-adjusted values for the futures price and the basis.

The relationship between the basis and the spread is an important one and deserves further explanation. The spread reflects the shape of the forward curve, which was discussed in Chapter 3. In a normal or contango market, the forward curve will be upward-sloping, so the spread – which we will define here as the later-to-expire price minus the sooner-to-expire price – will be positive. In an inverted or backwardated market, the forward curve will be downward-sloping, so the spread between two futures contracts will be negative.

The shape of the forward curve, and consequently the sign (i.e., + or −) of the spread, are useful indicators of future basis behavior. When the forward curve is upward-sloping and spreads are positive – conditions typical of a surplus – the basis is generally weak and is likely to strengthen. Under these conditions, a basis trader would prefer a long basis (i.e., short hedge) strategy, all else the same. Conversely, when the forward curve is downward-sloping and spreads are negative – conditions commonly observed in a shortage – the basis is generally strong and is likely to weaken, so a basis trader would prefer a short basis (i.e., long hedge) strategy, all else the same.

Recall that the futures price establishes the general price level, while the basis reflects local supply/demand conditions. In a surplus situation, both the futures market and the basis will be signaling buyers to make purchases now and simultaneously signaling sellers to make sales later. The futures market sends this message via an upward-sloping forward curve and positive spreads (i.e., lower prices now and higher prices later), and the basis sends this message via a weak basis relative to historical levels (i.e., weaker basis now and stronger basis later).

Conversely, in a shortage situation, both the futures market and the basis will be signaling buyers to make purchases later and simultaneously signaling sellers to make sales now. The futures market sends this message via a downward-sloping forward curve and negative spreads (i.e., lower prices now and higher prices later), and the basis sends this message via a strong basis relative to historical levels (i.e., stronger basis now and weaker basis later). Because futures prices and the basis work in tandem to convey this information to the market, knowing whether spreads are positive or negative can help a basis trader determine whether they should be long the basis or short the basis.

Spread Impact on Hedging Results

When a short hedge (i.e., long basis position) is rolled forward, the hedger buys a *nearby* or sooner-to-expire futures contract and simultaneously sells a *deferred* or later-to-expire futures contract. When a long hedge (i.e., short basis position) is rolled back, the hedger sells a deferred futures contract and simultaneously buys a nearby futures contract. Notice that both rolling actions involve buying a nearby contract and selling a deferred contract, which is commonly referred to as a *bull spread*. When a bull spread is held as a speculative position – covered in the next chapter – both futures positions will be held simultaneously, and the trader will profit if the nearby contract increases more (or decreases less) than the deferred contract, causing the spread to narrow or decrease. This narrowing of the spread is more likely to occur in a bull market, hence the name. From our discussion above, a narrowing of the spread is likely to occur in combination with a strengthening of the basis, all else the same.

Conversely, when a long hedge (i.e., short basis position) is rolled forward, the hedger sells a nearby futures contract and simultaneously buys a deferred futures contract. When a short hedge (i.e., long basis position) is rolled back, the hedger buys a deferred futures contract and simultaneously sells a nearby futures contract. Notice that both rolling actions involve selling the nearby contract and buying the deferred, which is commonly referred to as a *bear spread*. When a bear spread is held as a speculative position, both futures positions will be held simultaneously, and the trader will profit if the nearby contract decreases more (or increases less) than the deferred contract, causing the spread to widen or increase. This widening of the spread is more likely to occur in a bear market, hence the name. A widening of the spread is likely to occur in combination with a weakening of the basis, all else the same.

Notice that rolling a hedge does not actually create a bull spread or a bear spread, because the hedger holds only one futures position, not two, but bull/bear spreading is a useful way to think about the rolling process. By rolling the hedge, the hedger exchanges their current futures position and current basis for different ones, which is equivalent to establishing a new hedge. For this new hedge to be successful the basis needs to strengthen (for a short hedge), or the basis needs to weaken (for a long hedge).

Basis Impact of an Implicit Bear Spread

We can observe this in the following excerpt from Table 11.1 (renamed here Table 11.3).

Table 11.3 Excerpt of Results for Long Hedge: Rising Prices, Basis Positive and Weakens, Rolled Forward

	Futures +	Basis =	Cash
OctY1:	Long MarY2 at $3.00	Short at +$0.50	[Short at $3.50]
DecY1:	Short MarY2 at $3.90	Long at +$0.40	{$4.30}
DecY1:	Long MayY2 at $4.05	Short at +$0.25	{$4.30}
AprY2:	Short MayY2 at $4.55	Long at +$0.05	Long at $4.60

Notice that an implicit bear spread is created in December using short March futures (i.e., nearby) and long May futures (i.e., deferred). This is not an actual bear spread because the short March futures in December offsets the long March futures established in October, leaving the long May futures to make the price level adjustments for the hedge.

We can standardize all these values to the May futures, using the methods presented earlier in this chapter. The $0.15 spread between the March futures and May futures should be added to the $3.00 price of the March futures in October, resulting in a $3.15 (= $3.00 + $0.15) spread-adjusted futures price for the May futures in October. In addition, the $0.15 spread should be subtracted from the short +$0.50 basis for the March futures contract in October, resulting in a short +$0.35 (= +$0.50 − $0.15) spread-adjusted basis for the May futures in October. Then we can restate Table 11.3 with all positions expressed in terms of the May futures (see Table 11.3A).

Table 11.3A Excerpt of Results for Long Hedge: Rising Prices, Basis Positive and Weakens, Rolled Forward Using Spread-Adjusted Futures Prices and Basis Values

	Futures +	Basis =	Cash
OctY1:	Long MayY2 at $3.15 (= $3.00 + $0.15)	Short at +$0.35 (= +$0.50 − $0.15)	[Short at $3.50]
DecY1:			
DecY1:			
AprY2:	Short MayY2 at $4.55	Long at +$0.05	Long at $4.60

Notice that a larger (i.e., wider) spread would increase the spread-adjusted beginning futures price on the long futures position and decrease the spread-adjusted beginning basis value on the short basis position, all else the same. These results are consistent with a bear spread, in which a wider spread is associated with a weaker basis, and would reduce the potential profit of the rolled hedge. Conversely, a smaller (i.e., narrower) spread would decrease the spread-adjusted beginning futures price and increase the spread-adjusted beginning basis value, which would increase the potential profit of the rolled hedge.

Basis Impact of an Implicit Bull Spread

Example 11.2 and Table 11.2 involve rolling back a short hedge and therefore also contain an implicit bear spread. However, reversing the long and short positions in Table 11.2 will convert it into an example of rolling back a long hedge, which we will use to demonstrate an implicit bull spread (see Table 11.4).

Table 11.4 Excerpt of Results for Long Hedge: Falling Prices, Basis Negative and Strengthens, Rolled Back

	Futures +	Basis =	Cash
AugY1:	Long JulY2 at $4.00	Short at −$0.50	[Short at $3.50]
NovY1	Short JulY2 at $3.70	Long at −$0.40	{$3.30}
NovY1	Long MarY2 at $3.55	Short at −$0.25	{$3.30}
FebY2:	Short MarY2 at $3.15	Long at −$0.15	Long at $3.00

Notice that an implicit bull spread is created in November using short July futures (i.e., deferred) and long March futures (i.e., nearby). This is not an actual bull spread because the short July futures in November offsets the long July futures established in August, leaving the long March futures to make the price level adjustments for the hedge.

We can standardize all these values to the March futures. The $0.15 spread between the March futures and July futures should be subtracted from the $4.00 price of the July futures in August, resulting in a $3.85 (= $4.00 − $0.15) spread-adjusted futures price for the March futures in August. In addition, the $0.15 spread should be added to the short −$0.50 basis for the July futures contract in August, resulting in a short −$0.35 (= −$0.50 + $0.15) spread-adjusted basis for the July futures in August. Then we can restate Table 11.4 with all positions expressed in terms of the March futures (see Table 11.4A).

Table 11.4A Excerpt of Results for Long Hedge: Falling Prices, Basis Negative and Strengthens, Rolled Back Using Spread-Adjusted Futures Prices and Basis Values

	Futures +	Basis =	Cash
AugY1:	Long MarY2 at $3.85 (= $4.00 − $0.15)	Short at −$0.35 (= −$0.50 + $0.15)	[Short at $3.50]
NovY1			
NovY1			
FebY2:	Short MarY2 at $3.15	Long at −$0.15	Long at $3.00

Notice that in this case a larger (i.e., wider) spread would decrease (rather than increase) the spread-adjusted beginning futures price on the long futures position and increase (rather than decrease) the spread-adjusted beginning basis value on the short basis position, all else the same. These results are consistent with a bull spread, in which a wider spread is associated with a stronger basis, so a larger spread would increase the profit potential of rolled hedge. Conversely, a smaller (i.e., narrower) spread would increase the spread-adjusted beginning futures price and decrease the spread-adjusted beginning basis value, which would decrease the potential profit of the rolled hedge.

From these examples we can see why the spread must be incorporated into any decision about rolling a hedge. Basis trading allows commercial hedgers to protect themselves from changes in the general price level, and to speculate on basis changes as a way to enhance profits. Hedges can be rolled forward and back to take advantage of favorable basis opportunities, with the (i.e., narrower) spread between the two futures contracts being an important determinant of the profitability from rolling a hedge.

12 Speculating with Futures

The focus of this book until now has been on hedging with futures and the role of hedgers. Hedging is the use of futures positions with cash positions to manage price-level risk, and basis behavior determines hedging performance. Risk management is the primary motive for hedging, and is the reason why futures markets exist.

The other type of futures market activity is *speculation*, which is the use of futures positions to profit from favorable price changes. Normally there is no cash market position associated with a speculative futures position, so there is no basis and therefore no basis gain or loss. Speculators as a group hold a wide range of opinions about market direction and price relationships, so typically there is a speculator who is willing to buy or sell whenever a hedger wants to sell or buy. Stated differently, speculators provide *liquidity*, or the ability to enter and exit the market without affecting the price. Consequently, speculators are an essential component of a well-functioning market.

Speculation vs. Investment

Speculating is often contrasted negatively with investing. Investing (as in the purchase of securities such as stocks and bonds) is said to provide companies with capital for productive purposes that benefit society; in contrast, speculation is said to be nothing more than betting on prices and therefore serves no economic purpose. In fact, companies never see any of the money that investors spend on stocks and bonds in the secondary market. Only newly-issued securities generate new capital, so most of what is commonly called "investment" is really nothing more than betting on the prices of existing securities, possibly with the added bonus of periodic stock dividends or bond interest payments.

This raises an important question: Why is betting on commodity futures prices any different from – or any better than – betting on securities, or for that matter betting in a casino? To begin to answer this question, we should differentiate speculation, which deals with existing risks, from ordinary gambling, which creates risks where none exist. By itself, gambling serves no higher economic or societal purpose, beyond providing entertainment value to the participants. In contrast, futures speculation provides liquidity that assists hedgers in their risk-management efforts. (Similarly, securities speculation provides liquidity that facilitates the issuance of new securities.) In addition, speculation contributes to the price discovery process by helping to move prices to their economically justified values, thereby benefiting the broader economy.

Speculative Styles

Scalping

There are several different styles or types of futures speculation. At one extreme are traders commonly referred to as *scalpers* or *locals*. These speculators act as *market makers* who are always willing to make a market, or buy when someone wants to sell, and sell when someone wants to buy. The term "scalper" refers to the way that these traders take a small slice of the price, while the term "local" refers to how these traders lived in the cities where the exchanges were located, unlike most customers, who lived elsewhere. Under normal market conditions, scalpers are willing to buy at one or two ticks, or minimum price increments, below the current market price and willing to sell at one or two ticks above the current market price. Scalpers make trades hundreds or thousands of times a day in an effort to capture the bid-ask spread. Scalpers typically will hold a particular futures contract for only a brief time – seconds to minutes – and try to avoid accumulating a sizeable position, either long or short, to limit their exposure to sudden market moves. They also strive to end each day's trading session *flat*, or with no position. They generally have no opinion about the direction of the market, and as the market moves higher or lower they will constantly adjust their bid and ask prices accordingly, all in an effort to make a small profit on each trade. As long as the profitable trades outnumber the unprofitable ones, a scalper will make a profit.

Obviously, not every contract that a scalper buys will be profitable – the market may go down before it can be sold and liquidated – and not every contract that a scalper sells will be profitable – the market may go up before it can be bought and liquidated. This is particularly true when the market is volatile and prices are changing rapidly, or when the market is trending – either up or down – and the scalper accumulates an inventory of positions on one side of the market, either long or short. When a scalper is exposed to more risk, they typically will respond by widening, or increasing the *width*, or the size of the gap, of the bid-ask spread; they may also reduce the *depth*, or the number of contracts they are willing buy or sell at a particular price. Conversely, when the market is less volatile and scalpers are exposed to less risk, they generally will respond by narrowing the bid-ask spread and may also increase the number of contracts they will buy or sell at a particular price. This explains why the width of the bid-ask spread is often used as a measure of liquidity, with a *tighter* or narrower spread indicating greater liquidity, all else the same. In recent years, computerized trading programs have been developed to replicate the liquidity-providing role that scalpers perform. In many markets, these programs have largely replaced individual scalpers, particularly as electronic trading platforms have replaced trading pits.

Position Trading

At the other extreme of the trading style spectrum are *position traders*, who take *outright* long or short positions and hold them for a period of time in hopes of making a profit when the price moves up or down in their favor. Unlike scalpers, position traders may hold positions for days, weeks, or months – until either the trader's price objectives are reached or the trader gives up and exits the market. This description implies two other important differences between position traders and scalpers. First, position traders have a definite opinion about the direction of the market and frequently rely on forecasting tools to develop those opinions. These forecasting tools may be based on *fundamental analysis*, which uses supply and demand factors to determine the economic equilibrium price. Alternatively, they may be based on *technical analysis*, which uses trading signals from chart formations, equations, or computer programs to make timing decisions on when to buy or sell. Second, position traders must have the ability to maintain their positions for extended periods of time, and therefore require both patience and substantial trading capital to withstand losses when the market (temporarily) moves in the wrong direction. Position traders serve an important economic function by identifying situations where the market is mispriced, and buying (if the market is too low) or selling (if the market is too high) to help move the price level back to its equilibrium level.

Spreading

Somewhat intermediate in style are *spreaders*, who trade on price relationships or differences and hold simultaneous long and short positions in different markets or contracts. Spreaders serve an important economic function by identifying situations where one market or contract month is mispriced relative to another. Stated differently, spreaders look for situations where one market or contract is either too high or too low compared to the other, and consequently the difference between them is either wide or too narrow. Spread traders then take positions that help move the price relationship back to its equilibrium level, by buying the underpriced position and simultaneously selling the overpriced position.

Like position traders, spreaders may hold positions for days, weeks, or months, and they often use fundamentals to identify trading opportunities. But unlike position traders, spreaders are indifferent about the price level, and do not care whether prices move higher or lower. This is because holding simultaneous long and short positions in related contract months or markets acts as a hedge against changes in the price level, with gains in one position largely offsetting losses in the other. Consequently, spread positions typically involve less risk than outright long or short positions, all else the same.

Notice that hedging is a special case of spread trading, in which simultaneous short and long positions are held in the cash commodity and the corresponding futures contract, and the spread between them is the basis (i.e., cash minus futures). In the same way that basis traders think in terms of buying or selling the basis, spread traders think in terms of buying or selling the spread. As long as the spread widens (for a trader who buys the spread) or narrows (for a trader who sells the spread), the spreader will make a profit. Spreaders view the spread as a tangible value, so they ignore the price changes for the individual *legs* or components of the spread, and focus instead on the combined result or difference.

Intra-Market Spreads

There are a number of different types of spreads. *Intra-market spreads*, also called *calendar spreads*, involve long and short positions in different contract months of the same market. For example, a *carry spread* or *storage spread* involves two different contract months in the same production cycle of a storable commodity, such as March corn vs. May corn, and uses the cost of carry to determine whether the spread is too wide or too narrow.

Another example of a calendar spread is an *old crop-new crop spread* which involves two contract months in different production cycles, such as July corn vs. December corn. Because of the different production cycles, the cost of carry is not a factor, and historical price relationships may be used to determine whether the spread is too wide or too narrow. The same historical approach is used for calendar spreads on nonstorable and/or continuously-produced commodities, in which the spread relationships are driven by differences in supply/demand factors for the two different contract months.

Many – but not all – markets use the naming convention for calendar spreads in which the first leg is the nearby (i.e., sooner-to-expire) contract month and the second leg is the deferred (i.e., later-to-expire) contract month. Many – but not all – markets also use the naming convention in which *buying the spread* means buying the first leg and selling the second, and *selling the spread* means selling the first leg and buying the second.

Suppose that we have a market with an upward-sloping forward curve. In this scenario, buying the spread means buying the lower-priced contract (i.e., the first or nearby leg) and selling the higher-priced contract (i.e., the second or deferred leg). Buying the spread also implies that the spread will be profitable if it widens (i.e., becomes larger), but the strategy described here will be profitable only if the spread narrows (i.e., gets smaller). This simple example illustrates the sometimes confusing and inconsistent terminology associated with spread trading.

To avoid such problems, a trader can refer to buying a nearby contract and selling a deferred contract as a bull spread, a term introduced in Chapter 11 and one whose meaning is consistent and universally understood across all markets. A bull spread will be profitable if the nearby contract increases more (or decreases less) than the deferred contract, causing the spread to narrow or decrease, which is the scenario described in the previous paragraph. As noted in the previous chapter, this narrowing of the spread is more likely to occur in a bull market, hence the name. Conversely, the reader should refer to selling a nearby contract and buying a deferred contract as a bear spread. A bear spread will be profitable if the nearby contract decreases more (or increases less) than the deferred contract, causing the spread to widen or increase. This widening of the spread is more likely to occur in a bear market, hence the name.

Intra-market spreads are not limited to two legs. A *butterfly futures spread* has three legs, and uses a series of three contract months within a particular time period, where the middle contract month is mispriced relative to both the soonest-to-expire (i.e., first) and latest-to-expire (i.e., last) contract months in the series. For example, if the middle month is overpriced relative to the others, then the spreader would sell 2 of the middle contract months, and simultaneously buy 1 of the first contract month and buy 1 of the last contract month. Conversely, if the middle month is underpriced relative to the others, then the spreader would buy 2 of the middle contract month, and simultaneously sell 1 of the first contract month and sell 1 of the last contract month. Notice that a butterfly spread is balanced, with equal numbers of short and long positions. Also notice that the spreader will be indifferent about whether the contracts move up or down, or by how much, as long as the three contract months come into alignment with one another.

Inter-Market Spreads

Inter-market spreads can involve equal numbers of long and short positions, generally in the same contract months, but in different markets. Spreads may be created between commodities that are substitutes or complements. Examples of popular inter-market spreads, using the same contract months, include wheat vs. corn, live cattle vs. lean hogs, WTI crude oil vs. Brent crude oil, corn vs. soybeans, gold vs. silver, and any two of Chicago wheat, Kansas City wheat, and Minneapolis wheat. In all cases the respective commodities have overlapping supply or demand factors that affect the prices for both goods. Notice that these spreads are balanced, with equal numbers of long and short positions.

Inter-market spreads also include *processing spreads*, which reflect input–output relationships or other physical linkages, and often involve different numbers of contracts to represent the relative amounts of the respective commodities in the relationship. Popular examples include the soybean crush (10 contracts of soybeans vs. 9 contracts of soybean oil plus 12 contracts of soybean meal), the crack spread (3 contracts of crude oil vs. 2 contracts of gasoline plus 1 contract of heating oil or diesel fuel), and the cattle crush (2 contracts of feeder cattle plus 1 contract of corn vs. 4 contracts of live cattle). Notice that these spreads are not balanced in terms of the numbers of long and short positions, but they are balanced in terms of the dollar values of those long and short positions.

All of these spreads were described in detail in Chapter 9, but were presented as hedging strategies. Notice that these spreads also can be used as speculative strategies, in situations where the spread or processing margin is either too high or too low relative to historical norms. In each case, the value of the output(s) should reflect the value of the input(s) plus a processing cost to transform the input(s) into the final product(s). Commodity markets are characterized by zero long-run economic profits, so if the combined value of the outputs is substantially greater than the combined value of the inputs plus the processing cost, a trader might sell the outputs and buy the inputs. Conversely, if the combined value of the outputs is substantially less than the combined value of the inputs plus the processing cost, a trader might sell the outputs and buy the inputs.

At the beginning of this chapter we described how scalpers provide liquidity by their willingness to buy or sell at a slight difference from the current market price. Position traders and spreaders also provide liquidity, but in a much different manner. These traders have a wide spectrum of opinions about market direction and price relationships, and rely on countless numbers of forecasting methods and trading strategies with varying objectives, all of which leads to a constant stream of buying and selling activity. Consequently, there is almost always a speculator who is willing to buy or sell – either to create a new position or to liquidate an existing one – whenever a hedger needs to place or lift a hedge.

Speculators and Speculative Impact

Speculators account for the majority of trading activity in most futures markets, whether measured by the number of individual traders, percentage of volume, or percentage of open interest. While this high level of involvement in the markets further confirms the liquidity-providing role of speculators, it also helps to explain the negative connotation often associated with speculation. Over the years, speculators frequently have been blamed by hedgers and various public officials for "manipulating" the markets when prices move in the "wrong" direction. Upon closer examination these allegations typically turn out to be unfounded, particularly in recent decades since these markets have been better regulated. Nevertheless, it is important for the reader to appreciate the natural tension that exists between hedgers and speculators, much of which is due to the zero-sum-game nature of futures trading. This natural tension also explains much of the regulatory structure designed to monitor speculators and speculative activity.

Commitments of Traders

In Chapter 5 we introduced the concept of *reportable levels* for the number of contracts above which large traders – hedgers and speculators alike – must report the actual number of positions they hold and classify those positions as hedging or speculative. These reportable traders must disclose the positions they hold as of the close of business each Tuesday, and on the following Friday afternoon the CFTC publishes the *Commitments of Traders* report. This publication is a market-by-market compilation of the positions held by all reporting traders, for each market with 20 or more reporting traders. It provides a weekly summary of the types of traders and the numbers of long and short positions held by reportable traders in each trader category.

These data are reported to the public in various formats, with the *Disaggregated Commitments of Traders* providing the most detailed information. The *Disaggregated* report for corn futures as of Tuesday, December 27, 2016 was introduced in Chapter 5 as Table 5.1 and is reproduced here. The reportable threshold for corn futures is 250 contracts in all contract months combined, which are owned or controlled by an individual or entity. For the following discussion of Figure 5.1, we will refer to the rows designated "All." We will ignore the rows labeled "Old" and "Other," which allow comparisons to certain historical versions of the report.

Open Interest as the Measure of Commitment

The *Commitments of Traders* report uses open interest (i.e., the number of contracts owned or controlled as of the reporting date), not volume (i.e., the number of contracts bought or sold

CORN - CHICAGO BOARD OF TRADE
Disaggregated Commitments of Traders - Futures Only, December 27, 2016

Code-002602

	Open Interest	Producer/Merchant/ Processor/User		Swap Dealers			Managed Money			Other Reportables			Nonreportable Positions	
		Long	Short	Long	Short	Spreading	Long	Short	Spreading	Long	Short	Spreading	Long	Short
							Reportable Positions							

(CONTRACTS OF 5,000 BUSHELS)

Positions

	Open Interest	PM Long	PM Short	Swap Long	Swap Short	Swap Spreading	MM Long	MM Short	MM Spreading	Other Long	Other Short	Other Spreading	Nonrep Long	Nonrep Short
All	1,231,462	305,691	540,774	261,693	3,607	12,425	163,648	273,250	63,799	178,037	58,581	105,195	140,974	173,831
Old	1,096,404	257,766	476,872	246,591	3,576	4,688	154,925	261,315	59,126	168,693	65,929	80,757	123,858	144,141
Other	135,058	47,925	63,902	20,681	5,610	2,158	12,682	15,894	714	30,100	13,408	3,682	17,116	29,690

Changes in Commitments from: December 20, 2016

	Open Interest	PM Long	PM Short	Swap Long	Swap Short	Swap Spreading	MM Long	MM Short	MM Spreading	Other Long	Other Short	Other Spreading	Nonrep Long	Nonrep Short
	4,026	19,309	-13,684	-7,633	-383	-829	-117	13,959	3,024	-13,379	8,712	-1,982	5,633	-4,791

Percent of Open Interest Represented by Each Category of Trader

	Open Interest	PM Long	PM Short	Swap Long	Swap Short	Swap Spreading	MM Long	MM Short	MM Spreading	Other Long	Other Short	Other Spreading	Nonrep Long	Nonrep Short
All	100.0	24.8	43.9	21.3	0.3	1.0	13.3	22.2	5.2	14.5	4.8	8.5	11.4	14.1
Old	100.0	23.5	43.5	22.5	0.3	0.4	14.1	23.8	5.4	15.4	6.0	7.4	11.3	13.1
Other	100.0	35.5	47.3	15.3	4.2	1.6	9.4	11.8	0.5	22.3	9.9	2.7	12.7	22.0

Number of Traders in Each Category

	Open Interest	PM Long	PM Short	Swap Long	Swap Short	Swap Spreading	MM Long	MM Short	MM Spreading	Other Long	Other Short	Other Spreading
All	706	219	299	23	4	17	49	70	43	98	73	101
Old	698	214	284	23	4	13	48	71	39	102	79	83
Other	400	52	228	13	7	6	15	12	4	38	55	18

Percent of Open Interest Held by the Indicated Number of the Largest Traders

	By Gross Position				By Net Position			
	4 or Less Traders		8 or Less Traders		4 or Less Traders		8 or Less Traders	
	Long	Short	Long	Short	Long	Short	Long	Short
All	12.5	12.3	19.9	19.0	11.8	11.5	18.7	17.5
Old	13.5	13.3	21.5	20.4	13.2	12.6	21.0	18.4
Other	26.0	15.7	39.7	25.0	25.3	15.2	38.9	24.0

Figure 5.1 Disaggregated Commitments of Traders Report for Corn Futures as of December 27, 2016

over some period of time). Thus, the report provides a snapshot of the numbers of contracts and types of positions (i.e., long or short) held by each type of market participant in all contract months for that particular futures contract – hence the term "commitments of traders" – rather than a summary of the trading activity of those participants. These open interest values are then used to determine the change from the corresponding value in the previous week's report, the percent of total open interest represented by that category, and the number of individual traders in that category. Notice that on the reporting date the total open interest in corn futures was 1,231,462 contracts, and in this particular report there were 706 reporting traders, either individuals or firms, in the corn futures market that provided all of the detailed information contained in this table.

Reportable Traders by Specific Occupation or Activity

Producer/Merchant/Processor/User

The market participant types listed in the column headings along the top of the table are not simply "hedger" or "speculator" but specific occupations or activities. The first such reportable category is Producer/Merchant/Processor/User which describes types of traditional hedgers. In this particular report these participants held 305,691 long contracts and 540,774 short positions, which accounted for 24.8% of the long open interest and 43.9% of short open interest, respectively and were held by 219 and 299 reporting traders, respectively. Notice that traditional hedgers account for less than half of the market, and this hedging activity is conducted by a relatively small number of relatively large participants. These data also reveal a feature common to most commodity markets, namely that futures-related hedging activity by traditional hedgers tends to be concentrated on the short side of the market. This pattern suggests that futures-based hedging by producers is more prevalent than hedging by users, all else the same.

Swap Dealers

The next reportable category is Swap Dealers. Recall from Chapter 1 that swaps can be described as a series of forward contracts with different maturities. We will cover swaps more thoroughly in Chapter 18, but now we will simply state that most Swap Dealers use futures markets as hedging instruments for commercial risk management or investing purposes. Swap Dealers collectively held 261,693 long contracts, 3,607 short contracts, and 12,425 spread positions which each consisted of both a long and a short position. These positions accounted for 21.3%, 0.3%, and 1.0% of the total long, total short, and total open interest, respectively and were held by 23, 4, and 17 reporting traders, respectively. In contrast to the Producer/Merchant/Processor/User category, the Swap Dealers were heavily concentrated on the long side of the market. This concentration suggests that many of these swaps likely were specialized hedging products developed for end-users of corn-related products, and customized instruments to provide investors with long exposure to the corn market.

Managed Money

The third reportable category is Managed Money, which represents corn futures positions held exclusively for investment purposes, and is commonly referred to as speculative "fund" activity. The positions in this category tend to shift between long and short based on market trends, so changes in the Managed Money category are often used as a barometer of professional speculator opinion. The traders in this category collectively held 163,648 long contracts, 273,250 short contracts, and 63,799 spread positions which each consisted of both a long and a short position. These investors were predominantly short and increased their short exposure from the previous week's report (i.e., December 20, 2016). They reduced their long positions by 117 contracts and increased their short positions by 13,959 contracts, suggesting that managed-money investors were becoming more bearish toward the corn market. There were 49 individuals or entities with long positions, 70 with short positions, and 43 with spread positions, and their positions accounted for 13.3% of the long open interest, 22.2% of the short open interest, and 5.2% of the total open interest.

Other Reportables

The last reportable category is Other Reportables, which consists of traders whose occupations or activities do not fit within one of the other categories. Consequently, we do not know whether these traders are predominantly hedgers or speculators, but this category does include large individual speculators who trade for themselves, rather than for other investors. For corn futures this category accounted for a rather large proportion of the open interest. These traders held 178,037 long contracts, 58,581 short contracts, and 105,195 spreads which each consisted of both a long and a short position, and which accounted for 14.5% of the long open interest, 4.8% of the short open interest, and 8.5% of the total open interest. This category also accounted for a rather large proportion of the reporting traders in the corn market, with 98 individuals or entities holding long positions, 73 holding short positions, and 101 holding spread positions.

Total Reportable Positions

We can combine the positions held by the Producer/Merchant/Processor/User, Swap Dealers, Managed Money, and Other Reportables categories in the following manner to determine the long open interest and short open interest held by all reportable traders (see Table 12.1).

Recall that each spread is actually two positions – one long and one short – so we must combine the separate long and short components of the Total Spread value in Table 12.1 with the Total Outright Long and Short positions, respectively, to obtain the Total Reportables long and short positions.

Table 12.1 Calculation of Total Reportable Long and Short Open Interest from Disaggregated Commitments of Traders Report, Corn Futures, December 27, 2016

Reporting category	Long	Short	Spread
Producer/Merchant/ Processor/User	305,691	540,774	
Swap Dealers	261,693	3,607	12,425
Managed Money	163,648	273,250	63,799
Other Reportables	178,037	58,581	105,195
Total Spread			181,419
Total Outright Long and Short	909,069	876,212	
Spread (as separate Long and Short)	181,419	181,419	
Total Reportables	1,090,488	1,057,631	

Nonreportable Positions

The differences between these Total Reportables long and short values and the 1,231,462 total open interest are the Nonreportable Positions, which appear in the far right-hand columns in Figure 5.1. These nonreportable traders each hold less than 250 contracts in all months combined and therefore are not subject to large-trader reporting requirements. Consequently, the total numbers of contracts they hold – 140,974 long contracts (= 1,231,462 – 1,090,488) and 173,831 short contracts (= 1,231,462 – 1,057,631) – are simply calculated values. Nonreportables include both hedgers and speculators, and they are smaller traders with individual holdings as small as a single contract. As a group, nonreportable traders held 11.4% of the long open interest and 14.1% of the short open interest. However, we do not know how many individual traders are in this category, because they are not required to submit weekly position reports or other information like the reportable traders.

Percent of Open Interest Held by Largest Traders

The last block of information is located toward the bottom of the table under the heading "Percent of Open Interest Held by the Indicated Number of the Largest Traders." This is a measure of market share, and is modelled after the four-firm and eight-firm concentration ratios commonly used in market power studies. Gross Position is simply the total number of contracts held, both long and short, and measures a trader's total holdings of futures contracts irrespective of market direction. Net Position is equal to total long positions minus total short positions (or total short positions minus total long positions) and measures whether a trader's holdings lean toward the long or short side of the market. Notice that a position trader's gross and net positions will be equal or nearly so, while a spread trader could have a large gross position and a zero net position.

In terms of gross position, the four traders with the largest positions accounted for 12.5% of the long open interest and 12.3% of the short open interest; the eight traders with the largest positions accounted for 19.9% of the long open interest and 19.0% of the short open interest. In terms of net position, the four traders with the largest positions accounted for 11.8% of the long open interest and 11.5% of the short open interest; the eight traders with the largest positions accounted for 18.7% of the long open interest and 17.5% of the short open interest. The similarities of the corresponding gross and net position values suggests that these traders were predominantly position traders with a particular view about the market direction. Using either the gross or net measure, the four largest position holders on each side of the market owned or controlled approximately one-eighth of the total corn futures contracts, and the eight largest position holders on each side of the market owned or controlled between one-fifth and one-sixth of all the contracts.

Speculative Participation in Commodity Futures

Speculative Vehicles

There are several ways that an individual can participate as a speculator in commodity futures. The most direct method is to open an account with a futures commission merchant or FCM and begin trading. Alternatively, an individual may invest in a *commodity fund*, which is analogous to a mutual fund of actively managed stocks or bonds but which holds futures and other derivatives. The fund will be managed by a *commodity pool operator* (CPO) and trading decisions often will be delegated to a *commodity trading advisor* (CTA), both of which must be registered with the CFTC. A *hedge fund* has elements of both a commodity fund and a mutual fund, and may invest in derivatives as well as securities; participation is often limited to high net worth individuals. An individual might also invest in a commodity-focused *exchange traded fund* (ETF), which typically specializes in a specific commodity or set of commodities and generally has a highly structured, almost mechanical trading strategy. Unlike any of the other commodity investments listed here, ETFs are bought and sold like shares of common stocks and are traded on securities exchanges.

In terms of the Commitments of Traders report discussed above, an individual speculator's positions would appear under Nonreportable (if below the reporting threshold) or Other Reportables (if above the reporting threshold); a commodity fund's positions would appear under Managed Money; and the hedge fund and ETF positions would appear under Managed Money if traded as futures, or under Swap Dealers if customized futures-based instruments were held instead of the actual futures contracts.

Returns to Speculation

A number of studies on speculator returns have been conducted over the years. These studies, which examined individual trading accounts at FCMs, found that the distribution of gross profits for individual speculators resemble a bell-shaped curve with the mean (average) near zero. Except for a few large winners and a few large losers in the "tails" of the curve, most individuals make or lose relatively modest amounts. After adjusting for commissions and other transaction costs, net profits tend to be negative. Despite these discouraging results, every speculator believes they can be one of the "few large winners" identified in these studies, and everyone else benefits from the liquidity these speculators provide as a byproduct of their quest for profits.

13 Introduction to Options on Futures

An option is a type of derivative that gives the buyer the right, but not the obligation, to buy or sell a commodity at the expiration of the option. This is in contrast to a futures contract, which requires the buyer to buy a commodity at the expiration of the contract. Notice that an option replaces the buyer's obligation with a choice.

How Options Work

In general, an option gives the right, but not the obligation, to do something. Common examples outside of the commodity markets include real estate options which gives a buyer the right to purchase a property at an agreed-upon price by a specific date; auto leases which give the lessor the right to buy the vehicle at a specified price at the end of the leasing period; and full-fare airline tickets which give the traveler the right to change their departure date or to receive a refund.

An Example from Real Estate

Suppose that a real estate developer buys an option from the owner of a property, and pays the owner an up-front *premium*. In addition to establishing the purchase price for the property, the option provides a period of time before the *expiration* date for the developer to decide whether or not to *exercise*, or act on, the option and buy the property at the agreed-upon *strike price* or *exercise price*. The developer can use this time to arrange the financing to purchase and develop the property, pursue zoning changes, apply for building permits, and resolve many of the other issues and uncertainties that go along with such a project. If anything occurs during this time that puts the project in jeopardy, the developer can *abandon* the option and simply walk away with no further costs or obligations.

If the developer decides to exercise the option and purchase the property, then they must pay the strike price (i.e., the purchase price) to the seller, and the seller must transfer ownership to the buyer. Alternatively, if the developer changes their mind, or does nothing, or simply runs out of time, then the option expires and no longer exists. Regardless of whether or not the option is exercised, the buyer forfeits the premium and the seller keeps the premium. Notice that the premium is a payment for some time to decide and possibly change one's mind, not a deposit that is refunded if no action is taken. Also notice that the premium is not a down payment on the strike price in the event that the option is later exercised. If the buyer exercises the option, then they must pay the full strike price, not the strike price minus the premium. Stated differently, the premium is the price paid for the option, while the strike price is the price paid for the property if the option is exercised.

Options on Futures

Option Buyers and Sellers

This real estate example provides a useful introduction to options on commodity futures. A futures contracts is a derivative, and an option is a derivative, so an option on a futures contract is a derivative of a derivative.

The buyer – also called the *holder* – of a *call* option has the right to buy a specific futures contract for a specific contract month at a specific price; think of the option buyer "calling" or bringing in the *underlying* futures contract (i.e., the futures contract on which the option is based). The real estate option from above is an example of a call option. Conversely, the buyer or holder of a *put* option has the right to sell a specific futures contract for a specific contract month at a specific price; think of the option buyer "putting" or pushing away the underlying futures contract. Notice that a call option shares some similarities with a long futures position, and a put option shares some similarities with a short futures position. Also notice that only the buyer receives the right to exercise the option. The seller – also called the *writer* – is required to perform if the buyer exercises the option; this is covered in further detail in the following sections.

Consistent with futures terminology, buying an option results in a long option position and selling an option results in a short option position, so there are long and short calls, and long and short puts. Also consistent with futures, a trader with an existing short option position can buy that same option to close it out, and a trader with an existing long option position can sell that same option to close it out. Notice that calls and puts are separate and distinct instruments, so a put cannot be used to liquidate a call or vice versa. In yet another similarity with futures, a trader can sell a call or sell a put without having a position in the underlying futures contract. This is possible because options are derivatives, and a new option – either a call or a put – is created each time a new buyer and a new seller make a transaction.

Each option can be exercised at a specific price known as the exercise price or strike price, so named because this is the price at which the deal is struck. Typically there will be large number of strike prices available for each call and each put. Strike prices are listed at specific intervals and over specific price ranges for each contract month in a systematic process that is described in the rulebook for each option contract. The intervals are selected to be narrow enough to provide a degree of pricing precision, yet wide enough to concentrate trading activity and liquidity. Narrower intervals are commonly used around current price levels – for example, 5 cents per bushel or $0.50 per barrel – where there is the most trading interest, and wider intervals are used at higher and lower price levels – for example, 10 cents per bushel or $2.50 per barrel – where there is less activity. As the underlying futures price moves to higher or lower levels, additional strike prices will be listed within the applicable ranges. Consequently, for a call or put on a particular contract month, there may be dozens or even hundreds of strike prices eligible for trading.

Exercise or Abandon

The option buyer will make their decision to exercise based on the relationship between the strike price and the market price for the underlying futures contract. It will be profitable to exercise a call option if the strike price is below the market price, because the option buyer can exercise and buy the futures contract for less than the market price. Conversely, it will be profitable to exercise a put option if the strike price is above the market price, because the option buyer can sell the futures contract for more than the market price. An *American-style* option can be exercised at any time over the life of the option, while a *European-style* option can be exercised only at expiration, at the end of the life of the option.

Upon exercise, the option buyer receives a long (for a call) or short (for a put) futures contract at the strike price, and the option seller is assigned the opposite position (i.e., a short position at the strike price for a call that has been exercised, or a long position at the strike price for a put that has been exercised) in the same futures contract. Notice that if it is profitable for the buyer to exercise an option, it will be unprofitable for the seller to be exercised upon, so the seller will receive a losing futures position via the exercise process. Conversely, if the relationship between the strike price and the market price make it unprofitable to exercise, the option buyer can simply abandon the option without any penalty. Similar to futures contracts, options on futures are traded on exchanges, and all terms and conditions of an option are standardized except the premium, which is negotiated between the buyer and seller in the same manner as a futures price.

In the Money vs. Out of the Money

If an option would be profitable to exercise, it is said to be *in the money*. As described earlier, a call is in the money if the strike price is below the market price, because the option buyer can exercise and buy the futures contract for less than the market price. Conversely, a put is in the money if the strike price is above the market price, because the option buyer can exercise and sell the futures contract for more than the market price.

If an option would be unprofitable to exercise, it is said to be *out of the money*. A call is out of the money if the strike price is above the market price, because an option buyer who exercises would buy the futures contract for more than the market price. Conversely, a put is out of the money if the strike price is below the market price, because an option buyer who exercises would sell the futures contract for less than the market price. The strike price and futures price relationships for in-the-money and out-of-the-money options are demonstrated in Figure 13.1.

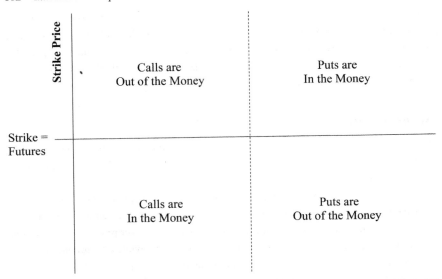

Figure 13.1 Relationship of Strike Price to Futures Price for In-The-Money and Out-Of-
The-Money Options

If the strike price of an option is equal to the market price, then exercising it would be a breakeven proposition, and the option is said to be *at the money*. For purposes of this book, at the money will be considered the same as out of the money, because it would be unprofitable to exercise an at-the-money option.

Intrinsic Value of an Option

The amount by which an option is in the money – or equivalently, the gross profit to the buyer from exercising an option – is called the *intrinsic value*. By definition, intrinsic value can be only positive or zero; it cannot be negative because an option buyer cannot be required to exercise an out-of-the-money option. An option that is out of the money at expiration will be abandoned, not exercised, so the maximum loss for an option buyer is the premium paid for the option. The gain or loss for the buyer of an option that is in the money at expiration is equal to the intrinsic value minus the premium paid for the option. Notice that an option may expire in the money and still result in a loss to the option buyer, if the intrinsic value is less than the premium paid for the option.

The maximum gain for an option seller occurs when the option expires out of the money, and is equal to the premium received. The gain or loss for the seller of an option that is in the money at expiration is equal to the premium received minus the intrinsic value of the option. Notice that an option may expire in the money and still result in a profit to the option seller, if the intrinsic value is less than the premium paid for the option.

Similarities between Options and Insurance

By this point the reader may have noticed a number of similarities between options and insurance: the strike price of an option corresponds to the level of coverage, the amount by which an option is out of the money corresponds to the deductible, and the time to expiration corresponds to the policy period. For an insurance policy, a higher coverage level, a smaller deductible, and/or a longer policy period will result in a higher insurance premium, all else the same. Likewise, greater intrinsic value and/or more time until expiration will result in a higher option premium, all else the same. Exercising an option is comparable to filing a claim, and abandoning an option is comparable to not filing a claim, but in both situations the issuer of the coverage (i.e., the option seller or the insurance company) keeps the premium.

Option Trading

Notice that it is not necessary for an option buyer to exercise an option that has moved in the money to capture the increase in value. Instead, the buyer can simply sell the option, because the current premium will reflect the higher intrinsic value. Similarly, it is not necessary for an option buyer to abandon an option that has moved out of the money to exit their position. If the option has not yet expired, the premium will not yet be zero, so the buyer can sell the option and salvage this remaining value. The premium will not yet be zero because there is still a chance – right up until expiration – of a change in the underlying futures price that will move the option in the money.

Likewise, an option seller can buy an option to liquidate an already-existing short option position. Option value can be determined throughout the life of an option, not just at the beginning when a buyer and seller agree to create an option. Consequently, options can be bought and sold at any time up to expiration, at the then-current premium. When options are traded in this manner, the difference between the purchase price and the sale price will result in a gain or loss without the option being exercised.

Time Value of an Option

Option premiums consist of two components: intrinsic value and *extrinsic value*, which is more commonly referred to as *time value*:

$$\text{Premium} = \text{Intrinsic Value} + \text{Time Value} \qquad \text{(Equation 13.1)}$$

Time value can be only positive or zero; it cannot be negative. Stated differently, an option will have time value if it has not yet expired, because the time value at expiration will be zero. From Equation 13.1, the premium for an in-the-money option at expiration will be equal to its intrinsic value, and the premium for an out-of-the-money option at expiration will be zero, since in both cases the time value will be zero.

Time value is normally calculated by subtracting the intrinsic value from the option premium:

$$\text{Time Value} = \text{Premium} - \text{Intrinsic Value} \qquad \text{(Equation 13.2)}$$

The time value component reflects the time remaining to expiration, plus the volatility of returns (i.e., price changes) on the underlying asset, plus an expression for the relationship between the strike price and the price of the underlying asset, plus the interest rate. The interest rate has such a small impact that it is usually ignored by practitioners. Notice that the remaining three items – time to expiration, volatility, and relationship between strike price and underlying price – all influence whether or not the option moves (or remains) in the money and will be worth exercising.

For example, as the time remaining to expiration increases, the greater will be the opportunity for an out-of-the-money option to move in the money, so the premium will be larger, all else the same. Likewise, as the volatility increases, the greater will be the opportunity for an out-of-the-money option to move in the money, so the premium will be larger, all else the same. Finally, as an out-of-the-money option moves closer to being in the money, or as an in-the-money option moves even farther or *deeper* in the money, the opportunity for an option to move (or remain) in the money will be greater, so the premium will be larger, all else the same.

Time Value Decay

The relationship between the amount of time remaining until expiration and time value is not linear (i.e., a straight line) but instead is exponential (i.e., a curved line). Time value decreases at an increasing rate as the expiration date approaches. This decrease, which is referred to as *time value erosion* or *time value decay*, accelerates as expiration approaches, as shown in Table 13.1. This erosion or decay occurs automatically, without any change in the underlying price, so the value of an option will decrease over time, even if everything else remains constant.

This decrease in the premium due to time value decay is harmful to the option buyer, because the buyer wants the premium (i.e., the price of the option) to increase. An increase in the premium typically requires the option to move (deeper) in the money, and the option must move (deeper) in the money (i.e., the intrinsic value must increase) by more than enough to offset the ongoing loss of time value. If the option instead moves (deeper) out of the money (i.e., the intrinsic value decreases), then the decrease in the premium will be even greater. For an option buyer, the best possible outcome is for an option to move in the money, and to do it quickly and by a substantial amount.

Conversely, the decrease in the premium due to time value decay is helpful to the option seller, because the seller wants the premium to decrease. This decrease occurs automatically,

Figure 13.2 Time Value and Time to Expiration: $3.50 Call Option, $3.60 Futures Prices, 30% Volatility

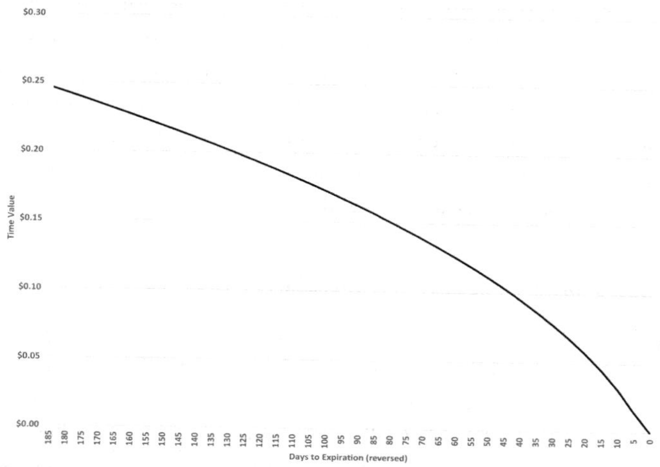

without any change in the intrinsic value, simply due to time value decay. However, the decrease in premium will be even greater if the option moves (deeper) out of the money (i.e., the intrinsic value decreases). The option seller will experience a loss only if the option moves (deeper) in the money (i.e., the intrinsic value increases) by more than enough to offset the loss of time value. For an option seller, the best possible outcome is for an option to expire out of the money.

Exercise and Assignment

When an option on a futures contract is exercised, the option seller does not obtain the underlying futures contract and transfer it to the option buyer. Instead, the clearing house creates a new futures contract for the contract month specified by the option, at a futures price equal to the strike price of the option. For each option that is exercised, the futures open interest increases by one contract, and the corresponding option open interest decreases by one contract.

When a call option is exercised, the option buyer receives a long position in the underlying futures contract, at a futures price equal to the strike price of the option. The corresponding short futures position is assigned randomly to a seller of that particular call option at that particular strike price, and the option positions for both parties are eliminated. Similarly, when a put option is exercised, the option buyer receives a short position in the underlying futures contract, at a futures price equal to the strike price of the option. The corresponding long futures position is assigned randomly to a seller of that particular put option at that particular strike price, and the option positions for both parties are eliminated. Notice that the option assignment process is different from the futures delivery and assignment process described in Chapter 4, in which assignment traditionally is made to the oldest long, based on the date the position was established. Because an option typically will not be exercised unless it is in the money, the futures position received by the option buyer will have an immediate gain, equal to the intrinsic value of the option that was exercised. Conversely, the futures position assigned to the option seller will have an immediate loss, equal to the intrinsic value of the option that was exercised.

Potential Gains and Losses, Margins, and Margin Calls

If the option is a call, the potential gain for the option buyer and the potential loss for the option seller are unlimited, because the price of the underlying futures contract can go up to infinity. If the option is a put, the potential gain for the option buyer and the potential loss for the option seller are finite but still large, because the price of the underlying futures contract cannot go below zero. The potential losses for the option seller are similar to the potential losses on a futures contract, so option sellers are required to post margins and may receive margin calls.

Conversely, the potential loss for the option buyer and the potential gain for the option seller, for either a call or a put, are limited to the premium paid/received when the option is created; recall that the option buyer can simply abandon the option if it is out of the money. The option buyer pays this premium when the option is created, and they have no further risk of loss, so option buyers are not required to post margins and do not receive margin calls.

When an option on a futures contract is abandoned, the abandoned option typically will be out of the money and therefore not worth exercising, so it is said to expire *worthless*. An abandoned option expires without being exercised and without any new futures contract being created, so the corresponding option open interest decreases by one contract for each option that is abandoned, and the futures open interest is unchanged.

Automatic Exercise

At many exchanges, an option that is in the money at expiration will be exercised automatically by the clearing house, and the underlying futures positions will be assigned to the option buyer and an option seller even if the option buyer does not formally exercise the option. Sometimes an expiring option will be slightly in the money, but the cost of liquidating the resulting futures contract would exceed the intrinsic value of the option and result in a net loss to the option buyer. At other times, an option buyer may want to exercise an expiring option that is at the money, and which otherwise would expire worthless, perhaps as part of a larger trading strategy. In both situations the option buyer can submit *contrary instructions*, also known as *counter instructions,* to the clearing house, and the clearing house will process the option exercise as directed.

Option Expiration Date and Futures Delivery

The expiration date for options on futures contracts which use physical delivery must occur before the beginning of the futures delivery process. This is necessary to prevent a put option from being exercised and causing an option seller, who is randomly assigned a long futures position at the strike price, from also being assigned a futures delivery. Recall from Chapter 4 that delivery assignment traditionally is made to the oldest long, based on the date the futures position was established. Normally a delivery would not be assigned to a newly created long, but there may be situations where most of the futures positions have been liquidated, and a newly created long position resulting from an option exercise would be in line for a futures delivery. In addition, some futures markets use random assignment in which a delivery may be assigned to any long position, irrespective of when the position was established.

In contrast, the expiration date for options on futures contracts which use cash settlement can occur at the same date and time as the expiration of the underlying futures contracts. Options that are in the money at expiration are automatically exercised by the clearing house, futures positions are created and assigned, and then those futures positions are immediately cash settled to the final settlement price.

Trading Venue and Method

An option on a futures contract is traded on the same exchange as the underlying futures contract, and the trading process for options is virtually identical to the trading process for futures that was described in Chapter 2. A substantial but declining share of option trading still takes place in trading pits, due to the complexity of many option strategies. The challenges of designing and programming a system for quick and efficient order entry of these complex strategies currently make pit trading the preferred method for executing many types of option trades. However, steady improvements to the technology mean that pit-based option trading likely will disappear, much like pit-based futures trading.

Clearing and Settlement

The clearing process for options on futures is identical to the clearing process for the underlying futures described in Chapter 4. However, the daily settlement process for options is slightly different. Because option premiums are based on the values of the underlying futures, and because options typically trade less actively than futures, the last price or premium at which an option traded may not accurately reflect the *fair value* or theoretically correct price of an option, even if it occurred at the end of the trading session.

Recall that an option premium consists of the intrinsic value – the amount by which it is in the money – plus its time value, which is based on the time to expiration, volatility, and other factors. This relationship can be expressed in an equation. While there are numerous option pricing equations or models, the most popular is the *Black-Scholes model*, which was designed for options on common stocks and includes the impact of dividend payments.

Futures contracts do not pay dividends, so a version known as the *Black model* was developed specifically for options on futures. Option pricing and the Black model will be discussed in detail in the next chapter, but for now the reader only needs to understand that option premiums can be estimated using an equation.

At the end of each trading day, the exchange uses the futures daily settlement prices plus one or more option pricing models to determine the option daily settlement prices (i.e., premiums). These calculations are performed separately for calls and puts, for each strike price, and for each contract month, so there may be hundreds or even thousands of individual calculations required to settle all the options on a particular futures contract. Once the daily settlement values have been determined, the clearing house calculates the total gains or losses for all options held by each clearing firm, nets those gains and losses into a single amount for each clearing firm, and uses the pays and collects process to transfer gains and losses among individual clearing firms. Each clearing firm then conducts a similar process for all accounts under its control, transferring funds from losing accounts to winning accounts at the end of each trading day. Like futures trading, option trading is a zero-sum game where every dollar lost by one trader is matched by a dollar gained by another trader. But unlike futures trading, where traders post margins representing a fraction of the full value of a futures contract, option buyers pay – and option sellers receive – the full value of the option when the position is created.

If the premium for an option decreases, the amount of the decrease is debited from the option buyer's account and credited to the option seller's account. Once the premium reaches zero, the full value paid by the option buyer at the beginning will have been transferred to the option seller, and the option buyer can experience no further losses on that particular option.

Conversely, if the premium for an option increases, the amount of the increase is debited from the option seller's account and credited to the option buyer's account. Once the premium has doubled, the full value received by the option seller at the beginning will have been transferred to the option buyer. Recall that an option premium represents only a fraction of the value of the underlying futures contract, so it is possible for premiums to increase by multiples of the beginning amount when the option moves in the money. Consequently, option sellers can lose much more than the premium received from the option buyer, and this is why option sellers must post margin and may receive margin calls.

Market Regulation

The entities responsible for regulating options on futures are the same as for the underlying futures contracts. Exchanges are the first-line regulators for the contracts they list for trading, the CFTC is the federal regulator, and the NFA is the industry self-regulator.

Chapter 2 described futures as contracts which require the buyer to take delivery – and the seller to make delivery – of a commodity at some future date, with the price of the commodity established today. An option is also a contract, which requires the option seller to provide the option buyer – if the buyer so chooses – with a long futures position for a call, or a short futures position for a put, at a futures price equal to the strike price of the option. Because they are contracts, options are legally enforceable agreements, and the option buyer has recourse if the option seller fails to perform their duties.

Like futures contracts, options have contract specifications which describe the underlying futures contract, and the number of contracts provided to the buyer upon exercise. The specifications also cover the minimum price increments used for the option premium, the ranges and intervals used for strike prices, the expiration date, option exercise procedures, and other option-specific details. There may or may not be daily price limits on the option premiums, depending on the particular option contract.

The contract specifications also include position limits which set the maximum number of options that an individual can own or control. Position limits on options are typically expressed in *futures-equivalent* terms. Option premiums do not move dollar-for-dollar with the price of the underlying futures contract, but instead change by smaller amounts. Consequently, each option contract has less impact, for hedging and speculative purposes, than the underlying futures contract. This impact factor, which is called the *delta* and will be discussed in the next chapter, varies for each strike price of the same contract month for puts and for calls. Multiplying an option position (i.e., number of option contracts) by its respective delta results in a futures equivalent value, which reflects the impact of that option position in terms of futures contracts. By definition, the delta is $+1$ for a long futures contract and -1 for a short futures contract. Position limit rules typically require all options and corresponding futures to be combined into a single futures equivalent value.

Options on Actuals

There are *options on actuals*, for which the underlying commodity is the physical commodity. Upon exercise of an option on actual, the option seller must obtain the actual commodity specified in the option and transfer it to the option buyer. Obtaining and delivering a physical commodity can be a complicated process, as was described in Chapter 4, and for this reason options on actuals are limited to commodities such as precious metals with relatively liquid cash markets, or to commercial participants such as energy companies that have ready access to, and the ability to handle, the underlying commodities.

14 Option Pricing

In Chapter 13 we introduced the concept that the price of an option, or premium, can be expressed as an equation. The most popular and well-known of these option pricing equations is the Black-Scholes model, but there is a version known as the Black model specifically designed for options on futures. The Black model, sometimes referred to as "Black '76" for the year it was published, is named for Fisher Black, the economist who developed it.

The Black Model

Call Option Formula

Recall that an option premium can be divided into intrinsic value and time value. Intrinsic value for a call is equal to the price of the underlying futures contract minus the strike price of the option. Time value is equal to some combination of the time remaining to expiration, the volatility of the underlying futures contract, and other factors. The Black model incorporates all of these variables into a single equation:

$$C = e^{-(rt)} \left\{ \left[F \times N(d_1) \right] - \left[K \times N(d_2) \right] \right\}$$

(Equation 14.1)

where

$$d_1 = \frac{\ln\left(\dfrac{F}{K}\right) + \left[\left(\dfrac{\sigma^2}{2}\right) \times t\right]}{\sigma \times \sqrt{t}}$$

(Equation 14.2)

and

$$d_2 = d_1 - \left(\sigma \times \sqrt{t}\right)$$

(Equation 14.3)

When we examine each variable and grouping of variables in Equation 14.1,

C = call option premium;

e = Euler's number ≈ 2.718282 · · ·, which is a constant that is frequently used in calculations involving compounding and discounting;

r = risk-free interest rate, typically Treasury bills or LIBOR, expressed as a decimal;

t = time remaining to expiration, as the percentage of a calendar year (i.e., number of calendar days divided by 365), expressed as a decimal;

so

$e^{-(r \times t)}$ = discount factor, which converts the premium from future value (i.e., the value at expiration) to present value (i.e., the value today):

F = futures price for the underlying contract;

$N(d_1)$ = normal distribution-based probability (i.e., cumulative normal density function value) of d_1. This step simply uses d_1 as the z-value in the "Area Under the Standard Normal Curve" table found in the back of any statistics book, or via the Excel function NORM.S.DIST;

K = strike price of the option;

$N(d_2)$ = normal distribution-based probability (i.e., cumulative normal density function value) of d_2. This step simply uses d_2 as the z-value in the "Area Under the Standard Normal Curve" table found in the back of any statistics book, or via the Excel function NORM.S.DIST;

so

$\{[F \times N(d_1)] - [K \times N(d_2)]\}$ = probability-adjusted intrinsic value, since F − K = intrinsic value for a call; and

σ = volatility (in percent) of futures returns (described in a later section below), expressed as a decimal.

Notice that in the equation for d_1 above, $\ln\left(\dfrac{F}{K}\right)$ is the natural logarithm of the ratio of the futures price and the strike price. This term reflects the relationship between the strike price and the price of the underlying asset, but in a manner different from intrinsic value. If the call option is in the money, F will be greater than K, and the ratio $\left(\dfrac{F}{K}\right)$ will be greater than one, so the natural log of $\left(\dfrac{F}{K}\right)$ will be positive. Conversely, if the option is out of the money, F will be less than K, and the ratio $\left(\dfrac{F}{K}\right)$ will be less than one, so the natural log of $\left(\dfrac{F}{K}\right)$ will be negative.

In addition, it can be shown that:

$N(d_1)$ = delta for a call option (i.e., the change in the option premium for a small change in price of the underlying futures contract), which was introduced in Chapter 13; and

$N(d_2)$ = probability that a call option expires in the money (i.e., F is greater than K).

Call Option Pricing Example

For example, suppose that we have a call option with a strike price of $3.50 and the underlying futures price is $3.60, so the option is 10 cents in the money. This option expires in

185 calendar days (i.e., t = 185 ÷ 365 = .5068 of a calendar year), the volatility is 30% (i.e., σ = .30), and the interest rate is 5% (i.e., r = .05). We can calculate the fair value for this call option using the Black model, with all values rounded to 4 decimals:

$$e^{-(r \times t)} = 0.9750$$

$$d_1 = \frac{\ln\left(\dfrac{F}{K}\right) + \left[\left(\dfrac{\sigma^2}{2}\right) \times t\right]}{\sigma \times \sqrt{t}} = (0.0282 + 0.0228) \div 0.2136 = 0.2388$$

$N(d_1) = 0.5944$ using Excel, or 0.5948 using the table value

so

$F \times N(d_1) = \$3.60 \times 0.5944 = \$2.1398$

$$d_2 = d_1 - \left(\sigma \times \sqrt{t}\right) = 0.2388 - 0.2136 = 0.0252$$

$N(d_2) = 0.5101$ using Excel, or 0.5120 using the table value

so

$K \times N(d_2) = \$3.50 \times 0.5101 = \$1.7854$

and

$$C = e^{-(r \times t)}\left\{\left[F \times N(d_1)\right] - \left[K \times N(d_2)\right]\right\} = 0.9750 \times (\$2.1398 - \$1.7854)$$
$$= 0.9750 \times \$0.3544 = \$0.3455$$

Put Option Formula

There is also a Black model for put options, which we have simplified for the reader by eliminating some statistical notation:

$$P = e^{-(r \times t)}\left\{K \times \left[1 - N(d_2)\right] - F \times \left[1 - N(d_1)\right]\right\} \qquad \text{(Equation 14.4)}$$

In this equation,

P = put option premium;

$1 - N(d_1)$ = normal distribution-based probability (i.e., cumulative normal density function value) of d_1 as described above, subtracted from 1. This represents the remaining area under the standard normal curve (i.e., probability) not assigned to the corresponding call option with the same strike price.

$1 - N(d_2)$ = normal distribution-based probability (i.e., cumulative normal density function value) of d_2 as described above, subtracted from 1. This represents the remaining area under the standard normal curve (i.e., probability) not assigned to the corresponding call option with the same strike price.

so

{K × [1 − N(d_2)] − F × [1 − N(d_1)]} = probability-adjusted intrinsic value, since K − F = intrinsic value for a put. Notice that the order of the futures price and strike price is reversed from the Black model for a call.

In addition, it can be shown that:

$1 - N(d_1)$ = absolute value of the delta for a put option, since put deltas are negative; and

$1 - N(d_2)$ = probability that a put option expires in the money (i.e., K is greater than F)

Put Option Pricing Example

For example, suppose that we have a put option with a strike price of $3.50 and the underlying futures price is $3.60, so the option is 10 cents out of the money. This option expires in 185 calendar days (i.e., t = 185 ÷ 365 = .5068 of a calendar year), the volatility is 30% (i.e., σ = .30), and the interest rate is 5% (i.e., r = .05), same as in our call option example above. We can calculate the fair value for this put option using the Black model (rounded to 4 decimals):

$e^{-(r \times t)}$ = 0.9750 (from the call option example above)
$N(d_2)$ = 0.5101 using Excel (from the call option example above)
$1 - N(d_2)$ = 0.4899

so

$K \times [1 - N(d_2)]$ = $3.50 × 0.4899 = $1.7147
$N(d_1)$ = 0.5944 using Excel (from the call option example above)
$1 - N(d_1)$ = 0.4056

so

$F \times [1 - N(d_1)]$ = $3.60 × 0.4056 = $1.4602
and

$$P = e^{-(r \times t)} \left\{ K \times \left[1 - N(d_2) \right] - F \times \left[1 - N(d_1) \right] \right\} = 0.9750 \times (\$1.7147 - \$1.4602)$$
$$= 0.9570 \times \$0.2545 = \$0.2481$$

Measuring Volatility

Notice the prominent role of volatility, represented by σ, which appears in several places in the Black model. Volatility is the single most important component of option pricing, but it is also the most difficult to measure. It is impossible to observe volatility directly, so two indirect methods are used. One method is *implied volatility*, which uses the current market value of the premium as an input and rearranges Equation 14.1 to solve the Black model for σ. Implied volatility represents the volatility indicated by the current market price. It is a real-time value that changes constantly as premiums and other market conditions change, so it can be viewed as a snapshot of volatility for a particular option at a particular point in time.

The other method is *historical volatility*, also sometimes referred to as *realized volatility*, which uses the annualized standard deviation of daily returns. Notice that there is a specific method for calculating historical volatility. First, calculate the continuously-compounded daily returns (i.e., percentage daily price changes) over some period of n calendar days, using the formula:

$$r_t = \ln\left(\frac{F_t}{F_{t-1}}\right)$$

(Equation 14.5)

where

r_t = percentage return for a particular day;

F_t = futures price on a particular day; and

F_{t-1} = futures price on the previous day

Next, find the standard deviation of the r_t values. Finally, annualize the standard deviation by multiplying it by the square root of the number of calendar days in the calculation period (i.e., $\sqrt{n}$). This annualized value, which is written as a decimal, is commonly expressed as the *percent volatility*. Historical volatility is sensitive to the number of observations used in the calculation, which implies a tradeoff. A longer time period provides a more robust sample, but will include older observations that may not reflect current market conditions. Conversely, a shorter time period eliminates the stale data problem, but the sample may be too small to be statistically reliable.

As noted in Chapter 13, the Black model can be used to determine daily settlement values for option premiums. It also can be used by option traders to calculate theoretical values, on which they can base their bid and ask prices. Notice that the Black formula is referred to as a model, so actual market prices may differ from theoretical values. Nevertheless, theoretical values are useful benchmarks for establishing and evaluating market values for premiums.

Model Assumptions and Shortcomings

Like all models, the Black model and the Black-Scholes model from which it is derived make certain assumptions about the statistical relationships between option premiums and each of the various inputs. These assumptions can lead to discrepancies between model values and market values. For example, the models typically assume that returns are normally distributed, but studies have found that actual returns typically have a bell-shaped distribution with *fat tails* which indicate a larger number of extremely high returns and extremely low returns than would be observed in a normal distribution. The models also assume that volatility is constant across all strike prices, but empirical evidence suggests that the market assigns higher implied volatilities to the at-the-money options, and lower implied volatilities to the in-the-money and out-of-the-money options. These differences between model estimates of volatility and market reality can produce a gap between the estimated and actual premiums known as the *volatility smile*. One reason for the volatility smile is the fat-tailed distribution of actual returns.

In addition, the models assume that all options are European-style, which cannot be exercised except at expiration. However, virtually all options on futures are American-style, which can be exercised at any time up to and including expiration. This additional exercise ability is known as the *early exercise option*, so an American option can be viewed as a European option combined with an early exercise option. Because this early exercise option will have some positive value, an American option should have a higher premium than a European option, all else the same. Although the Black model tends to undervalue American-style options, the value of the early exercise option turns out to be quite small. Consequently the Black model provides a reasonable approximation of American-style option values.

Put–Call Parity

The Black model shows that the premiums for calls and puts on the same underlying futures contract are interrelated. Furthermore, if the call and put have the same strike price, then the premiums will be related to the underlying futures price by the *put-call parity* formula:

$$\text{Call premium} - \text{Put premium} + \text{Strike price} = \text{Futures price} \qquad \text{(Equation 14.6)}$$

Pricing with Put–Call Parity

The put-call parity formula can be used to find any of these four values, provided we have the prices for the other three. This can greatly simplify the process of finding the fair-value price for a call premium, assuming the put premium is known, and vice versa. For example, recall the lengthy calculation process (above) using Equation 14.4 to find the premium for a put using the Black model. Instead, we could use put-call parity to find the put premium. First, we can rearrange the put-call parity equation to solve for the put premium:

$$\text{Call premium} - \text{Put premium} + \text{Strike price} = \text{Futures price} \qquad \text{(Equation 14.6)}$$

so

$$\text{Call premium} + \text{Strike price} = \text{Futures price} + \text{Put Premium} \qquad \text{(Equation 14.7)}$$

and

$$\text{Call premium} + \text{Strike price} - \text{Futures price} = \text{Put Premium} \qquad \text{(Equation 14.8)}$$

Then we can insert the values for the call premium, the strike price, and the underlying futures price into this equation:

Call premium = $0.3455
Strike price = $3.50
Futures price = $3.60

so

Put premium = $0.3455 + $3.50 − $3.60 = $0.2455 ≈ $0.2481 using the Black model. Notice that the difference between these two solutions is $0.0026, which is approximately equal to one tick, or minimum price increment ($0.0025) for the futures contract.

Indeed, many option professionals use a model only to calculate call premiums, and then use put-call parity to find the corresponding put premiums.

Identifying and Arbitraging Price Discrepancies

The put-call parity formula also can be used to find pricing discrepancies in the call option, put option, or underlying futures; notice that the strike price is effectively a constant. Because these prices are interdependent, put-call parity cannot be used to identify the mis-priced component; this can be done only by checking each one with a pricing model. However, any discrepancies greater than one tick can be profitably arbitraged by taking offsetting positions. For example, suppose that we have the following values, from our Black model option pricing examples above:

Call premium = $0.3455, which when rounded to the nearest tick = $0.3450
Put premium = $0.2481, which when rounded to the nearest tick = $0.2475
Strike price = $3.50
Futures price = $3.60
Using put-call parity, $0.3450 − $0.2475 + $3.50 = $3.5975, which is within 1 tick (i.e., $0.0025) of $3.60, so there are no arbitrage opportunities.

Instead, suppose that we have the following values:

Call premium = $0.3400 (vs. $0.3450 above)
Put premium = $0.2475 (same as above)
Strike price = $3.50 (same as above)
Futures price = $3.60 (same as above)

Using put-call parity, $0.3400 − $0.2475 + $3.50 = $3.5925, which differs from $3.60 by 3 ticks ($0.0075). Since $3.5925 is less than $3.60, we can arbitrage this difference by buying the left side of Equation 14.6, selling the right side, and then waiting for prices to adjust. Buying the left side of the equation involves buying the call at $0.3400 and simultaneously selling the put at $0.2475; we do nothing with the strike price because it is fixed at $3.60. Selling the right side of the equation involves only one step, which is selling the futures at $3.60. Notice that selling the left side of the equation is done simultaneously with buying the right side. Market forces will eventually move these prices into alignment, and cause the left side and right side of the equation to become equal. When this alignment happens, we will have a risk-free profit of $0.0075, ignoring commissions and other transaction costs.

Option Sensitivity and the Greeks

With any type of model, it is important to know the sensitivity of the results to changes in each of the variables. Sensitivity analysis − how much the final value will change if a particular input value changes by a certain amount − allows the user to understand beforehand how the final values may be affected by various events, and consequently how much reliance should be placed on the results. For example, an impact multiplier measures the change in the final value from a one-unit change in an input, while the first derivative from calculus measures the change in the final value from an infinitesimally small change in an input, and an elasticity measures the final value and input changes in percentage terms.

In the Black model there are interactions among the variables that make it difficult to determine the impact of a particular change on the premium simply by visually examining the formula. Consequently, they must be determined via simulations or calculus. These measures are known as the *Greeks* because most are denoted by Greek letters. The most commonly used Greeks are:

Delta: change in the premium from a one-cent change in the underlying futures price;
Theta: change in the premium from a one-day change in the time to expiration;
Vega: change in the premium from a one-percent change in the volatility. Notice that there is no Greek letter vega, but there also is no Greek letter beginning with a "v" corresponding to volatility, so a quasi-Greek-sounding name was created for this purpose; and
Rho: change in the premium from a one-percent change in the interest rate.

Other Greeks measure the sensitivity of the Greeks listed above to various changes. The most commonly used of these second-order Greeks is:

Gamma: change in Delta from a one-cent change in the underlying futures price.

Properties of Delta and Trading Applications

Delta is the most widely used of all the Greeks, and appeared briefly in our discussion of the Black model where it was shown that $N(d_1)$ is equivalent to delta. In graphical terms, delta is the slope of the line that results when the premium is plotted against the underlying futures price, shown in Figure 14.1 for a call option. Because higher futures prices cause call options to move (deeper) in the money and premiums to increase, we would expect call option premiums and futures prices to move in the same direction (i.e., futures prices and call premiums are positively correlated). Consequently, the delta for a call option is positive, and ranges between 0 and +1. Conversely, because higher futures prices cause put options to move (deeper) out of the money and premiums to decrease, we would expect put option premiums and futures prices to move in the opposite direction (i.e., futures prices and put premiums are negatively correlated). Consequently, the delta for a put option is negative, and ranges between 0 and −1.

When an option moves (deeper) in the money, it behaves more like the underlying futures contract, and its delta moves closer to +1 for a call, or closer to −1 for a put. Conversely, when an option moves (deeper) out of the money, it behaves less like the underlying futures contract, and its delta moves closer to 0. Finally, when an option is at the money, its delta will be approximately .5 for a call, or −.5 for a put. The opposite behavior of call deltas

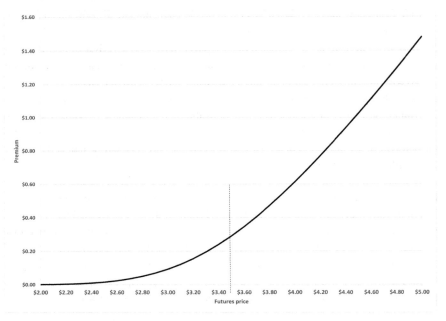

Figure 14.1 Premium Over a Range of Futures Prices: Slope = Delta, $3.50 Call Option, 30% Volatility, 185 Days to Expiration

and put deltas leads to some useful relationships. For example, the delta for a call with a particular strike, plus the absolute value of the delta for a put with the same strike, equals +1. Stated differently, a long call plus a short put, both with the same strike, is equivalent to a "synthetic" long futures position. We will discuss synthetic futures and options in Chapter 16.

Delta also can be used to determine how many options are required to provide the same hedging or speculative performance as a certain number of the underlying futures contracts. For example, suppose that a particular application requires 6 short futures contracts. Instead, the user decides to use put options that each have a delta of −.40. By definition, a short futures contract has a delta of −1, so 6 short futures contracts would have a combined delta of −6. Instead, the user could buy 15 (= −6 ÷ −.40) of these put options to obtain the same outcome as 6 short futures contracts over the relevant price range. A similar procedure was used in Chapter 13 to calculate futures-equivalent values for position limits on options.

In a related application, delta can be used to determine how many futures are required to hedge a certain number of options, or vice versa, which is often called the *option hedge ratio*. For example, suppose that an option seller has sold 100 call options and wants to collect the premium without any risk of the options being exercised. The call options each have a delta of +.2, but because the trader has short positions the sign on the delta must be reversed. Consequently, the short calls each have a delta of −.2, for a combined delta of −20 (= 100 × −.2).

To offset this exposure, the option seller would need to buy 20 futures contracts, each with a delta of +1, for a combined delta of +20. The +20 delta from the futures offsets the −20 delta from the calls, making the option seller *delta neutral*. We will cover delta neutral hedging more fully in Chapter 16.

Another common application – or mis-application, because this one happens to be incorrect – is to interpret delta as the probability that the option will expire in the money and/or be exercised. In our discussion of the Black model above, we saw that $N(d_1)$ is delta, and $N(d_2)$ is the probability that the option expires in the money. We also saw that d_2 in the Black model is equal to d_1 minus the volatility adjusted for the time to maturity:

$$d_2 = d_1 - \left(\sigma \times \sqrt{t} \right)$$

(Equation 14.3)

The only way that $N(d_2)$ can equal $N(d_1)$ is if d_2 equals d_1. The only way that d_2 can equal d_1 is if either volatility (σ) is zero – which is highly unlikely – or if the time to expiration (t) is zero – in which case the option has expired, and the probability that the option will expire in the money and/or be exercised no longer matters. Instead, because d_2 typically will be less than d_1, $N(d_2)$ typically will be less than $N(d_1)$, and consequently the delta value typically will overestimate the probability that an option will expire in the money.

Properties of Gamma

From Figure 14.1, we can see that the slope or delta for a particular option is not constant, but changes as the underlying futures price changes. Furthermore, the changes in the slope are greatest around the at-the-money futures price, and decrease as we move either in the money or out of the money. The change in the slope, which in calculus terms is the second derivative of the option premium with respect to the underlying futures price, is represented by *gamma*. Gamma, or the change in the delta from a change in the futures price, is important to market participants because it indicates how frequently a delta-based strategy will need to be rebalanced. The delta will change more for a large gamma than a small gamma, all else the same. In addition, gamma may be positive or negative, so a positive gamma will result in a larger positive delta and a smaller (in absolute terms) negative delta, all else the same.

Properties of Theta

The concept of time value decay was introduced in Chapter 13 with Figure 13.1. Notice that Figure 14.2 is the same graphical representation, but without reversing the time-to-expiration scale along the bottom axis. We can see that the slope or theta for a particular option is not constant, but changes with the time to expiration. The change in the slope (i.e., time value decay) is greatest at expiration, and becomes smaller as the time to expiration increases. In addition, when we compare theta at different strikes for the same underlying futures, as in Figure 14.3, we find that time value decay – and therefore theta – is greatest for the at-the-money option, and decreases as we move either in the money or out of the money.

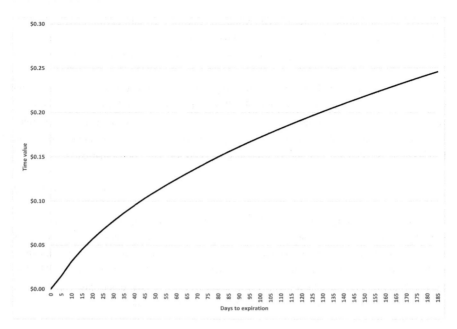

Figure 14.2 Time Value Over a Range of Times to Expiration: Slope = Theta, $3.50 Call Option, $3.60 Futures Price, 30% Volatility

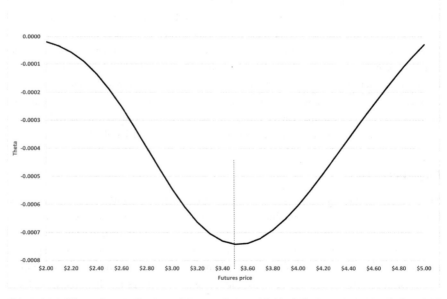

Figure 14.3 Theta Over a Range of Futures Prices: $3.50 Call Option, 30% Volatility, 185 Days to Expiration

By convention, theta is always negative for both calls and puts, because it represents the loss in premium from holding the option for one day.

Properties of Rho

As noted earlier in this chapter, the interest rate has such a small impact on option premiums that in practice it is usually ignored. In contrast to all the other components of the Black model, the interest rate is the only one with a linear relationship, shown in Figure 14.4. Furthermore, the slope of the premium relative to the interest rate is virtually flat, confirming that changes in the interest rate, represented by *rho*, have a negligible impact on option prices. Recall that the interest rate is used in the Black model as part of the discount factor, $e^{-(r \times t)}$, which explains the slightly negative or downward slope.

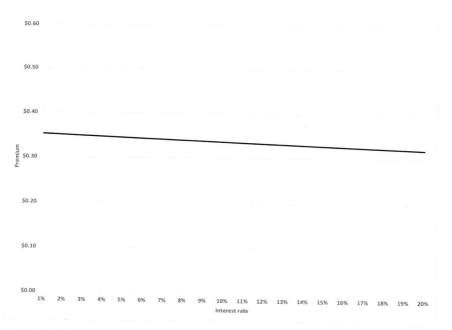

Figure 14.4 Premium Over a Range of Interest Rates: Slope = Rho, $3.50 Call Option, 30% Volatility, 185 Days to Expiration

Properties of Vega

Volatility is the most important component of option pricing, and consequently *vega* is one of the most important of the Greeks. Higher volatility results in higher premiums for both calls and puts, all else the same, so vega is always positive, as shown in Figure 14.5. However, vega is not uniform across all strikes, as shown in Figure 14.6. Vega is highest for at-the-money

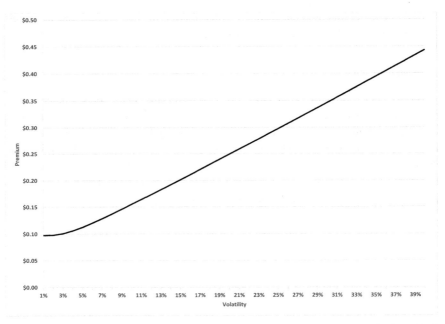

Figure 14.5 Premium Over a Range of Volatilities: Slope = Vega, $3.50 Call Option, $3.60 Futures Price, 185 Days to Expiration

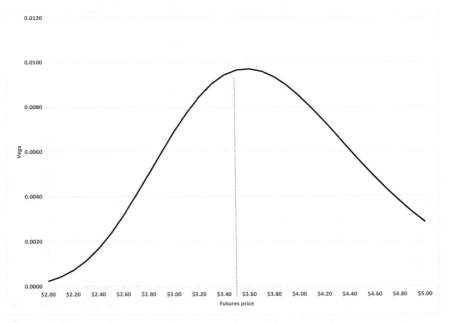

Figure 14.6 Vega Over a Range of Futures Prices: $3.50 Call Option, 30% Volatility, 185 Days to Expiration

options, because any change will cause the options to move either in the money or out of the money. Conversely, volatility has less impact on in-the-money and out-of-the-money options, because they can change and still remain in the money or out of the money.

Summary

This chapter has presented two ways to price an option: directly, using the Black model, and indirectly, using put-call parity. Put-call parity is based on the principle that the premium for a particular option must be consistent with the premium for the opposite option (i.e., the put option if we are pricing a call, and vice versa), the strike price for both options, and the underlying futures price. Even if all of these other instruments are individually mispriced, put-call parity will find a value for the fourth instrument that is consistent with the other three.

In contrast, the Black model allows us to calculate the premium for an option "from scratch" using data from external sources that are largely independent from – and therefore not easily influenced by – the option being priced. Despite some shortcomings, the Black model provides reliable benchmarks for premiums established in the marketplace by the forces of supply and demand. Market conditions are constantly changing, and these changes often affect option premiums. Another useful feature of the Black model are the Greeks, which measure the change in the premium due to a change in the price of the underlying futures price (i.e., delta), the volatility of the underlying futures price (i.e., vega), the time to expiration (i.e., theta), or the interest rate (i.e., rho).

Option pricing can be highly complex, and this chapter has limited the mathematical and statistical material to only the essentials necessary for an effective understanding of premium behavior. In the next chapter we will use a purely graphical approach to further explore option premiums under a range of outcomes, including profits and losses from various option trading strategies.

15 Profit Tables and Profit Diagrams

A *profit diagram* – also known as a payoff diagram – shows how a range of prices affects the profitability of a position or combination of positions, typically at expiration. These positions can involve options, futures, and/or cash commodities, but they are particularly useful for options, given the variation in outcomes depending on whether an option is in the money, at the money or out of the money.

Futures and Cash Positions: Linear Profits

Long Futures

For example, suppose that we buy a futures contract at $3.50, and we want to construct a profit diagram for this long futures position, using a range of prices at expiration from $3.00 to $4.00 in 5-cent increments. First, we need to construct a *profit table* with the calculated profit at each price (see Table 15.1).

Table 15.1 Profit on Long Futures Position Established at $3.50

Price	Profit on long $3.50 futures
$3.00	−$0.50
$3.05	−$0.45
$3.10	−$0.40
$3.15	−$0.35
$3.20	−$0.30
$3.25	−$0.25
$3.30	−$0.20
$3.35	−$0.15
$3.40	−$0.10
$3.45	−$0.05
$3.50	$0.00
$3.55	$0.05
$3.60	$0.10
$3.65	$0.15
$3.70	$0.20
$3.75	$0.25
$3.80	$0.30
$3.85	$0.35
$3.90	$0.40
$3.95	$0.45
$4.00	$0.50

Notice that the values shown in Table 15.1 are gross profits (i.e., selling price minus buying price), without any commissions or other transaction costs, and without any time-value-of-money adjustments to correct for the different times at which these revenues and expenses occur. While it is possible to construct a profit table with additional columns for these items, the simplified version with gross profits is sufficient for our purposes here. Strictly speaking, a profit table includes revenues and expenses while a payoff table includes only revenues, but the terms are often used interchangeably.

We can construct a profit diagram for this long futures position using the data in Table 15.1 (see Figure 15.1).

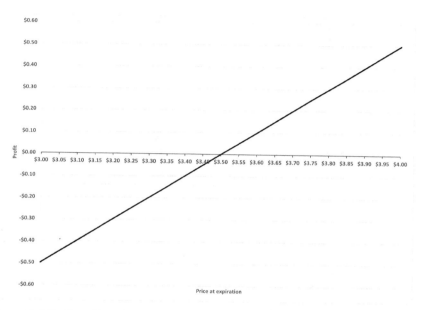

Figure 15.1 Profit on Long Futures Position Established at $3.50

Notice that for this long futures position, there are profits at prices above $3.50 and losses at prices below $3.50. In addition, there is a positive linear relationship between profits and prices because profits increase dollar-for-dollar as prices increase, up to a price of infinity, and losses increase dollar-for-dollar as prices decrease, down to a price of zero. Consequently the slope of the profit diagram is +1, corresponding to a delta of +1. We can see how futures contracts offer unlimited profits and (virtually) unlimited losses, which is why futures contracts require margins and have margin calls.

Short Futures

Conversely, suppose that we sell a futures contract at $3.50, and we want to construct a profit diagram for this short futures position, using a range of prices at expiration from $3.00 to $4.00 in 5-cent increments. As in the previous example, we first need to construct a profit table with the calculated profit at each price (see Table 15.2).

Then, using the data in Table 15.2, we can construct a profit diagram for this short futures position (see Figure 15.2).

Table 15.2 Profit on Short Futures Position Established at $3.50

Price	Profit on short $3.50 futures
$3.00	$0.50
$3.05	$0.45
$3.10	$0.40
$3.15	$0.35
$3.20	$0.30
$3.25	$0.25
$3.30	$0.20
$3.35	$0.15
$3.40	$0.10
$3.45	$0.05
$3.50	$0.00
$3.55	−$0.05
$3.60	−$0.10
$3.65	−$0.15
$3.70	−$0.20
$3.75	−$0.25
$3.80	−$0.30
$3.85	−$0.35
$3.90	−$0.40
$3.95	−$0.45
$4.00	−$0.50

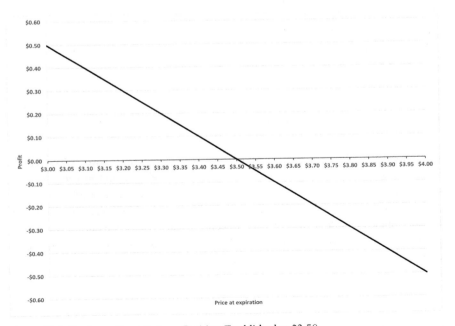

Figure 15.2 Profit on Short Futures Position Established at $3.50

Notice that for this short futures position, there are profits at prices below $3.50 and losses at prices above $3.50. In addition, there is a negative linear relationship between profits and prices because profits increase dollar-for-dollar as prices decrease, down to a price of zero, and losses increase dollar-for-dollar as prices increase, up to a price of infinity. Consequently, the slope of the profit diagram is −1, corresponding to a delta of −1. Once again, we can see how futures contracts provide (virtually) unlimited profits and unlimited losses.

Comparing Figure 15.2 to Figure 15.1, we can see that a short position is the mirror image of the corresponding long position. Stated differently, if we invert or "flip" these diagrams top for bottom, we can convert the profit diagram for a short futures position into the profit diagram for the corresponding long futures position and vice versa.

Long Cash

Profit tables for cash positions are constructed in the same manner as for futures positions. Likewise, profit diagrams for cash positions have the same shapes as the profit diagrams for futures positions: upward-sloping straight lines for long positions and downward-sloping straight lines for short positions, with profits that change dollar-for-dollar with the cash price. For example, Table 15.3 shows that the profit table for a long cash position established at $3.50 is identical to the profit table for a long futures position established at $3.50, presented earlier as Table 15.1.

Table 15.3 Profit on Long Cash Position Established at $3.50

Price	Profit on long $3.50 cash
$3.00	−$0.50
$3.05	−$0.45
$3.10	−$0.40
$3.15	−$0.35
$3.20	−$0.30
$3.25	−$0.25
$3.30	−$0.20
$3.35	−$0.15
$3.40	−$0.10
$3.45	−$0.05
$3.50	$0.00
$3.55	$0.05
$3.60	$0.10
$3.65	$0.15
$3.70	$0.20
$3.75	$0.25
$3.80	$0.30
$3.85	$0.35
$3.90	$0.40
$3.95	$0.45
$4.00	$0.50

Similarly, Figure 15.3 shows that the profit diagram for a long cash position established at $3.50 is identical to the profit diagram for a long futures position established at $3.50, presented earlier as Figure 15.1.

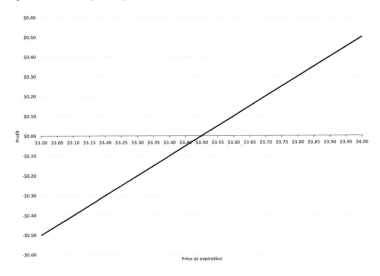

Figure 15.3 Profit on Long Cash Position Established at $3.50

Hedging Long Cash with Short Futures

Now suppose that we hedge the long cash position in Figure 15.3 with the short futures position in Figure 15.2. We can create a profit table (see Table 15.4) with separate columns for the profits from the individual cash and futures positions, and then add the cash and futures profits at each price to find the profit for the combined cash plus futures position.

Table 15.4 Profit on Long Cash Position Established at $3.50 Hedged with Short Futures Position Established at $3.50

Price	Profit on long $3.50 cash	Profit on short $3.50 futures	Combined profit
$3.00	−$0.50	$0.50	$0.00
$3.05	−$0.45	$0.45	$0.00
$3.10	−$0.40	$0.40	$0.00
$3.15	−$0.35	$0.35	$0.00
$3.20	−$0.30	$0.30	$0.00
$3.25	−$0.25	$0.25	$0.00
$3.30	−$0.20	$0.20	$0.00
$3.35	−$0.15	$0.15	$0.00
$3.40	−$0.10	$0.10	$0.00
$3.45	−$0.05	$0.05	$0.00
$3.50	$0.00	$0.00	$0.00
$3.55	$0.05	−$0.05	$0.00
$3.60	$0.10	−$0.10	$0.00
$3.65	$0.15	−$0.15	$0.00
$3.70	$0.20	−$0.20	$0.00
$3.75	$0.25	−$0.25	$0.00
$3.80	$0.30	−$0.30	$0.00
$3.85	$0.35	−$0.35	$0.00
$3.90	$0.40	−$0.40	$0.00
$3.95	$0.45	−$0.45	$0.00
$4.00	$0.50	−$0.50	$0.00

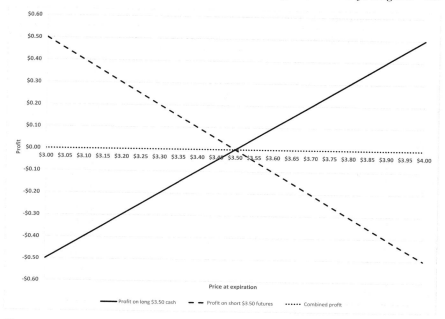

Figure 15.4 Profit on Long Cash Position Established at $3.50 Hedged with Short Futures Position Established at $3.50

Then we can use the data in Table 15.4 to construct a profit diagram for this hedged position (see Figure 15.4).

Notice that the combined result from hedging a long cash position established at $3.50 with a short futures position established at $3.50 is a zero profit or loss on the hedge at all price levels, shown by the last column in Table 15.4 and the horizontal dotted line in Figure 15.4. This example demonstrates numerically and graphically one of key the points from Chapter 6: that hedging with futures uses gains in one market to offset losses in the other. The result is a stable purchase or sale price, which in this example is $3.50.

Options Positions: Nonlinear Profits

Long Calls

Profit diagrams for options are nonlinear, unlike cash and futures positions, and this non-linearity is the reason why options are so flexible. The profit diagrams for calls and puts are shaped like a hockey stick, with a horizontal segment and an upward- or downward-sloping diagonal segment, resulting in a sharp bend or "kink" at the strike price. For example, suppose that we buy a call option with a $3.50 strike price and pay a premium of $0.35. We can construct a profit diagram for this long call position, using a range of futures prices at expiration from $3.00 to $4.00 in 5-cent increments, but first we need to construct a profit table (see Table 15.5) with the calculated profit at each futures price.

Table 15.5 Profit on Long $3.50 Call, $0.35 Premium

Price	Intrinsic value for long $3.50 call	Premium for long $3.50 call	Profit on long $3.50 call
$3.00	$0.00	−$0.35	−$0.35
$3.05	$0.00	−$0.35	−$0.35
$3.10	$0.00	−$0.35	−$0.35
$3.15	$0.00	−$0.35	−$0.35
$3.20	$0.00	−$0.35	−$0.35
$3.25	$0.00	−$0.35	−$0.35
$3.30	$0.00	−$0.35	−$0.35
$3.35	$0.00	−$0.35	−$0.35
$3.40	$0.00	−$0.35	−$0.35
$3.45	$0.00	−$0.35	−$0.35
$3.50	$0.00	−$0.35	−$0.35
$3.55	$0.05	−$0.35	−$0.30
$3.60	$0.10	−$0.35	−$0.25
$3.65	$0.15	−$0.35	−$0.20
$3.70	$0.20	−$0.35	−$0.15
$3.75	$0.25	−$0.35	−$0.10
$3.80	$0.30	−$0.35	−$0.05
$3.85	$0.35	−$0.35	$0.00
$3.90	$0.40	−$0.35	$0.05
$3.95	$0.45	−$0.35	$0.10
$4.00	$0.50	−$0.35	$0.15

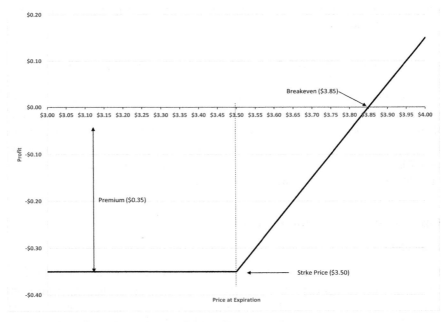

Figure 15.5 Profit on Long $3.50 Call, $0.35 Premium

Then, using the profit data in Table 15.5, we can construct a profit diagram for this long call (see Figure 15.5).

The horizontal segment of an option profit diagram represents the profits for the range of futures prices where the option is out of the money. An option that is out of the money has zero intrinsic value; consequently, the profit is constant for all futures prices in this range, and the slope of this segment is zero. Notice that for the long call in Figure 15.5 this segment includes futures prices below the $3.50 strike price. The vertical distance between the horizontal segment of the profit diagram and the zero-profit axis represents the option premium. For a long option position, the horizontal segment is below the zero-profit axis (i.e., negative gross profit), reflecting the premium paid by the option buyer (i.e., an outflow of funds). Notice that in Figure 15.5 this vertical distance is −$0.35, which is the amount of the premium paid by the buyer, as well as the maximum loss that can be experienced by the option buyer. Conversely, for a short option position, the horizontal segment is above the zero-profit axis (i.e., positive gross profit), reflecting the premium received by the option seller (i.e., an inflow of funds). Readers may find it useful to think of premiums received or paid as cash flows in (+) or out (−), respectively.

The diagonal segment of the option profit diagram represents the profits for the range of futures prices where the option is in the money. Notice that for the long call in Figure 15.5 this segment includes futures prices above the $3.50 strike price. An option that is in the money has intrinsic value, and consequently the slope is non-zero. For a long option position, profits increase as the option moves in the money and the intrinsic value increases. The profit diagram in Figure 15.5 crosses the zero-profit axis at $3.85. This is the breakeven futures price for the option buyer, and is equal to the $3.50 strike price plus the $0.35 premium. At futures prices above $3.85 the profits on the long call option position become positive.

Because profit tables and profit diagrams typically are calculated at expiration, a long call (i.e., buying the right to buy a futures contract) that is in the money will have a delta of +1. This means profits on a long call that is in the money will increase dollar-for-dollar as futures prices increase, and the slope of the diagonal segment will be +1. The delta of a long futures position also is +1, so for prices above the strike price, the profit on a long call option is equivalent to the profit on a long futures position established at the $3.85 breakeven price.

Short Calls

Conversely, for a short option position, profits decrease and eventually turn negative as the option moves in the money (recall that gains for the option buyer are matched by losses for the option seller). We can see this in the profit table for a short $3.50 call option (see Table 15.6), with a premium of $0.35 which is received by the option seller.

The profit data in Table 15.6 can be used to construct a profit diagram for this short call (see Figure 15.6).

As in the previous example, the horizontal segment in Figure 15.6 represents the profits for the range of futures prices where the option is out of the money. Because the profit is constant for all futures prices below the $3.50 strike price, the slope of this segment is zero. The horizontal segment is above the zero-profit axis (i.e., positive gross profit), reflecting the

Table 15.6 Profit on Short $3.50 Call, $0.35 Premium

Price	Intrinsic value for short $3.50 call	Premium for short $3.50 call	Profit on short $3.50 call
$3.00	$0.00	$0.35	$0.35
$3.05	$0.00	$0.35	$0.35
$3.10	$0.00	$0.35	$0.35
$3.15	$0.00	$0.35	$0.35
$3.20	$0.00	$0.35	$0.35
$3.25	$0.00	$0.35	$0.35
$3.30	$0.00	$0.35	$0.35
$3.35	$0.00	$0.35	$0.35
$3.40	$0.00	$0.35	$0.35
$3.45	$0.00	$0.35	$0.35
$3.50	$0.00	$0.35	$0.35
$3.55	−$0.05	$0.35	$0.30
$3.60	−$0.10	$0.35	$0.25
$3.65	−$0.15	$0.35	$0.20
$3.70	−$0.20	$0.35	$0.15
$3.75	−$0.25	$0.35	$0.10
$3.80	−$0.30	$0.35	$0.05
$3.85	−$0.35	$0.35	$0.00
$3.90	−$0.40	$0.35	−$0.05
$3.95	−$0.45	$0.35	−$0.10
$4.00	−$0.50	$0.35	−$0.15

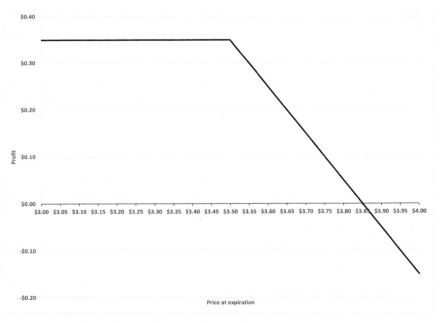

Figure 15.6 Profit on Short $3.50 Call, $0.35 Premium

premium received by the option seller (i.e., an inflow of funds). Notice that in Figure 15.6 this vertical distance is +$0.35, which is the amount of the premium received by the seller, as well as the maximum profit that can be experienced by the option seller.

At futures prices above the $3.50 strike price, the option moves in the money and the profits decrease, as shown by the diagonal segment of the profit diagram in Figure 15.6. The profit diagram crosses the zero-profit axis at $3.85. This is the breakeven futures price for the option seller, and is equal to the $3.50 strike price plus the $0.35 premium, same as for the option buyer. At futures prices above $3.85 the profits on a short call option position become negative.

Because profit tables and diagrams are calculated at expiration, a short call (i.e., selling the right to buy a futures contract) that is in the money will have a delta of −1. This means profits on a short call that is in the money will decrease dollar-for-dollar as futures prices increase, and the slope of the diagonal segment will be −1. Recall from above that the delta of a short futures position also is −1, so for prices above the strike price, the profit on a short call option is equivalent to the profit on a short futures position established at the $3.85 breakeven price.

Notice that the profit diagram for a short call in Figure 15.6 is the mirror image of the corresponding long call in Figure 15.5. Stated differently, if we invert or "flip" the profit diagram top for bottom, we can convert the profit diagram for a long call into the diagram for the corresponding short call and vice versa. Alternatively, we can switch between long and short positions by reversing the signs (i.e., + or −) on the intrinsic value, premium, and profit entries in the profit tables, presented earlier as Table 15.5 and Table 15.6.

Long Puts

The same principles described above for calls also apply to puts. Suppose that we buy a put option with a $3.50 strike price and pay a premium of $0.25. To construct a profit diagram for this long put position using a range of futures prices at expiration from $3.00 to $4.00 in 5-cent increments, we need to first construct a profit table with the calculated profit at each futures price (see Table 15.7).

Then, using the profit data in Table 15.7, we can construct a profit diagram for this long put (see Figure 15.7).

As described earlier, the horizontal segment of the option profit diagram represents the profits for the range of futures prices where the option is out of the money, so the slope of this segment is zero at futures prices above the $3.50 strike price. This horizontal segment is below the zero-profit axis (i.e., negative gross profit), reflecting the premium paid by the option buyer (i.e., an outflow of funds), and the vertical distance below the axis is −$0.25, which is the amount of the premium paid by the buyer, as well as the maximum loss for the option buyer.

The diagonal segment of the option profit diagram represents the profits for the range of futures prices where the option is in the money. This segment includes futures prices below the $3.50 strike price. The profit diagram in Figure 15.7 crosses the zero-profit axis at $3.25.

Table 15.7 Profit on Long $3.50 Put, $0.25 Premium

Price	Intrinsic value for long $3.50 put	Premium for long $3.50 put	Profit on long $3.50 put
$3.00	$0.50	−$0.25	$0.25
$3.05	$0.45	−$0.25	$0.20
$3.10	$0.40	−$0.25	$0.15
$3.15	$0.35	−$0.25	$0.10
$3.20	$0.30	−$0.25	$0.05
$3.25	$0.25	−$0.25	$0.00
$3.30	$0.20	−$0.25	−$0.05
$3.35	$0.15	−$0.25	−$0.10
$3.40	$0.10	−$0.25	−$0.15
$3.45	$0.05	−$0.25	−$0.20
$3.50	$0.00	−$0.25	−$0.25
$3.55	$0.00	−$0.25	−$0.25
$3.60	$0.00	−$0.25	−$0.25
$3.65	$0.00	−$0.25	−$0.25
$3.70	$0.00	−$0.25	−$0.25
$3.75	$0.00	−$0.25	−$0.25
$3.80	$0.00	−$0.25	−$0.25
$3.85	$0.00	−$0.25	−$0.25
$3.90	$0.00	−$0.25	−$0.25
$3.95	$0.00	−$0.25	−$0.25
$4.00	$0.00	−$0.25	−$0.25

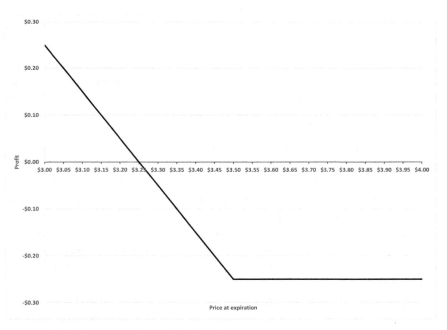

Figure 15.7 Profit on Long $3.50 Put, $0.25 Premium

This is the breakeven futures price for the option buyer, and is equal to the $3.50 strike price minus the $0.25 premium. At futures prices below $3.25 the profits on the long put option position become positive.

For a long option position, profits increase as the option moves in the money and the intrinsic value increases, so a long put (i.e., buying the right to sell a futures contract) that is in the money will have a delta of −1. This means profits on a long put that is in the money will increase dollar-for-dollar as futures prices decrease, and the slope of the diagonal segment will be −1. The delta of a short futures position also is −1, so for prices below the strike price, the profit on a long put option is equivalent to the profit on a short futures position established at the $3.25 breakeven price.

Short Puts

Conversely, the profit table for a short $3.50 put option, with a premium of $0.25 which is received by the option seller, is presented in Table 15.8.

Table 15.8 Profit on Short $3.50 Put, $0.25 Premium

Price	Intrinsic value for short $3.50 put	Premium for short $3.50 put	Profit on short $3.50 put
$3.00	−$0.50	$0.25	−$0.25
$3.05	−$0.45	$0.25	−$0.20
$3.10	−$0.40	$0.25	−$0.15
$3.15	−$0.35	$0.25	−$0.10
$3.20	−$0.30	$0.25	−$0.05
$3.25	−$0.25	$0.25	$0.00
$3.30	−$0.20	$0.25	$0.05
$3.35	−$0.15	$0.25	$0.10
$3.40	−$0.10	$0.25	$0.15
$3.45	−$0.05	$0.25	$0.20
$3.50	$0.00	$0.25	$0.25
$3.55	$0.00	$0.25	$0.25
$3.60	$0.00	$0.25	$0.25
$3.65	$0.00	$0.25	$0.25
$3.70	$0.00	$0.25	$0.25
$3.75	$0.00	$0.25	$0.25
$3.80	$0.00	$0.25	$0.25
$3.85	$0.00	$0.25	$0.25
$3.90	$0.00	$0.25	$0.25
$3.95	$0.00	$0.25	$0.25
$4.00	$0.00	$0.25	$0.25

Using the profit data in Table 15.8, we can construct a profit diagram for this short put (see Figure 15.8).

As in the previous option profit diagrams, the horizontal segment in Figure 15.8 represents the range of futures prices where the option is out of the money, which in this case includes futures prices above the $3.50 strike price. The horizontal segment is above the zero-profit axis (i.e., positive gross profit), reflecting the premium received by the option seller (i.e., an inflow of funds), and the vertical distance is +$0.25, which is the amount of the premium received by the seller, as well as the maximum profit for the option seller.

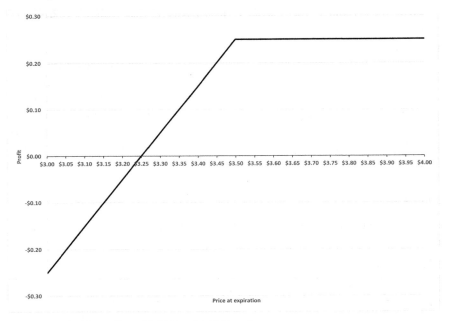

Figure 15.8 Profit on Short $3.50 Put, $0.25 Premium

At futures prices below the $3.50 strike price, the short put moves in the money and the profits decline for the option seller, as shown by the diagonal segment of the profit diagram in Figure 15.8. The profit diagram crosses the zero-profit axis at $3.25. This is the breakeven futures price for the option seller, and is equal to the $3.50 strike price minus the $0.25 premium, same as for the option buyer. At futures prices below $3.25 the profits on a short option position become negative.

The delta for an in-the-money short put (i.e., selling the right to sell a futures contract) is +1, same as the delta for a long futures position. For prices below the strike price, the profit on a short put option is equivalent to the profit on a long futures position established at the $3.25 breakeven price.

The profit diagram for a short put in Figure 15.8 is the mirror image of the corresponding long put in Figure 15.7, just as the profit diagram for a short call is the mirror image of the corresponding long call. We can invert or "flip" the option profit diagram top for bottom and convert the profit diagram for a long put into the diagram for the corresponding short put and vice versa. Similarly, we can switch between long and short positions in the profit tables by reversing the signs (i.e., + or −) on the intrinsic value, premium, and profit entries in Table 15.7 and Table 15.8.

In the discussion above, we have shown that the profit diagrams for options have some similarities to futures, but also some important differences. The ability of an option buyer to abandon an option when the underlying price is unfavorable is reflected by the horizontal segment of the profit diagram. Abandoning the option limits the option buyer's losses to the amount paid for the premium, which is a sunk cost that is incurred regardless of the eventual outcome for the option.

Hedging Long Cash with Long Puts

We can illustrate the practical value of this ability of the option buyer to abandon an unfavorable position by modifying the hedging example in Table 15.4 and Figure 15.4. Instead of hedging a long cash position established at $3.50 with a short futures position established at $3.50, we will hedge the long cash position using a long put option with a $3.50 strike price and a premium of $0.25. Using the profits for the long put position from Table 15.7, we can construct the profit table (see Table 15.9).

Table 15.9 Profit on Long Cash Position Established at $3.50, Hedged with Long $3.50 Put, $0.25 Premium

Price	Profit on long cash at $3.50	Profit on long $3.50 put	Combined profit
$3.00	−$0.50	$0.25	−$0.25
$3.05	−$0.45	$0.20	−$0.25
$3.10	−$0.40	$0.15	−$0.25
$3.15	−$0.35	$0.10	−$0.25
$3.20	−$0.30	$0.05	−$0.25
$3.25	−$0.25	$0.00	−$0.25
$3.30	−$0.20	−$0.05	−$0.25
$3.35	−$0.15	−$0.10	−$0.25
$3.40	−$0.10	−$0.15	−$0.25
$3.45	−$0.05	−$0.20	−$0.25
$3.50	$0.00	−$0.25	−$0.25
$3.55	$0.05	−$0.25	−$0.20
$3.60	$0.10	−$0.25	−$0.15
$3.65	$0.15	−$0.25	−$0.10
$3.70	$0.20	−$0.25	−$0.05
$3.75	$0.25	−$0.25	$0.00
$3.80	$0.30	−$0.25	$0.05
$3.85	$0.35	−$0.25	$0.10
$3.90	$0.40	−$0.25	$0.15
$3.95	$0.45	−$0.25	$0.20
$4.00	$0.50	−$0.25	$0.25

Then a profit diagram can be constructed for the hedged position, using the data from Table 15.9 (see Figure 15.9).

A hedger with a long cash position wants to be protected against lower prices, but a futures hedge also prevents them from benefitting from higher prices. Futures gains offset cash losses at lower prices, and futures losses offset cash gains at higher prices. As was shown in Table 15.4 and Figure 15.4, hedging this long cash position with a short futures position produces a combined profit of zero and a constant price of $3.50.

Using a long put instead of short futures protects the hedger against lower prices, but allows the hedger to benefit from higher prices. Notice that the dotted line representing combined profits in Figure 15.9 is horizontal at prices below $3.50, at a profit level of −$0.25 which represents the premium paid for the option. At prices above the $3.50 strike price, the

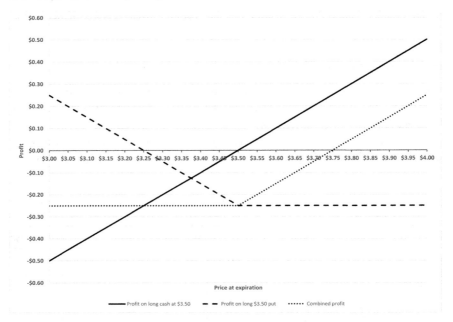

Figure 15.9 Long Cash Position at $3.50 Hedged with Long $3.50 Put, $0.25 Premium

combined profit line is parallel to the long cash profit line, and it moves higher dollar-for-dollar with increases in the underlying price. The combined profit line in Figure 15.9 crosses the zero-profit axis at $3.75, which is equal to the $3.50 strike price plus the $0.25 premium, above which the hedger receives profits on the combined cash-plus-option position.

Short Hedging with Long Puts vs. Short Futures

Comparing the combined profit lines in Figure 15.9 and Figure 15.4, we can see that the hedger is better off with the long put at prices above $3.75, and better off with short futures at prices below $3.75, all else the same. However, the hedger does not know beforehand what the price will be at expiration, so it is impossible to know in advance which hedging approach will be better in a particular situation. Instead, the hedger likely will base their decision on the likelihood of various price levels. In terms of the tradeoffs involved, the hedger using long put options instead of short futures must be willing to accept losses of $0.25 at prices below $3.50, and smaller losses at prices between $3.50 and $3.75, in return for profits at prices above $3.75.

Hedging Long Cash with Short Calls

The option hedger also could use a short call instead of a long put. Recall that the maximum profit for an option seller is the premium received from the option buyer, so a hedge using a short option position will cover losses on the cash position only if those losses do not exceed the amount of premium received. In addition, the seller of the option may be assigned a short futures position at the strike price if the option moves in the money and is exercised. To examine these properties, we can modify Table 15.9 so it hedges the long cash position using the short call option with a $3.50 strike price and a premium of $0.35 from Table 15.6 (see Table 15.10).

Table 15.10 Profit on Long Cash Position Established at $3.50, Hedged with Short $3.50 Call, $0.25 Premium

Price	Profit on long cash at $3.50	Profit on short $3.50 call	Combined profit
$3.00	−$0.50	$0.35	−$0.15
$3.05	−$0.45	$0.35	−$0.10
$3.10	−$0.40	$0.35	−$0.05
$3.15	−$0.35	$0.35	$0.00
$3.20	−$0.30	$0.35	$0.05
$3.25	−$0.25	$0.35	$0.10
$3.30	−$0.20	$0.35	$0.15
$3.35	−$0.15	$0.35	$0.20
$3.40	−$0.10	$0.35	$0.25
$3.45	−$0.05	$0.35	$0.30
$3.50	$0.00	$0.35	$0.35
$3.55	$0.05	$0.30	$0.35
$3.60	$0.10	$0.25	$0.35
$3.65	$0.15	$0.20	$0.35
$3.70	$0.20	$0.15	$0.35
$3.75	$0.25	$0.10	$0.35
$3.80	$0.30	$0.05	$0.35
$3.85	$0.35	$0.00	$0.35
$3.90	$0.40	−$0.05	$0.35
$3.95	$0.45	−$0.10	$0.35
$4.00	$0.50	−$0.15	$0.35

Then we construct a profit diagram for the hedged position, using the data in Table 15.10 (see Figure 15.10).

Notice that the dotted line representing combined profits in Figure 15.10 is horizontal at prices above $3.50. This horizontal segment occurs at a profit level of +$0.35 which represents the premium received for the option. At prices below the $3.50 strike price, the combined profit line is parallel to the long cash profit line, and it moves lower dollar-for-dollar with decreases in the underlying price. The combined profit line at prices between $3.50 and $3.15 shows how the $0.35 premium received from selling the call option can be used to cover the first $0.35 of losses on the long cash position. The dotted line crosses the zero-profit axis at $3.15, and at prices below $3.15 − corresponding to cash position losses greater than $0.35 − the hedger incurs losses on the combined cash-plus-option position.

Short Hedging with Short Calls vs. Short Futures

Comparing the combined profit lines in Figure 15.10 and Figure 15.4, we can see that the hedger is better off with the short call at prices above $3.15, and better off with short futures at prices below $3.15. However, the hedger does not know beforehand what the price will

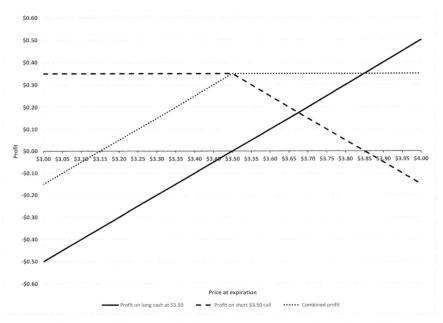

Figure 15.10 Long Cash Position at $3.50 Hedged with Short $3.50 Call, $0.35 Premium

be at expiration. It is impossible to know in advance which hedging approach will be better, so the decision between an option hedge and a futures hedge will be based on the hedger's expectations about the likelihood of various price levels. In terms of the tradeoffs involved, the hedger using short call options instead of short futures must be willing to accept steadily increasing losses at prices below $3.15, in return for profits that begin at prices above $3.15 and reach a maximum of $0.35 at a price of $3.50.

Hedging Short Cash with Long Futures

We can develop similar hedging examples using options with a short cash position. If we hedge a short cash position with a long futures position, the profits and losses will offset, and the combined profit will be zero. Table 15.11 hedges a short cash position established at $3.50 with a long futures position established at $3.50.

Consequently, when we use the data in the profit table to construct a profit diagram (see Figure 15.11), the combined profit line will be horizontal, similar to the results in Figure 15.4 for a long cash position hedged with a short futures position.

Hedging Short Cash with Long Calls

A hedger with a short cash position wants to be protected against higher prices, but a futures hedge also prevents them from benefitting from lower prices. Futures gains offset cash losses

Table 15.11 Profit on Short Cash Position Established at $3.50, Hedged with Long Futures Position Established at $3.50

Price	Profit on short cash at $3.50	Profit on long futures at $3.50	Combined profit
$3.00	$0.50	−$0.50	$0.00
$3.05	$0.45	−$0.45	$0.00
$3.10	$0.40	−$0.40	$0.00
$3.15	$0.35	−$0.35	$0.00
$3.20	$0.30	−$0.30	$0.00
$3.25	$0.25	−$0.25	$0.00
$3.30	$0.20	−$0.20	$0.00
$3.35	$0.15	−$0.15	$0.00
$3.40	$0.10	−$0.10	$0.00
$3.45	$0.05	−$0.05	$0.00
$3.50	$0.00	$0.00	$0.00
$3.55	−$0.05	$0.05	$0.00
$3.60	−$0.10	$0.10	$0.00
$3.65	−$0.15	$0.15	$0.00
$3.70	−$0.20	$0.20	$0.00
$3.75	−$0.25	$0.25	$0.00
$3.80	−$0.30	$0.30	$0.00
$3.85	−$0.35	$0.35	$0.00
$3.90	−$0.40	$0.40	$0.00
$3.95	−$0.45	$0.45	$0.00
$4.00	−$0.50	$0.50	$0.00

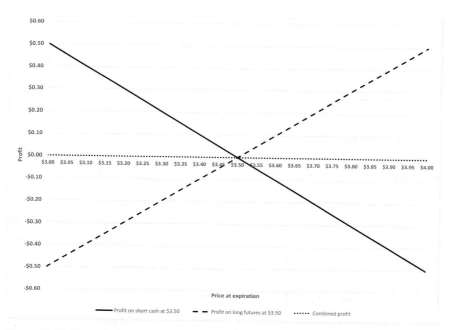

Figure 15.11 Short Cash Position Established at $3.50 Hedged with Long Futures Position Established at $.350

at higher prices, and futures losses offset cash gains at lower prices. Hedging this short cash position with a long futures position, as shown in Table 15.11 and Figure 15.11, produces a combined profit of zero and a constant price of $3.50.

Using a long call instead of long futures protects the hedger against higher prices, but allows the hedger to benefit from lower prices. We can demonstrate this by modifying Table 15.11, replacing the profit on the long futures with the profit on a long $3.50 call from Table 15.5, and then calculating the profit on the combined position (see Table 15.12).

Table 15.12 Profit on Short Cash Position Established at $3.50, Hedged with Long $3.50 Call, $0.35 Premium

Price	Profit on short cash at $3.50	Profit on long $3.50 call	Combined profit
$3.00	$0.50	−$0.35	$0.15
$3.05	$0.45	−$0.35	$0.10
$3.10	$0.40	−$0.35	$0.05
$3.15	$0.35	−$0.35	$0.00
$3.20	$0.30	−$0.35	−$0.05
$3.25	$0.25	−$0.35	−$0.10
$3.30	$0.20	−$0.35	−$0.15
$3.35	$0.15	−$0.35	−$0.20
$3.40	$0.10	−$0.35	−$0.25
$3.45	$0.05	−$0.35	−$0.30
$3.50	$0.00	−$0.35	−$0.35
$3.55	−$0.05	−$0.30	−$0.35
$3.60	−$0.10	−$0.25	−$0.35
$3.65	−$0.15	−$0.20	−$0.35
$3.70	−$0.20	−$0.15	−$0.35
$3.75	−$0.25	−$0.10	−$0.35
$3.80	−$0.30	−$0.05	−$0.35
$3.85	−$0.35	$0.00	−$0.35
$3.90	−$0.40	$0.05	−$0.35
$3.95	−$0.45	$0.10	−$0.35
$4.00	−$0.50	$0.15	−$0.35

We can see this more clearly in the profit diagram shown in Figure 15.12, which is constructed from the data in Table 15.12.

Notice that the dotted line representing combined profits in Figure 15.12 is horizontal at prices above $3.50, at a profit level of −$0.35 which represents the premium paid for the option. At prices below the $3.50 strike price, the combined profit line is parallel to the short cash profit line, and it moves higher dollar-for-dollar with decreases in the underlying price. The combined profit line in Figure 15.12 crosses the zero-profit axis at $3.15, which is equal to the $3.50 strike price minus the $0.35 premium, below which the hedger receives profits on the combined cash-plus-option position.

Long Hedging with Long Calls vs. Long Futures

When we compare the combined profit lines in Figure 15.11 and Figure 15.12, we can see that the hedger is better off with the long call at prices below $3.15, and better off with long futures at prices above $3.15, all else the same. In terms of the tradeoffs involved, the hedger

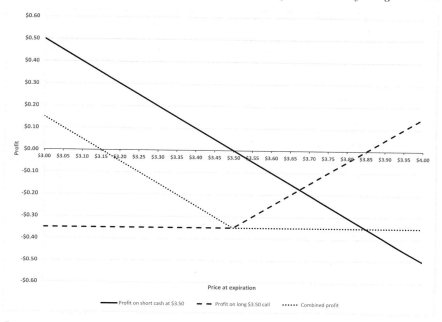

Figure 15.12 Short Cash Position at $3.50 Hedged with Long $3.50 Call, $0.35 Premium

using long call options instead of long futures must be willing to accept losses of $0.35 at prices above $3.50, and smaller losses at prices between $3.50 and $3.15, in return for profits at prices below $3.15.

Hedging Short Cash with Short Puts

The option hedger also could use a short put instead of a long call. A hedge using a short option position will cover losses on the cash position only if those losses do not exceed the amount of premium received. In addition, the seller of the option may be assigned a long futures position at the strike price if the option moves in the money and is exercised. We can modify Table 15.12 so it hedges the short cash position using the short put option from Table 15.8 (see Table 15.13).

Then, we can use the data in Table 15.13 to construct a profit diagram (see Figure 15.13). Notice that the dotted line representing combined profits in Figure 15.13 is horizontal at prices below $3.50. This horizontal segment occurs at a profit level of +$0.25 which represents the premium received for the option. At prices above the $3.50 strike price, the combined profit line is parallel to the short cash profit line, and it moves lower dollar-for-dollar with increases in the underlying price. The combined profit line at prices between $3.50 and $3.75 shows how the $0.25 premium received from selling the put option can be used to cover the first $0.25 of losses on the short cash position. The dotted line crosses the

Table 15.13 Profit on Short Cash Position Established at $3.50, Hedged with Short $3.50 Put, $0.25 Premium

Price	Profit on short cash at $3.50	Profit on short $3.50 put	Combined profit
$3.00	$0.50	−$0.25	$0.25
$3.05	$0.45	−$0.20	$0.25
$3.10	$0.40	−$0.15	$0.25
$3.15	$0.35	−$0.10	$0.25
$3.20	$0.30	−$0.05	$0.25
$3.25	$0.25	$0.00	$0.25
$3.30	$0.20	$0.05	$0.25
$3.35	$0.15	$0.10	$0.25
$3.40	$0.10	$0.15	$0.25
$3.45	$0.05	$0.20	$0.25
$3.50	$0.00	$0.25	$0.25
$3.55	−$0.05	$0.25	$0.20
$3.60	−$0.10	$0.25	$0.15
$3.65	−$0.15	$0.25	$0.10
$3.70	−$0.20	$0.25	$0.05
$3.75	−$0.25	$0.25	$0.00
$3.80	−$0.30	$0.25	−$0.05
$3.85	−$0.35	$0.25	−$0.10
$3.90	−$0.40	$0.25	−$0.15
$3.95	−$0.45	$0.25	−$0.20
$4.00	−$0.50	$0.25	−$0.25

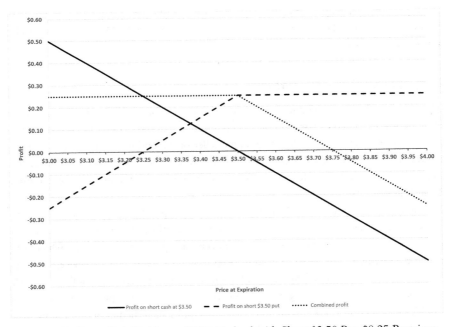

Figure 15.13 Short Cash Position at $3.50 Hedged with Short $3.50 Put, $0.25 Premium

zero-profit axis at \$3.75, and at prices above \$3.75 – corresponding to cash position losses greater than \$0.25 – the hedger incurs losses on the combined cash-plus-option position.

Long Hedging with Short Puts vs. Long Futures

Comparing the combined profit lines in Figure 15.13 and Figure 15.11, we can see that the hedger in these examples is better off with the short put at prices below \$3.75, and better off with long futures at prices above \$3.75. However, the hedger does not know beforehand what the price will be at expiration. In terms of the tradeoffs involved, the hedger using short put options instead of long futures must be willing to accept losses at prices above \$3.75, in return for profits that begin at prices below \$3.75 and reach a maximum of \$0.25 at a price of \$3.50.

Discussion

Hedging with futures is very straightforward, but also relatively inflexible. In a typical scenario, the hedger has a particular cash position and takes an offsetting futures position, with most of the decisions involving when to place the hedge and when to lift or roll. In contrast, hedging with options is extremely flexible, but requires more decisions. The hedger must decide whether to use a call or a put, and which of the many strike prices to use. For purposes of simplicity the examples presented in this chapter used only at-the-money options, but a call or put on a particular futures contract month will have dozens or even hundreds of strike prices to choose from, each with its own premium value and Greeks. Consequently, selecting a particular option can be an intimidating task.

Fortunately – or perhaps unfortunately, depending on one's point of view – there is no single call or put/strike price combination that is the all-around "best" in all market situations. As shown by the examples in this chapter, sometimes the best outcome will be obtained from a futures contract, at other times it will be a call, and at still other times it will be a put. Only in hindsight can a hedger know whether they made the "right" hedging decision. However, profit tables and profit diagrams are useful for narrowing the number of choices, and for knowing in advance the results from a particular choice over a range of market prices, all of which help the hedger to make more informed decisions.

Options allow the hedger to participate in favorable prices and avoid unfavorable prices, giving them the best of both worlds. However, the premium plays an important role in these outcomes. For a long option position, the premium represents a cost that may shift the hedger's breakeven price to an undesirable level; for a short option position, the premium is a lump-sum revenue item that may not be sufficient to cover losses from a large change in the market price. Profit tables and profit diagrams can be used to analyze these factors for individual positions and combinations of positions, both to identify potential opportunities and to avoid unpleasant surprises.

16 Hedging with Options

Hedging a cash position with a long option protects the hedger against unfavorable price changes, but allows them to benefit from favorable price changes. While this might appear to be the best of both worlds, the cost of the premium may be so large that it outweighs any potential benefit that might occur from a favorable price change. In addition, we discovered in Chapter 14 that the delta is not constant over the life of an option, so the number of options required to hedge a particular cash position will change over the duration of the hedge. Consequently, a hedge using a long option must be managed more carefully and actively than a futures hedge, all else the same. Notice that the basis issues described for futures hedges in Chapter 7 apply equally to option hedges, but for simplicity they will be ignored here. Also notice that the examples in this chapter will ignore commissions and other transaction costs, as well as time-value-of-money adjustments to correct for differences in the timing of cash flows.

Also recall from Chapter 15 that hedging a cash position with a short option provides only limited protection against unfavorable prices. Hedging by selling an option will offset losses on the cash position up to the point where cash losses equal the amount of premium received. Beyond that point, where cash losses exceed the amount of premium received, the hedge provides no further protection. In addition, if the short option moves in the money and is exercised by the option buyer, the hedger (i.e., option seller) will not benefit from favorable price changes. Consequently, selling an option is often considered to be more of a profit-enhancing strategy than a risk-reducing strategy.

Option-Based Hedging Strategies

Floor

With these points in mind, let's take a closer look at each of the option hedging strategies from the previous chapter, beginning with the use of a long put to hedge a long cash position from Figure 15.9, reproduced here.

We can see that the combined profit (i.e., dotted line) is horizontal at $3.50 and below, which is the strike price of the long put. Consequently, this hedging strategy is known as a *floor*

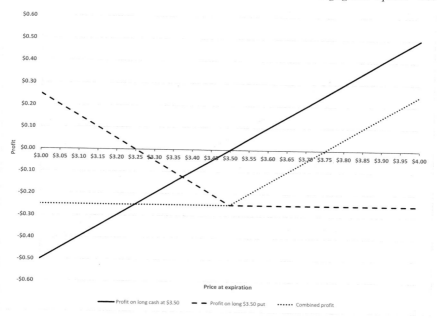

Figure 15.9 Long Cash Position at $3.50 Hedged with Long $3.50 Put, $0.25 Premium

because it places a lower bound on the net price (i.e., cash price received plus gain or loss on the option position) for the cash commodity. Alternatively, it establishes a limit on the combined losses (i.e., negative profits) received by the hedger at lower prices. The maximum loss is equal to the premium paid for the long put. This strategy is also known as a *protective put* because the long put acts like an insurance policy on the long cash position.

Ceiling

Similarly, the profit diagram for a long call used to hedge a short cash position was presented in Figure 15.12, reproduced here.

We can see that the combined profit (i.e., dotted line) is horizontal at $3.50 and above, which is the strike price of the long call. Consequently, this hedging strategy is known as a *ceiling* or *cap* because it places an upper bound on the net price (i.e., cash price paid minus gain or loss on the option position) for the cash commodity. Stated differently, it establishes a limit on the combined losses (i.e., negative profits) received by the hedger at higher prices. This loss is equal to the premium paid for the long call. This strategy is also known as a *protective call* because the long call acts like an insurance policy on the short cash position.

Collar

For both the floor and the ceiling, the amount paid for the premium represents a cost, and therefore it plays an important role in the profit or loss received by the hedger. When hedging

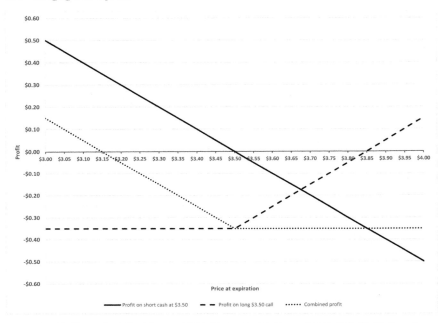

Figure 15.12 Short Cash Position at $3.50 Hedged with Long $3.50 Call, $0.35 Premium

a long cash position, one way to reduce the cost of the long put is to sell a call option at a higher strike price, in a common hedging strategy known as a *collar* or *fence*. Consequently, a collar establishes a band or range around the profits and losses on the hedged position.

For example, suppose that we use the long cash position at $3.50 hedged with a long $3.50 put in Figure 15.9 as a starting point. Recall that hedging with an option protects the hedger against unfavorable price changes but allows them to benefit from favorable price changes. For prices below $3.50, the $0.25 premium reduces the price at which the hedged position is more profitable – or less unprofitable – than the unhedged position to $3.25 (i.e., where the dotted line moves above the solid line). For prices above $3.50, the $0.25 premium makes the hedged position less profitable (by $0.25) than the unhedged position, and increases the price at which the hedged position becomes profitable to $3.75 (i.e., where the dotted line crosses the zero-profit axis).

To reduce the impact of the put premium, suppose that we add a short $4.00 call option with a premium of $0.1575. The profit table for this combined position is presented as Table 16.1.

We can use the data in Table 16.1 to create a profit diagram for the combined position, presented as Figure 16.1.

Notice that we extended the scaling for the horizontal axis to the $2.50 to $4.50 price range to show the key details for the short $4.00 call position and the combined profit line. To simplify comparison of the profit diagrams for this collar strategy and the original option

Table 16.1 Profit on Long Cash Position Established at $3.50, Hedged with Long $3.50 Put, $0.25 Premium and Short $4.00 Call, $0.1575 Premium

Price	Profit on long cash at $3.50	Profit on long $3.50 put	Profit on short $4.00 call	Combined profit
$2.50	−$1.0000	$0.7500	$0.1575	−$0.0925
$2.55	−$0.9500	$0.7000	$0.1575	−$0.0925
$2.60	−$0.9000	$0.6500	$0.1575	−$0.0925
$2.65	−$0.8500	$0.6000	$0.1575	−$0.0925
$2.70	−$0.8000	$0.5500	$0.1575	−$0.0925
$2.75	−$0.7500	$0.5000	$0.1575	−$0.0925
$2.80	−$0.7000	$0.4500	$0.1575	−$0.0925
$2.85	−$0.6500	$0.4000	$0.1575	−$0.0925
$2.90	−$0.6000	$0.3500	$0.1575	−$0.0925
$2.95	−$0.5500	$0.3000	$0.1575	−$0.0925
$3.00	−$0.5000	$0.2500	$0.1575	−$0.0925
$3.05	−$0.4500	$0.2000	$0.1575	−$0.0925
$3.10	−$0.4000	$0.1500	$0.1575	−$0.0925
$3.15	−$0.3500	$0.1000	$0.1575	−$0.0925
$3.20	−$0.3000	$0.0500	$0.1575	−$0.0925
$3.25	−$0.2500	$0.0000	$0.1575	−$0.0925
$3.30	−$0.2000	−$0.0500	$0.1575	−$0.0925
$3.35	−$0.1500	−$0.1000	$0.1575	−$0.0925
$3.40	−$0.1000	−$0.1500	$0.1575	−$0.0925
$3.45	−$0.0500	−$0.2000	$0.1575	−$0.0925
$3.50	$0.0000	−$0.2500	$0.1575	−$0.0925
$3.55	$0.0500	−$0.2500	$0.1575	−$0.0425
$3.60	$0.1000	−$0.2500	$0.1575	$0.0075
$3.65	$0.1500	−$0.2500	$0.1575	$0.0575
$3.70	$0.2000	−$0.2500	$0.1575	$0.1075
$3.75	$0.2500	−$0.2500	$0.1575	$0.1575
$3.80	$0.3000	−$0.2500	$0.1575	$0.2075
$3.85	$0.3500	−$0.2500	$0.1575	$0.2575
$3.90	$0.4000	−$0.2500	$0.1575	$0.3075
$3.95	$0.4500	−$0.2500	$0.1575	$0.3575
$4.00	$0.5000	−$0.2500	$0.1575	$0.4075
$4.05	$0.5500	−$0.2500	$0.1075	$0.4075
$4.10	$0.6000	−$0.2500	$0.0575	$0.4075
$4.15	$0.6500	−$0.2500	$0.0075	$0.4075
$4.20	$0.7000	−$0.2500	−$0.0425	$0.4075
$4.25	$0.7500	−$0.2500	−$0.0925	$0.4075
$4.30	$0.8000	−$0.2500	−$0.1425	$0.4075
$4.35	$0.8500	−$0.2500	−$0.1925	$0.4075
$4.40	$0.9000	−$0.2500	−$0.2425	$0.4075
$4.45	$0.9500	−$0.2500	−$0.2925	$0.4075
$4.50	$1.0000	−$0.2500	−$0.3425	$0.4075

hedge in Figure 15.9, we will re-scale Figure 16.1 so that both profit diagrams use the same $3.00 to $4.00 range, denoted as Figure 16.1A.

Notice that the combined profit line in Figure 16.1A for prices below $3.50 resembles the profit diagram in Figure 15.9 except that it has been shifted up by $0.1575. This vertical shift reflects the premium received for the short $4.00 call, and reduces the loss on the combined positions to $0.0925 (= $0.25 − $0.1575) at prices below $3.50. Also notice that the breakeven cash price (i.e., where the dotted line crosses the zero-profit axis) has been shifted

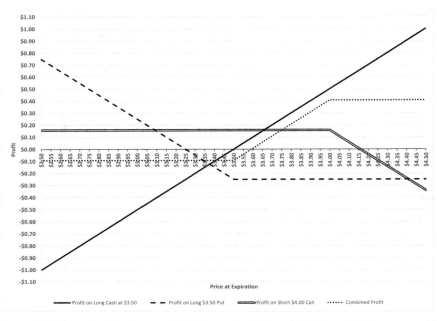

Figure 16.1 Long Cash Position at $3.50 Hedged with Long $3.50 Put, $0.25 Premium and Short $4.00 Call, $0.1575 Premium

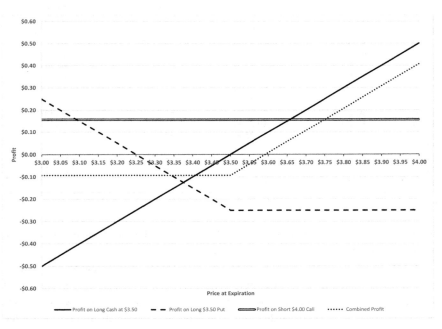

Figure 16.1A Long Cash Position at $3.50 Hedged with Long $3.50 Put, $0.25 Premium and Short $4.00 Call, $0.1575 Premium (Rescaled)

to the left by $0.1575, from $3.75 to $3.5925. This horizontal shift reflects the premium received for the short $4.00 call, and reduces the price at which the strategy becomes profitable to $3.5925 (= $3.75 − $0.1575). Stated differently, the collar reduces the cost of hedging a long cash position with a long put option from $0.25 to $0.0925 (= $0.25 − $0.1575), which is the net premium paid for the combined option position.

Zero-Cost Collar

It follows that selling a second out-of-the-money call option – not necessarily another $4.00 call – would further reduce this cost. If the additional premium received from this second short call happened to be $0.0925, then the cost of the collar strategy would be zero, and the result is known as a *zero-cost collar* because the net cost of the options is zero. Alternatively, selling a second $4.00 call for $0.1575 would cause the combined premium for the collar strategy to change from a *net debit* value of −$0.0925 to a *net credit* value of +$0.0650 (= −$0.0925 + $0.1575). Notice that with a net credit the hedger not only would be protected against lower prices, but also would receive a premium for doing it.

At this point the reader might be thinking that this is too good to be true, and they would be correct – there are some important drawbacks. We can create a profit table for the collar strategy in Table 16.2.

Then we can use the data in Table 16.2 to create a profit diagram for the combined position, presented in Figure 16.2.

By extending the scaling for the horizontal axis to $2.50 to $4.50, we can compare these results to Figure 16.1 to determine the impact of adding the second $4.00 short call. Notice that at prices below $3.50, the second short call shifted up the combined profit line (i.e., dotted line) by an additional $0.1575, which is the premium received for the second short call, and the combined profit is positive at all price levels. Also notice that at prices between $3.50 and $4.00, the second short call shifted up the combined profit line by an additional $0.1575.

However, at prices above $4.00, where the short calls are in the money, adding the second short call changed the direction of the combined profit line (i.e., dotted line) from horizontal to downward-sloping. The long cash position offsets the impact of the first short call, but there is nothing to offset the impact of the second short call. Consequently, at prices above $4.00, the collar with two short calls is equivalent to having a naked (i.e., unhedged) short position in a $4.00 call at an effective premium of $0.5650 (from Table 16.2). In addition, at prices above $4.5650 (= $4.00 strike price + $0.5650 effective premium) the combined profit declines due to the negative impact of the second short $4.00 call, which is moving deeper in the money. This is in contrast to the collar with one short call in Figure 16.1, which had constant net profits at prices above $4.00, and in contrast to the long cash position hedged with a long put in Figure 15.9.

A different choice of strike price(s) for the out-of-the-money calls would change the collar strategy results somewhat, but it would not alter the basic point that selling one or more options can reduce the net cost of the option hedge. Selling options that are deeper

Table 16.2 Profit on Long Cash Position Established at $3.50, Hedged with Long $3.50 Put, $0.25 Premium and 2 Short $4.00 Calls, Each $0.1575 Premium

Price	Profit on long cash at $3.50	Profit on long $3.50 put	Profit on 2 × short $4.00 call	Combined profit
$2.50	−$1.0000	$0.7500	$0.3150	$0.0650
$2.55	−$0.9500	$0.7000	$0.3150	$0.0650
$2.60	−$0.9000	$0.6500	$0.3150	$0.0650
$2.65	−$0.8500	$0.6000	$0.3150	$0.0650
$2.70	−$0.8000	$0.5500	$0.3150	$0.0650
$2.75	−$0.7500	$0.5000	$0.3150	$0.0650
$2.80	−$0.7000	$0.4500	$0.3150	$0.0650
$2.85	−$0.6500	$0.4000	$0.3150	$0.0650
$2.90	−$0.6000	$0.3500	$0.3150	$0.0650
$2.95	−$0.5500	$0.3000	$0.3150	$0.0650
$3.00	−$0.5000	$0.2500	$0.3150	$0.0650
$3.05	−$0.4500	$0.2000	$0.3150	$0.0650
$3.10	−$0.4000	$0.1500	$0.3150	$0.0650
$3.15	−$0.3500	$0.1000	$0.3150	$0.0650
$3.20	−$0.3000	$0.0500	$0.3150	$0.0650
$3.25	−$0.2500	$0.0000	$0.3150	$0.0650
$3.30	−$0.2000	−$0.0500	$0.3150	$0.0650
$3.35	−$0.1500	−$0.1000	$0.3150	$0.0650
$3.40	−$0.1000	−$0.1500	$0.3150	$0.0650
$3.45	−$0.0500	−$0.2000	$0.3150	$0.0650
$3.50	$0.0000	−$0.2500	$0.3150	$0.0650
$3.55	$0.0500	−$0.2500	$0.3150	$0.1150
$3.60	$0.1000	−$0.2500	$0.3150	$0.1650
$3.65	$0.1500	−$0.2500	$0.3150	$0.2150
$3.70	$0.2000	−$0.2500	$0.3150	$0.2650
$3.75	$0.2500	−$0.2500	$0.3150	$0.3150
$3.80	$0.3000	−$0.2500	$0.3150	$0.3650
$3.85	$0.3500	−$0.2500	$0.3150	$0.4150
$3.90	$0.4000	−$0.2500	$0.3150	$0.4650
$3.95	$0.4500	−$0.2500	$0.3150	$0.5150
$4.00	$0.5000	−$0.2500	$0.3150	$0.5650
$4.05	$0.5500	−$0.2500	$0.2150	$0.5150
$4.10	$0.6000	−$0.2500	$0.1150	$0.4650
$4.15	$0.6500	−$0.2500	$0.0150	$0.4150
$4.20	$0.7000	−$0.2500	−$0.0850	$0.3650
$4.25	$0.7500	−$0.2500	−$0.1850	$0.3150
$4.30	$0.8000	−$0.2500	−$0.2850	$0.2650
$4.35	$0.8500	−$0.2500	−$0.3850	$0.2150
$4.40	$0.9000	−$0.2500	−$0.4850	$0.1650
$4.45	$0.9500	−$0.2500	−$0.5850	$0.1150
$4.50	$1.0000	−$0.2500	−$0.6850	$0.0650

out of the money reduces the risk of exercise, and shifts the downward-sloping segment of the combined profit line farther to the right, but requires more options to be sold to generate a given amount of premium. Conversely, selling options that are closer to being in the money requires fewer options to be sold, but increases the risk of exercise, and moves the downward-sloping segment of the combined profit line closer to current price levels. The choice of specific strike(s) – because more than one strike price can be used if multiple

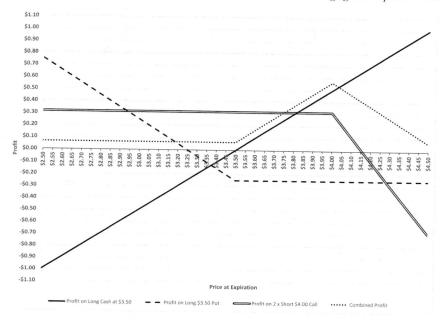

Figure 16.2 Long Cash Position at $3.50 Hedged with Long $3.50 Put, $0.25 Premium and 2 Short $4.00 Calls, Each $0.1575 Premium

options are sold – and the number(s) of options sold will depend on the hedger's desired net premium for the collar, their appetite for risk, their assessment of future price trends, and market conditions. As is always the case when using options, there are many tradeoffs involved in making these decisions, and there is no single combination of option positions that is "best" for all market scenarios. The examples presented in this section demonstrate why it is important for an option hedger to examine the combined profits at all price levels, and not just those near current price levels.

Inverse Collar

The collar strategy described above is used for hedging long cash positions. There is a counterpart strategy for hedging short cash positions known as the *inverse collar* or *reverse collar* which uses a long call as the hedging instrument, and reduces the net cost of the premium by selling one or more out-of-the-money puts.

For example, suppose that we begin with the short cash position at $3.50 hedged with a long $3.50 call in Figure 15.12. For prices above $3.50, the $0.35 premium increases the price at which the hedged position is more profitable – or less unprofitable – than the unhedged position to $3.85 (i.e., where the dotted line crosses the solid line). For prices below $3.50, the $0.35 premium makes the hedged position less profitable (by $0.35) than the unhedged position, and decreases the price at which the hedged position becomes profitable to $3.15 (i.e., where the dotted line crosses the zero-profit axis).

To reduce the impact of the call premium, suppose that we add a short $3.00 put option with a premium of $0.0750. The profit table for this inverse collar strategy is presented as Table 16.3.

We can use the data in Table 16.3 to create a profit diagram for the inverse collar, presented as Figure 16.3.

Table 16.3 Profit on Short Cash Position Established at $3.50, Hedged with Long $3.50 Call, $0.35 Premium and Short $3.00 Put, $0.0750 Premium

Price	Profit on short cash at $3.50	Profit on long $3.50 call	Profit on short $3.00 put	Combined profit
$2.50	$1.00	−$0.35	−$0.4250	$0.2250
$2.55	$0.95	−$0.35	−$0.3750	$0.2250
$2.60	$0.90	−$0.35	−$0.3250	$0.2250
$2.65	$0.85	−$0.35	−$0.2750	$0.2250
$2.70	$0.80	−$0.35	−$0.2250	$0.2250
$2.75	$0.75	−$0.35	−$0.1750	$0.2250
$2.80	$0.70	−$0.35	−$0.1250	$0.2250
$2.85	$0.65	−$0.35	−$0.0750	$0.2250
$2.90	$0.60	−$0.35	−$0.0250	$0.2250
$2.95	$0.55	−$0.35	$0.0250	$0.2250
$3.00	$0.50	−$0.35	$0.0750	$0.2250
$3.05	$0.45	−$0.35	$0.0750	$0.1750
$3.10	$0.40	−$0.35	$0.0750	$0.1250
$3.15	$0.35	−$0.35	$0.0750	$0.0750
$3.20	$0.30	−$0.35	$0.0750	$0.0250
$3.25	$0.25	−$0.35	$0.0750	−$0.0250
$3.30	$0.20	−$0.35	$0.0750	−$0.0750
$3.35	$0.15	−$0.35	$0.0750	−$0.1250
$3.40	$0.10	−$0.35	$0.0750	−$0.1750
$3.45	$0.05	−$0.35	$0.0750	−$0.2250
$3.50	$0.00	−$0.35	$0.0750	−$0.2750
$3.55	−$0.05	−$0.30	$0.0750	−$0.2750
$3.60	−$0.10	−$0.25	$0.0750	−$0.2750
$3.65	−$0.15	−$0.20	$0.0750	−$0.2750
$3.70	−$0.20	−$0.15	$0.0750	−$0.2750
$3.75	−$0.25	−$0.10	$0.0750	−$0.2750
$3.80	−$0.30	−$0.05	$0.0750	−$0.2750
$3.85	−$0.35	$0.00	$0.0750	−$0.2750
$3.90	−$0.40	$0.05	$0.0750	−$0.2750
$3.95	−$0.45	$0.10	$0.0750	−$0.2750
$4.00	−$0.50	$0.15	$0.0750	−$0.2750
$4.05	−$0.55	$0.20	$0.0750	−$0.2750
$4.10	−$0.60	$0.25	$0.0750	−$0.2750
$4.15	−$0.65	$0.30	$0.0750	−$0.2750
$4.20	−$0.70	$0.35	$0.0750	−$0.2750
$4.25	−$0.75	$0.40	$0.0750	−$0.2750
$4.30	−$0.80	$0.45	$0.0750	−$0.2750
$4.35	−$0.85	$0.50	$0.0750	−$0.2750
$4.40	−$0.90	$0.55	$0.0750	−$0.2750
$4.45	−$0.95	$0.60	$0.0750	−$0.2750
$4.50	−$1.00	$0.65	$0.0750	−$0.2750

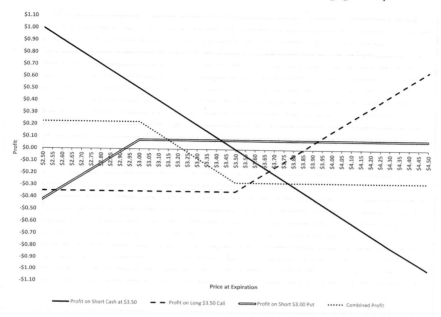

Figure 16.3 Short Cash Position at $3.50 Hedged with Long $3.50 Call, $0.35 Premium and Short $3.00 Put, $0.0750 Premium

Notice that the combined profit line in Figure 16.3 for prices above $3.50 resembles the profit diagram in Figure 15.12 except that it has been shifted up by $0.0750. This vertical shift reflects the premium received for the short $3.00 put, and reduces the loss on the combined positions to $0.2750 (= $0.35 − $0.0750) at prices above $3.50. Likewise, the breakeven cash price – where the dotted line crosses the zero-profit axis – has been shifted to the right by $0.0750, from $3.15 to $3.2250. This horizontal shift reflects the premium received for the short $3.00 put, and increases the price at which the strategy becomes profitable to $3.2250 (= $3.15 + $0.0750). Stated differently, the inverse collar reduces the cost of hedging a short cash position with a long call option by $0.0750. This cost could be further reduced by selling additional out-of-the-money puts, but at the risk that a lower cash price could cause the puts to move in the money and reduce the combined profits on the inverse collar at lower prices.

Covered Call and Covered Put

Chapter 15 also described the use of short options as hedging instruments. Going back to our insurance analogy, if buying an option is comparable to buying an insurance policy, then selling an option is analogous to selling an insurance policy. More specifically, a short call is similar to selling coverage against a long position (i.e., higher prices) and a short put is similar to selling coverage against a short position (i.e., lower prices), where the insurer collects a premium and pays the policyholder if a particular event occurs.

For example, a long cash position can be hedged using a short call, as shown in Figure 15.10, reproduced here.

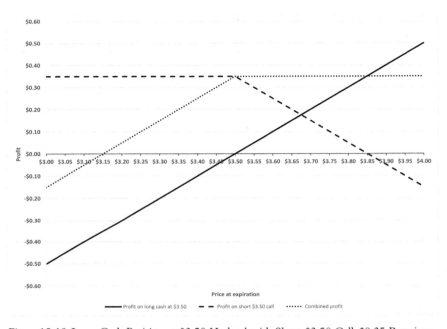

Figure 15.10 Long Cash Position at $3.50 Hedged with Short $3.50 Call, $0.35 Premium

This strategy is known as a *covered call* because the premium received from the sale of the call can be used to offset or "cover" losses from a decrease in the cash price, provided the decrease does not exceed the amount of premium received. In contrast, gains on the long cash position can be used to cover losses on the short call position dollar-for-dollar as the short call moves in the money. If the short call is exercised by the option buyer, the hedger will be assigned a short futures position at the strike price, and the hedge will perform like a standard futures hedge.

Similarly, Figure 15.13, which is reproduced here, illustrates the use of a short put to hedge a short cash position, which is known as a *covered put*.

The premium received from the sale of the put can be used to cover losses from an increase in the cash price, provided the price increase does not exceed the amount of premium received. Conversely, gains on the short cash position can be used to cover losses dollar-for-dollar on the short put position, or on the resulting long futures position if the option is exercised.

Due to the lump-sum nature of the premium received by an option seller, many observers classify covered calls and covered puts as speculative strategies rather than hedging strategies.

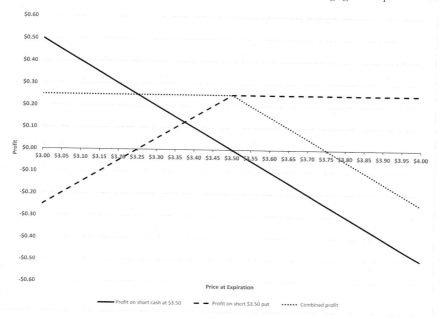

Figure 15.13 Short Cash Position at $3.50 Hedged with Short $3.50 Put, $0.25 Premium

However, the premium received from a short option can be used to offset limited losses on a cash position, so we have chosen to treat short options as a potential risk management tool. This approach is consistent with the use of short options in collars and inverse collars described earlier in this chapter. It is also consistent with the approach taken by many practitioners, who frequently sell options as a way to reduce or "cheapen up" the cost of buying other options as part of a comprehensive risk management program.

Delta–Neutral Hedging

Recall from Chapter 14 that delta is the change in the premium from a one-cent change in the underlying futures price. In addition, the delta for a call option is positive and ranges between 0 and +1; the delta for a put option is negative and ranges between 0 and −1. By definition, the delta is +1 for a long futures contract or long cash position, and −1 for a short futures contract or short cash position. A futures hedge uses opposite long and short positions in cash and futures, so one side of the hedge will have a delta of +1 and the other side of the hedge will have a delta of −1, for a delta of zero on the combined cash plus futures position. Stated differently, when the combined delta is zero, the combined position is *delta neutral*, and the gains on one side of the hedge will exactly offset losses on the other side and vice versa.

Impact of Changing Intrinsic Value and Time Value

When hedging with options, creating and maintaining a delta-neutral position can be challenging because the delta for an option changes each time the underlying futures price changes. In addition, even if the underlying futures price is stable, the delta will change simply due to time value decay. When an option has a long time to expiration, there is some probability that it will move in the money (or, conversely, move out of the money) by the expiration date. As expiration approaches, it becomes increasingly likely that the option will remain either in the money or out of the money, particularly for strikes far above and below the current price. This causes call deltas to move toward either +1 or 0 as expiration approaches, and put deltas to move toward either −1 or 0 as expiration approaches, and it eventually affects strikes close to the current price. At expiration, all options will be either in the money or out of the money and all deltas will be either +1 or 0 for calls, and −1 or 0 for puts. There cannot be any intermediate delta values at expiration.

Profit Diagrams Prior to Expiration

The combined effects of time decay and changing underlying prices are shown in Figure 16.4. It shows the profit that would result if a long $3.50 call purchased at an initial premium of $0.35 were liquidated at various times prior to expiration (the hockey-stick-shaped profit diagram at expiration is provided for reference). For example, at 180 days before expiration and an underlying futures price of $3.60, the premium would be approximately $0.35 and the profit would be zero (i.e., where the double line crosses the zero-profit axis). Each curve represents the range of profits (i.e., changes in premium) at a different time prior to expiration. Each curve also represents the range of premiums at a different time prior to expiration, minus the $0.35 initial premium paid for the $3.50 call. Consequently, the slope of each curve at a particular point corresponds to the delta of the call option at a particular time to expiration and at a particular underlying futures price. This is illustrated in Figure 16.4.

Moving along each curve, there is a range of delta values (i.e., slopes) for different underlying futures prices at a particular time to expiration. Moving vertically across the curves, there also is a range of delta values (i.e., slopes) for the same underlying futures price at different times to expiration. With this example in mind, the reader can understand how the delta can vary for a particular option. This variation of the delta means that a hedger must constantly monitor the delta of their positions, and make adjustments to keep the combined delta as close to zero as possible. This adjustment process is known as *delta-neutral hedging* or *dynamic hedging* and refers to the frequent addition or liquidation of options in response to changing delta values.

Dynamic Hedging Example

Suppose that we want to use options to hedge an expected purchase of 100,000 bushels of corn, which we plan to make in five months. Prices have fallen substantially in the past several weeks, so we want to be protected against any price increases while retaining the

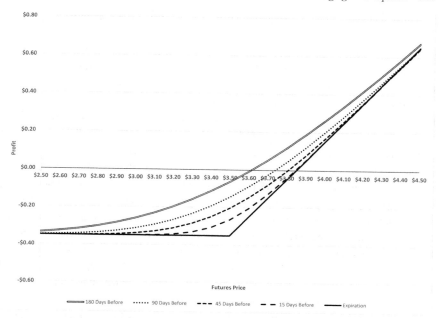

Figure 16.4 Profit Diagrams at Various Times Before Expiration: Long $3.50 Call, $0.35 Premium

ability to take advantage of any further price decreases. The futures price for the contract that expires around the time of the expected purchase is $3.4975, so we decide to use $3.50 calls as part of a ceiling strategy. The premium for a $3.50 call is $0.2625 per bushel, and the delta is +.5259. In this example, which uses actual futures prices from July 2016, we will ignore the basis and assume that the cash price is equal to the futures price. We also will ignore commissions and other transaction costs.

Each futures contract represents 5,000 bushels, so if we were hedging with futures we would need 20 futures contracts (= 100,000 ÷ 5,000). However, the delta of each call option is +.5259 while the delta of a long futures contract is +1.0, so we need to use 38 long calls (≈ 20 ÷ .5259) to have the same results as 20 long futures contracts. These 38 long calls require a total premium of $49,875 (= $0.2625 per bushel × 5,000 bushels per option × 38 options).

End of Day 1: At the end of the first day, the futures price is $3.6575, up $0.16 from the day before. Consequently, the cost of our expected purchase has increased, and the value of our short cash position has decreased by $0.16 per bushel, or $16,000 (= $0.16 per bushel × 100,000 bushels). However, our long calls have moved in the money, and the premium is now $0.3525 per bushel, for a gain of $0.09 per bushel (= $0.3525 − $0.2625), or $17,100 (= $0.09 per bushel × 5,000 bushels per option × 38 options) on our long call position. Our combined cash plus option position has a gain of $1,100 (= $17,100 − $16,000).

Because the options have moved in the money, the delta for each call is now +0.6149, or +23.3662 (= +0.6149 deltas per option × 38 options) for our long call position. The combined delta for our short cash position is −20 (= −1 × 20 futures-equivalent contracts), so we are over-hedged by +3.3662 deltas (= +23.3662 − 20), or approximately 5 call options (≈ +3.3662 deltas ÷ +0.6149 deltas per option); recall that there are no fractional options, so we must round to the nearest whole number. Once we have liquidated these 5 calls, our option position becomes long 33 calls, and our hedged position is delta neutral again.

End of Day 2: At the end of the second day, the futures price is $3.6225, down $0.0350 from the day before, so the cost of our expected purchase has decreased, and the value of our short cash position has increased by $0.0350 per bushel, or $3,500 (= $0.0350 per bushel × 100,000 bushels). At the same time, the premium for our long calls has decreased to $0.3300 per bushel. This is a loss for the day of $0.0225 per bushel (= $0.3300 − $0.3525), or $3,712.50 (= $0.0225 per bushel × 5,000 bushels per option × 33 options) on our long call position. Our combined cash plus option position has a loss on Day 2 of $212.50 (= $3,500 − $3,712.50).

The options have moved out of the money (or, more accurately, less in the money) on Day 2, and the delta for each call is now +0.5964, or +19.6812 (= +0.5964 deltas per option × 33 options) for our long call position. The delta for our short cash position is unchanged at −20, so we are under-hedged by −0.3188 deltas (= +19.6812 − 20), or approximately 1 call option (≈ −0.3188 deltas ÷ +0.5964 deltas per option). Adding this 1 long call brings our option position to 34 long calls, and makes our hedged position delta neutral again.

End of Day 3: At the end of the third day, the futures price is $3.5225, down $0.10 from the day before. Once again, the cost of our expected purchase has decreased, and the value of our short cash position has increased, this time by $0.10 per bushel, or $10,000 (= $0.10 per bushel × 100,000 bushels). This lower futures price makes the call options less valuable, so the premium has decreased to $0.2725 per bushel. For Day 3, this is a loss of $0.0575 per bushel (= $0.2725 − $0.3300), or $9,775 (= $0.0575 per bushel × 5,000 bushels per option × 34 options) on our long call position. The combined cash plus option position has a gain for the day of $225 (= +$10,000 − $9,775).

The options are only slightly in the money at the end of Day 3, and the delta for each call is now +0.5403, or +18.3702 (= +0.5403 deltas per option × 34 options) for our long call position. The delta for our short cash position is unchanged at −20, so once again we are under-hedged, this time by −1.6298 deltas (= +18.3702 − 20), or approximately 3 call options (≈ −1.6298 deltas ÷ +0.5403 deltas per option). Adding 3 more long calls to our option position brings us to 37 long calls, and makes our hedged position delta neutral again.

Discussion

The procedure described above is repeated each day for the duration of the option hedge. Notice that unless an option is held until expiration, an option-based strategy will not perform like the profit diagrams presented in this book. In practice, few cash purchases or sales align exactly with option expiration dates, which occur on a handful of dates each year. Consequently, most option positions are liquidated early, so the applicable profit diagrams will be more like the curves in Figure 16.4 than the customary angular, hockey stick-shaped figures used in most of our examples.

Option premiums adjust to market changes more slowly than the corresponding futures contracts, and consequently more option contracts are required to provide the same hedging performance as a given number of futures contracts, all else the same. Assuming that one option is equivalent to one futures contract is a common mistake made by first-time option hedgers – particularly individuals familiar with futures hedges who are new to using options – who are then disappointed by the results.

Also notice that the daily gains and losses for the cash position being hedged and the option position do not offset completely, even though the option position is adjusted each day. This mismatch occurs in large part because of the large daily price changes in our example – up $0.16 on Day 1, down $0.0350 on Day 2, down $0.10 on Day 3 – while the delta assumes small (i.e., one cent) price changes. This problem can be corrected by incorporating gamma – the change in delta from a one-cent change in the underlying futures price – into the dynamic hedging process. It also can be corrected by making more frequent (i.e., intra-day rather than end-of-day) adjustments to the option position.

At the beginning of this chapter, we noted that an option hedge must be managed more carefully and actively than a futures hedge, all else the same. The option hedging example presented in the previous section provides a realistic look at the dynamic hedging process. Despite its hands-on nature, option hedging is a valuable tool that offers greater flexibility and the potential for higher profits.

Delta Hedging by Option Market Makers

Market makers are the primary liquidity providers in the option markets. Unlike the locals or scalpers in the futures markets, who are willing to buy at prices slightly below the market price and sell at prices slightly above the market price, option market makers use the Black model and other option pricing programs to determine the premiums at which they are willing to buy or sell. There are hundreds or even thousands of put or call/expiration date/strike price combinations for the options on any particular futures contract, so it is highly unlikely that a market maker will buy or sell particular option and then trade it to someone else a few seconds later at a better price. Instead, the typical market maker will accumulate an inventory of short or long positions for a variety of strikes and expirations. This inventory typically consists of many thousands of individual option contracts.

The market maker is not a speculator on market direction, so they are indifferent regarding whether the market moves higher or lower, and they attempt to maintain a balanced position for the entire inventory that is neither net long nor net short. They accomplish this by constantly monitoring the deltas of the options for each underlying futures contract, and then buying or selling the underlying futures contract to make the inventory delta neutral. The market maker performs this re-balancing process throughout the trading day, and makes more frequent adjustments when the markets are more volatile or after large option transactions. Notice that the market maker buys or sells futures to make an option position delta neutral. This is the reverse of the process described above for an option hedger, who buys or sells options to make a cash (or futures) position delta neutral.

Synthetic Futures and Options

Synthetic Options

Recall from Chapter 15 that the profit diagrams for cash positions and futures positions are linear, and are upward-sloping for long positions and downward-sloping for short positions. It was shown that a long futures position (i.e., Figure 15.1) and a long cash position (i.e., Figure 15.3), both established at the same price, will have identical profit diagrams. It follows that a short cash position and a short futures position, both established at the same price, also will have identical profit diagrams.

Let's begin by taking a closer look at the profit diagrams for the four cash/option positions in Chapter 15. Figure 15.9 can be modified by replacing the cash position with a futures position, presented here as Figure 16.5.

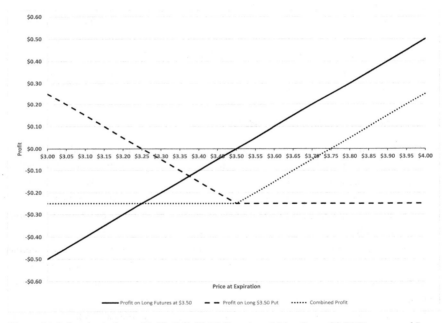

Figure 16.5 Synthetic Long $3.50 Call, $0.25 Premium Using Long $3.50 Futures and Long $3.50 Put, $0.25 Premium

The modified version shows the profits from a long futures position established at $3.50 (solid line) and a long $3.50 put with a premium of $0.25 (dashed line). Notice that the combined profit (dotted line) is equivalent to a long call with a strike price of $3.50 – the location of the bend – and a premium of $0.25 – the vertical distance between the horizontal segment and the zero-profit axis. This is an example of a *synthetic option* – in this particular case, a synthetic long call – in which the combined profits from positions in two or more other instruments are identical to the profits from an actual option position. We can express the formula for a synthetic long call (omitting the "synthetic" designation) as a long futures plus a long put, or:

Long Call = Long Futures + Long Put   (Equation 16.1)

In the same manner, we can modify Figure 15.10 by replacing the cash position with a futures position, presented here as Figure 16.6.

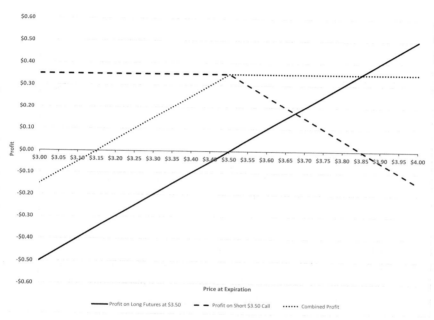

Figure 16.6 Synthetic Short $3.50 Put, $0.35 Premium Using Long $3.50 Futures and Short $3.50 Call, $0.35 Premium

The modified version shows the profits from a long futures position established at $3.50 (solid line) and a short $3.50 call with a premium of $0.35 (dashed line). The combined profit (dotted line) is equivalent to a short put with a strike price at $3.50 and a premium of $0.35, making this a synthetic $3.50 short put with a premium of $0.35. We can express the formula for a synthetic short put (omitting the "synthetic" designation) as a long futures plus a short call, or:

Short Put = Long Futures + Short Call   (Equation 16.2)

Likewise, the cash position in Figure 15.12 can be replaced with an equivalent futures position, presented here as Figure 16.7.

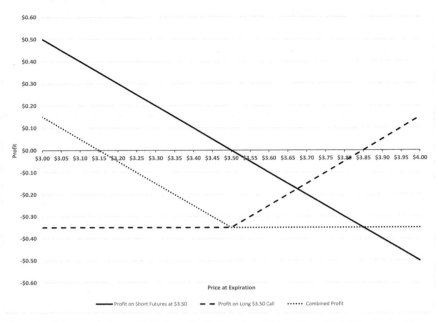

Figure 16.7 Synthetic Long $3.50 Put, $0.35 Premium Using Short $3.50 Futures and Long
$3.50 Call, $0.35 Premium

The result combines a short futures position established at $3.50 (solid line) with a long
$3.50 call at a premium of $0.35 (dashed line), for a synthetic $3.50 long put with a premium
of $0.35 (dotted line). We can express the formula for a synthetic long put (omitting the
"synthetic" designation) as a short futures plus a long call, or:

$$\text{Long Put} = \text{Short Futures} + \text{Long Call} \qquad \text{(Equation 16.3)}$$

Finally, Figure 15.13 can be modified to use a short futures position established at $3.50
(solid line) and a short $3.50 put at a premium of $0.25 (dashed line), presented here as
Figure 16.8.

The combined result (dotted line) is a synthetic $3.50 short call with a premium of $0.25.
We can express the formula for a synthetic short call (omitting the "synthetic" designation)
as a short futures plus a short put, or:

$$\text{Short Call} = \text{Short Futures} + \text{Short Put} \qquad \text{(Equation 16.4)}$$

For simplicity, these examples use a consistent $3.50 for cash, futures, and option strikes, and
premiums of either $0.25 or $0.35. Other combinations of actual cash/futures purchase or

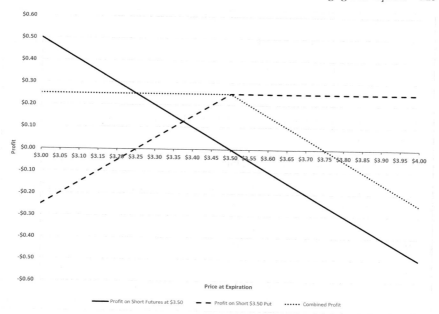

Figure 16.8 Synthetic Short $3.50 Call, $0.25 Premium Using Short $3.50 Futures and Short $3.50 Put, $0.25 Premium

sale prices, actual option strike prices, and actual option premiums can be used to produce different synthetic option strike prices and synthetic option premium values.

Synthetic Futures

We also can combine options positions to create *synthetic futures*, in which the combined profits from positions in two or more options are identical to the profits from an actual position in a futures contract. Recall from Chapter 10 that we introduced the convention of using a positive sign (+) for long positions and a negative sign (−) for short positions. Gains and losses on long and short positions are equal in magnitude but opposite in direction, and the normal rules for positive and negative signs apply. Consequently, subtracting (i.e., −) a long (i.e., +) position is equivalent to adding (i.e., +) a short (i.e., −) position, and subtracting (i.e., −) a short (i.e., −) position is equivalent to adding (i.e., +) a long (i.e., +) position. Using this notation, we can begin with Equation 16.1:

$$\text{Long Call} = \text{Long Futures} + \text{Long Put} \qquad \text{(Equation 16.1)}$$

and subtract a long put from both sides:

$$\text{Long Call} - \text{Long Put} = \text{Long Futures} \qquad \text{(Equation 16.5)}$$

However, subtracting a long put is the same as adding a short put, so:

Long Call + Short Put = Long Futures   (Equation 16.6)

which can be rearranged to produce:

Long Futures = Long Call + Short Put   (Equation 16.7)

which is the equation for a synthetic long futures. Then we can reverse the long and short positions for all the terms to produce:

Short Futures = Short Call + Long Put   (Equation 16.8)

which is the equation for a synthetic short futures. Notice that Equation 16.7 and Equation 16.8 can be derived from any of the synthetic option formulas.

Profit Diagram for Synthetic Long Futures

We can confirm Equation 16.7 for a synthetic long futures position by combining the $3.50 call and $3.50 puts from the previous chapter to construct the profit table in Table 16.4.

Then we can use the data in Table 16.4 to create a profit diagram for the synthetic long futures position, presented in Figure 16.9.

Table 16.4 Profit on Long $3.50 Call, $0.35 Premium Combined with Short $3.50 Put, $0.25 Premium

Price	Profit on long $3.50 call	Profit on short $3.50 put	Combined profit
$3.00	−$0.35	−$0.25	−$0.60
$3.05	−$0.35	−$0.20	−$0.55
$3.10	−$0.35	−$0.15	−$0.50
$3.15	−$0.35	−$0.10	−$0.45
$3.20	−$0.35	−$0.05	−$0.40
$3.25	−$0.35	$0.00	−$0.35
$3.30	−$0.35	$0.05	−$0.30
$3.35	−$0.35	$0.10	−$0.25
$3.40	−$0.35	$0.15	−$0.20
$3.45	−$0.35	$0.20	−$0.15
$3.50	−$0.35	$0.25	−$0.10
$3.55	−$0.30	$0.25	−$0.05
$3.60	−$0.25	$0.25	$0.00
$3.65	−$0.20	$0.25	$0.05
$3.70	−$0.15	$0.25	$0.10
$3.75	−$0.10	$0.25	$0.15
$3.80	−$0.05	$0.25	$0.20
$3.85	$0.00	$0.25	$0.25
$3.90	$0.05	$0.25	$0.30
$3.95	$0.10	$0.25	$0.35
$4.00	$0.15	$0.25	$0.40

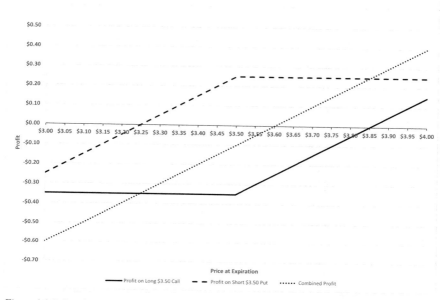

Figure 16.9 Synthetic Long $3.60 Futures Using Long $3.50 Call, $0.35 Premium and Short $3.50 Put, $0.25 Premium

Notice that the combined profit line in Figure 16.9 resembles the profit diagram for a long futures position in Figure 15.1. However, our synthetic long futures position in Figure 16.9 crosses the zero-profit axis at $3.60, unlike the actual long futures position in Figure 15.1 which crosses at $3.50. This $0.10 difference reflects the different premiums for the two options used to construct the synthetic position. Buying a call at $0.35 and selling a put at $0.25 results in a difference, or debit, of −$0.10 (= −$0.35 + $0.25). This $0.10 cost is added to the $3.50 strike price (i.e., the buying price of the long futures position if the option is exercised), resulting in a breakeven price for the synthetic long futures position of $3.60 (= $3.50 + $0.10).

Profit Diagram for Synthetic Short Futures

Similarly, we can confirm Equation 16.8 for a synthetic short futures position by combining the $3.50 strike calls and puts from the previous chapter to construct the profit table in Table 16.5.

We can use the data in Table 16.5 to create a profit diagram for the synthetic short futures position, presented here as Figure 16.10.

Table 16.5 Profit on Short $3.50 Call, $0.35 Premium Combined with Long $3.50 Put, $0.25 Premium

Price	Profit on short $3.50 call	Profit on long $3.50 put	Combined profit
$3.00	$0.35	$0.25	$0.60
$3.05	$0.35	$0.20	$0.55
$3.10	$0.35	$0.15	$0.50
$3.15	$0.35	$0.10	$0.45
$3.20	$0.35	$0.05	$0.40
$3.25	$0.35	$0.00	$0.35
$3.30	$0.35	−$0.05	$0.30
$3.35	$0.35	−$0.10	$0.25
$3.40	$0.35	−$0.15	$0.20
$3.45	$0.35	−$0.20	$0.15
$3.50	$0.35	−$0.25	$0.10
$3.55	$0.30	−$0.25	$0.05
$3.60	$0.25	−$0.25	$0.00
$3.65	$0.20	−$0.25	−$0.05
$3.70	$0.15	−$0.25	−$0.10
$3.75	$0.10	−$0.25	−$0.15
$3.80	$0.05	−$0.25	−$0.20
$3.85	$0.00	−$0.25	−$0.25
$3.90	−$0.05	−$0.25	−$0.30
$3.95	−$0.10	−$0.25	−$0.35
$4.00	−$0.15	−$0.25	−$0.40

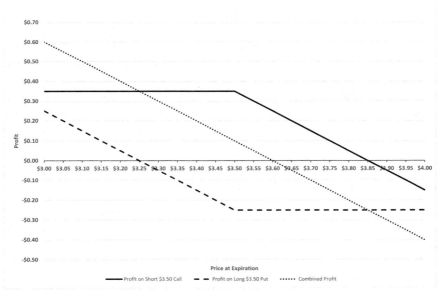

Figure 16.10 Synthetic Short $3.60 Futures Using Short $3.50 Call, $0.35 Premium and Long $3.50 Put, $0.25 Premium

Notice that the combined profit line in Figure 16.10 resembles the profit diagram for a short futures position in Figure 15.2. However, the synthetic short futures position in Figure 16.10 crosses the zero-profit axis at $3.60, unlike the actual short futures position in Figure 15.2 which crosses at $3.50. This $0.10 difference reflects the relative premiums for the two options used to construct the synthetic position. Selling a call at $0.35 and buying a put at $0.25 results in a difference, or credit, of +$0.10 (= +$0.35 − $0.25). This $0.10 revenue is added to the $3.50 strike price (i.e., the selling price of the short futures position if the option is exercised), resulting in a breakeven price for the synthetic short futures position of $3.60 (= $3.50 + $0.10).

Other Uses for Synthetic Positions

Every position or combination of positions, regardless of whether they are cash, futures, and/or options, will have a particular profit diagram. The profitability of a combination of positions should be viewed an integrated unit, rather than focusing on the behaviors of the individual components. Sometimes a number of seemingly unrelated positions will form a synthetic position that produces combined results far different from what the user is expecting.

Most commodity futures have daily price limits, which restrict the amount that prices can move up or down in a single trading session. In contrast, most options on futures do not have these limits. Suppose that a user wanted to liquidate a futures position that has moved against them, but the futures market is locked-limit and trading has halted. Depending on the reason for the limit move, the futures market may not resume trading until the following day, or perhaps even several days later, at a substantially more unfavorable price. The trader can avoid further losses by constructing an offsetting synthetic futures position. The synthetic futures position effectively serves as a hedge on the actual futures position, thereby limiting the trader's futures losses to those that have already been incurred. Later on, when futures trading resumes, the trader can liquidate both the actual and synthetic futures positions. Notice that a synthetic position and an actual position are equivalent in terms of profitability and cash flows, but a synthetic position cannot be used to liquidate an actual position or vice versa.

Synthetic futures and options also provide the foundation for *financial engineering*, in which new and unique financial products can be created by combining various positions in cash, futures, and options. These customized products typically have profit diagrams and other properties that are unavailable from standard derivatives.

17 Speculating with Options

There are four option characteristics that can be used as the focus for various trading strategies:

- changes in intrinsic value
- changes in time value
- changes in volatility
- changes in price relationships, or spreads, with other options or with underlying instruments.

In this chapter we will examine a number of trading strategies that are designed to take advantage of these option characteristics, using profit diagrams where applicable to illustrate how each strategy functions.

Intrinsic Value Strategies

Changes in intrinsic value are often called *directional trades* because any move up or down in the price of the underlying futures will affect the option premium. For example, if the underlying futures price increases, the premium for a call will increase and the premium for a put will decrease, all else the same. Conversely, if the underlying futures price decreases, the premium for a call will decrease and the premium for a put will increase, all else the same. This method of speculating on options is similar to speculating on futures, because both depend on being correct about the direction of futures prices. Option traders describe directional trades as being long premium or short premium, because the trader expects the premium to increase or decrease, respectively.

The final result for a directional trade also depends on the delta of the option, and on the amount of time it takes for the change in the underlying futures contract to occur. If the delta is small (i.e., close to zero), then a change in the underlying futures price will have relatively little impact on the option premium. Conversely, if the delta is large (i.e., close to +1 for a call or close to −1 for a put), then a change in the underlying futures price will have a relatively large impact on the premium. In addition, for a long option position, if the change in the underlying futures price occurs relatively slowly, then the loss in time value due to time decay may be greater than the gain in intrinsic value from the favorable change in the underlying futures price. In this situation the option trader will incur a loss on the long option position, despite being correct about the direction of the underlying futures price.

Time Value Strategies

Time value decay works to the advantage of option sellers (i.e., short option positions) and to the disadvantage of option buyers (i.e., long option positions). Time value is part of the premium that option buyers pay to option sellers, and more time to expiration results in greater time value, all else the same. As expiration approaches, the time value component of the option premium decreases – regardless of any changes to the intrinsic value – and eventually reaches zero at expiration. This decay occurs without any change in the underlying price, so the value of an option will decrease over time, even if everything else remains constant. Consequently, time decay can be described as a steady transfer of funds from the option buyer to the option seller over the life of the option.

Based on this description of time decay, option sellers can be viewed as time value speculators who are focused on collecting the time value component of the option premium. They typically are not concerned about market direction because they are delta neutral (delta neutral hedging was covered in the previous chapter). Recall that short option positions require margins and receive margin calls. If an option is exercised, the seller is assigned a futures position that results in an immediate loss. However, much of this loss already will have been realized via losses posted to the margin account, so the financial impact on the seller at the time of exercise and assignment will be minimal.

Volatility Strategies

Volatility is generally considered to be the single most important factor in option pricing. For both calls and puts higher volatility results in higher premiums, and lower volatility results in lower premiums, all else the same. Option traders describe volatility trades as being long volatility or short volatility, because the trader expects the volatility to increase or decrease, respectively. For example, a trader who wants to be long volatility and has no opinion about market direction would be indifferent about whether to be long calls or long puts. In contrast, a trader who wants to be long volatility and expects higher prices would prefer to be long calls, while a trader who wants to be long volatility and expects lower prices would prefer to be long puts, all else the same.

Straddle

Notice that a trader who wants to be long volatility and has no opinion about market direction could buy a call, but if the market drops suddenly they would be on the wrong side of the market. Similarly, the same trader could buy a put, but if the market rises suddenly they would be on the wrong side of the market. In both cases, the trader would be correct about increasing volatility, but would incur a loss because they took a position on what turned out to be the wrong side of the market. To neutralize the directional nature of these trades, the trader instead could use a long *straddle*, which consists of a long call and a long put, both with the same strike price, as shown in Figure 17.1.

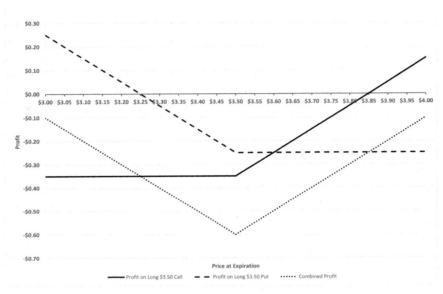

Figure 17.1 Long Straddle Using Long $3.50 Call, $0.35 Premium and Long $3.50 Put, $0.25 Premium

Having both a long call and a long put eliminates the risk of being on the wrong side of the market, but at the cost of paying an additional premium. In this example, instead of paying $0.35 for the long call, or paying $0.25 for the long put, the trader would pay $0.60 (= $0.35 + $0.25) for both options. The cost of this additional premium affects the breakeven price; notice that the dotted line does not cross the zero-profit axis within the $3.00 to $4.00 scale for the horizontal axis shown in Figure 17.1, so we must extend the scaling to the $2.50 to $4.50 price range shown in Figure 17.1A.

When we use this extended price range, we find that the dotted line crosses the zero-profit axis at $2.90 and at $4.10. These breakeven prices are equivalent to the $3.50 strike price for the long put minus the $0.60 combined premium, and the $3.50 strike price for the long call plus the $0.60 combined premium, respectively. Recall that increased volatility may result from wider price swings in both directions, but also from a sudden price move up or down in a particular direction. Unlike a long call or a long put, a straddle does not

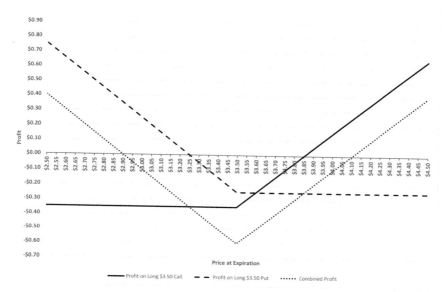

Figure 17.1A Long Straddle Using Long $3.50 Call, $0.35 Premium and Long $3.50 Put, $0.25 Premium (Rescaled)

require a price change in a particular direction to be profitable. However, the premiums for coverage in both directions can be costly (i.e., $0.60 in this particular case) and consequently the resulting price change necessary for a straddle to be profitable may be sizeable (i.e., $0.60 in either direction, in this particular case). Stated differently, the straddle in our example is unprofitable over a $1.20 price range, between $2.90 and $4.10.

Strangle

One way to reduce the premium cost is to use different strike prices for the long call and the long put, where both options are out of the money. This volatility strategy using different strikes is called a long *strangle*, and it operates on the same principle as a long strangle using a single strike for both option positions, as shown in Figure 17.2.

Using out-of-the-money strikes – $3.60 instead of $3.50 for the call, and $3.40 instead of $3.50 for the put – reduces the premiums paid to $0.30 instead of $0.35 for the call, and to $0.20 instead of $0.25 for the put, for a combined premium of $0.50 (= $0.30 + $0.20). However, notice that in this particular case the breakeven prices are unchanged at $2.90 (= $3.40 put strike minus $0.50 combined premium) and $4.10 (= $3.60 call strike plus $0.50 combined premium). Other scenarios may result in different breakeven prices, depending on the particular strikes chosen and their respective premiums.

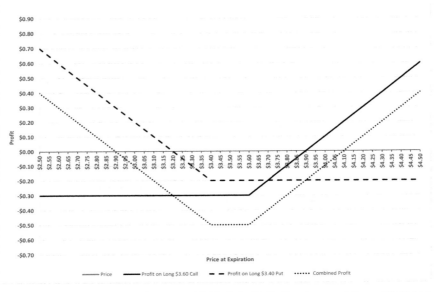

Figure 17.2 Long Strangle Using Long $3.60 Call, $0.30 Premium and Long $3.40 Put, $0.20 Premium

Other Volatility Strategies

In addition, the premiums for these volatility trades can be reduced by selling out-of-the-money calls and puts, which reduces the net cost of the combined premiums. When this is done with a straddle, the resulting strategy is called a *butterfly*; when this is done with a strangle, the resulting strategy is called a *condor*. The number of possible options strategies is virtually unlimited, and the strategies often have similarly descriptive or colorful names.

Similar option positions can be developed for short volatility scenarios, in which the trader expects volatility to decrease, and consequently premiums to decrease. A trader who wants to be short volatility and has no opinion about market direction would be indifferent about whether to be short calls or short puts. In contrast, a trader who wants to be short volatility and expects lower prices would prefer to be short calls, while a trader who wants to be short volatility and expects higher prices would prefer to be short puts, all else the same. To eliminate the directional nature of these trades, the trader could use a short straddle, which consists of a short call and a short put, both with the same strike price, as shown in Figure 17.3.

Having both a short call and a short put eliminates the risk of being on the wrong side of the market, and results in the collection of an additional premium. In this example, instead of receiving $0.35 for the short call, or receiving $0.25 for the short put, the trader receives $0.60 (= $0.35 + $0.25) for both options. This maximum profit of $0.60 occurs at the

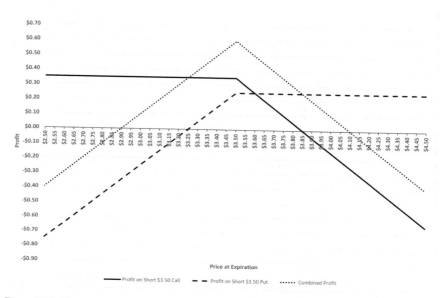

Figure 17.3 Short Straddle Using Long $3.50 Call, $0.35 Premium and Long $3.50 Put, $0.25 Premium

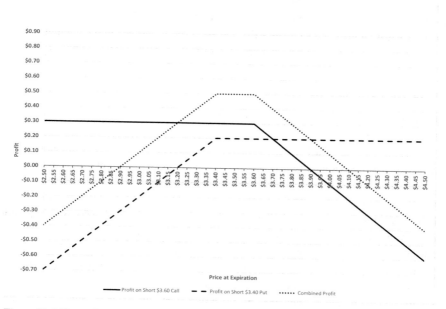

Figure 17.4 Short Strangle Using Long $3.60 Call, $0.30 Premium and Long $3.40 Put, $0.20 Premium

$3.50 strike price, and decreases steadily until the dotted line crosses the zero-profit axis in Figure 17.3 at $2.90 and at $4.10. These breakeven prices are equivalent to the $3.50 strike price for the short put minus the $0.60 combined premium, and the $3.50 strike price for the short call plus the $0.60 combined premium, respectively. As long as prices do not fall below $2.90 or rise above $4.10, the trader will have a profit on the short straddle.

Alternatively, the trader could use a short strangle, using different strike prices for the short call and the short put, where both options are out of the money. In Figure 17.4, using out-of-the-money strikes – $3.60 instead of $3.50 for the call, and $3.40 instead of $3.50 for the put – reduces the premiums received to $0.30 instead of $0.35 for the call, and to $0.20 instead of $0.25 for the put, for a combined premium of $0.50 (= $0.30 + $0.20). However, notice that in this particular case the breakeven prices are unchanged at $2.90 (= $3.40 put strike minus $0.50 combined premium) and $4.10 (= $3.60 call strike plus $0.50 combined premium). Other scenarios may result in different breakeven prices, depending on the particular strikes chosen and their respective premiums.

Spread Strategies

The large number of strike prices for calls and puts on a particular futures contract month, with the potential for pricing discrepancies on each of those individual options, translates into countless spread trading opportunities in options. Recall from Chapter 12 that we can trade the spread between two different futures contracts. Also recall from Chapter 16 that we can create a synthetic futures contract using opposite positions in puts and calls with the same strike price. Consequently, it is possible to trade the spread between a synthetic futures and an actual futures contract. Notice that the examples in this section use premium values at expiration, so positions that are liquidated prior to expiration may have different results.

Conversion and Reversal

Recall the synthetic short futures contract at $3.60, created in Table 16.5 and presented in Figure 16.10, reproduced here.

Suppose that the actual futures contract which corresponds to this synthetic position is trading at $3.58. Using a strategy known as a *conversion*, we could buy an actual futures contract at $3.58 and simultaneously create a synthetic short futures position at $3.60, for a risk-free profit of $0.02 at all price levels, ignoring commissions and other transaction costs. Notice that this profit is due to small pricing discrepancies among the three components, and does not require the trader to have any opinion about market direction. The profit table for this strategy is shown in Table 17.1 and the profit diagram is shown in Figure 17.5.

Alternatively, we could create a synthetic long futures contract, using a long $3.20 call with a premium of $0.5175 and a short $3.20 put with a premium of $0.1275. This results in a synthetic long futures position at $3.59; the profit table is presented as Table 17.2 and the profit diagram is presented in Figure 17.6.

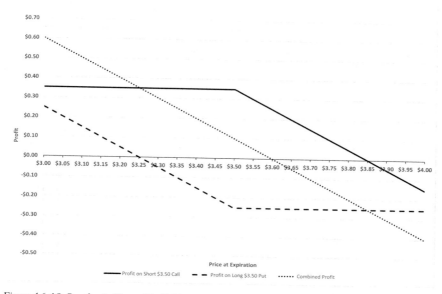

Figure 16.10 Synthetic Short $3.60 Using Short $3.50 Call, $0.35 Premium and Long $3.50 Put, $0.25 Premium

Table 17.1 Profit on Actual Long Futures at $3.58 Combined with Synthetic Short Futures at $3.60

Price	Profit on actual long futures at $3.58	Profit on synthetic short futures at $3.60	Combined profit
$3.00	−$0.58	$0.60	$0.02
$3.05	−$0.53	$0.55	$0.02
$3.10	−$0.48	$0.50	$0.02
$3.15	−$0.43	$0.45	$0.02
$3.20	−$0.38	$0.40	$0.02
$3.25	−$0.33	$0.35	$0.02
$3.30	−$0.28	$0.30	$0.02
$3.35	−$0.23	$0.25	$0.02
$3.40	−$0.18	$0.20	$0.02
$3.45	−$0.13	$0.15	$0.02
$3.50	−$0.08	$0.10	$0.02
$3.55	−$0.03	$0.05	$0.02
$3.60	$0.02	$0.00	$0.02
$3.65	$0.07	−$0.05	$0.02
$3.70	$0.12	−$0.10	$0.02
$3.75	$0.17	−$0.15	$0.02
$3.80	$0.22	−$0.20	$0.02
$3.85	$0.27	−$0.25	$0.02
$3.90	$0.32	−$0.30	$0.02
$3.95	$0.37	−$0.35	$0.02
$4.00	$0.42	−$0.40	$0.02

Table 17.2 Profit on Long $3.20 Call, $0.5175 Premium Combined with Short $3.20 Put, $0.1275 Premium

Price	Profit on long $3.20 call	Profit on short $3.20 put	Combined profit
$2.50	−$0.5175	−$0.5725	−$1.0900
$2.55	−$0.5175	−$0.5225	−$1.0400
$2.60	−$0.5175	−$0.4725	−$0.9900
$2.65	−$0.5175	−$0.4225	−$0.9400
$2.70	−$0.5175	−$0.3725	−$0.8900
$2.75	−$0.5175	−$0.3225	−$0.8400
$2.80	−$0.5175	−$0.2725	−$0.7900
$2.85	−$0.5175	−$0.2225	−$0.7400
$2.90	−$0.5175	−$0.1725	−$0.6900
$2.95	−$0.5175	−$0.1225	−$0.6400
$3.00	−$0.5175	−$0.0725	−$0.5900
$3.05	−$0.5175	−$0.0225	−$0.5400
$3.10	−$0.5175	$0.0275	−$0.4900
$3.15	−$0.5175	$0.0775	−$0.4400
$3.20	−$0.5175	$0.1275	−$0.3900
$3.25	−$0.4675	$0.1275	−$0.3400
$3.30	−$0.4175	$0.1275	−$0.2900
$3.35	−$0.3675	$0.1275	−$0.2400
$3.40	−$0.3175	$0.1275	−$0.1900
$3.45	−$0.2675	$0.1275	−$0.1400
$3.50	−$0.2175	$0.1275	−$0.0900
$3.55	−$0.1675	$0.1275	−$0.0400
$3.60	−$0.1175	$0.1275	$0.0100
$3.65	−$0.0675	$0.1275	$0.0600
$3.70	−$0.0175	$0.1275	$0.1100
$3.75	$0.0325	$0.1275	$0.1600
$3.80	$0.0825	$0.1275	$0.2100
$3.85	$0.1325	$0.1275	$0.2600
$3.90	$0.1825	$0.1275	$0.3100
$3.95	$0.2325	$0.1275	$0.3600
$4.00	$0.2825	$0.1275	$0.4100
$4.05	$0.3325	$0.1275	$0.4600
$4.10	$0.3825	$0.1275	$0.5100
$4.15	$0.4325	$0.1275	$0.5600
$4.20	$0.4825	$0.1275	$0.6100
$4.25	$0.5325	$0.1275	$0.6600
$4.30	$0.5825	$0.1275	$0.7100
$4.35	$0.6325	$0.1275	$0.7600
$4.40	$0.6825	$0.1275	$0.8100
$4.45	$0.7325	$0.1275	$0.8600
$4.50	$0.7825	$0.1275	$0.9100

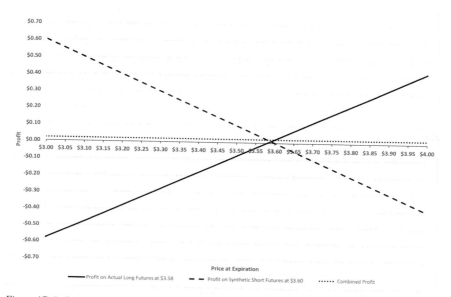

Figure 17.5 Conversion Using Actual Long Futures at $3.58 and Synthetic Short Futures at $3.60

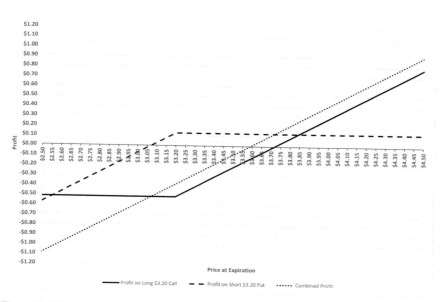

Figure 17.6 Synthetic Long $3.59 Futures Using Long $3.20 Call, $0.5175 Premium and Short $3.20 Put, $0.1275 Premium

Now suppose that the actual futures contract is trading at $3.60. Using a strategy known as a *reverse conversion* or *reversal*, we could short an actual futures contract at $3.60 and simultaneously create a synthetic long futures position at $3.59, for a risk-free profit of $0.01 at all price levels, ignoring commissions and other transaction costs. Notice that this profit is due to small pricing discrepancies among the three and does not require the trader to have any opinion about market direction. The profit table is shown in Table 17.3 and the profit diagram is shown in Figure 17.7.

Box Spread

It is also possible to trade the spread between two or more options, or two different synthetic futures contracts, using put–call parity (discussed in Chapter 14) to identify pricing discrepancies. For example, we could combine the short $3.50 call and long $3.50 put from Table 16.5 and Figure 16.10, with the long $3.20 call and short $3.20 put from Table 17.2 and Figure 17.6. These four positions produce the profit diagram shown in Figure 17.8.

This strategy is called a *box spread* because of the "box" formed by the intersection of the four option profit diagrams, which in Figure 17.8 resembles an inverted triangle. However, in this particular case, our box spread is equivalent to a synthetic long futures position at $3.59 (i.e., long $3.20 call plus short $3.20 put, plus $0.5175 premium paid minus $0.1275 premium received) plus a synthetic short futures position at $3.60 (i.e., short $3.50 call plus long $3.50 put, plus $0.35 premium received minus $0.25 premium paid), shown in Figure 17.8A.

Table 17.3 Profit on Actual Short Futures at $3.60 Combined with Synthetic Long Futures at $3.59

Price	Profit on actual short futures at $3.60	Profit on synthetic long futures at $3.59	Combined profit
$3.00	$0.60	−$0.59	$0.01
$3.05	$0.55	−$0.54	$0.01
$3.10	$0.50	−$0.49	$0.01
$3.15	$0.45	−$0.44	$0.01
$3.20	$0.40	−$0.39	$0.01
$3.25	$0.35	−$0.34	$0.01
$3.30	$0.30	−$0.29	$0.01
$3.35	$0.25	−$0.24	$0.01
$3.40	$0.20	−$0.19	$0.01
$3.45	$0.15	−$0.14	$0.01
$3.50	$0.10	−$0.09	$0.01
$3.55	$0.05	−$0.04	$0.01
$3.60	$0.00	$0.01	$0.01
$3.65	−$0.05	$0.06	$0.01
$3.70	−$0.10	$0.11	$0.01
$3.75	−$0.15	$0.16	$0.01
$3.80	−$0.20	$0.21	$0.01
$3.85	−$0.25	$0.26	$0.01
$3.90	−$0.30	$0.31	$0.01
$3.95	−$0.35	$0.36	$0.01
$4.00	−$0.40	$0.41	$0.01

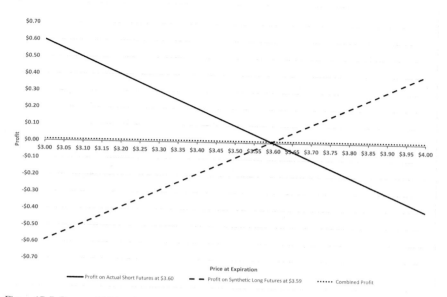

Figure 17.7 Reversal Using Actual Short Futures at $3.60 and Synthetic Long Futures at $3.59

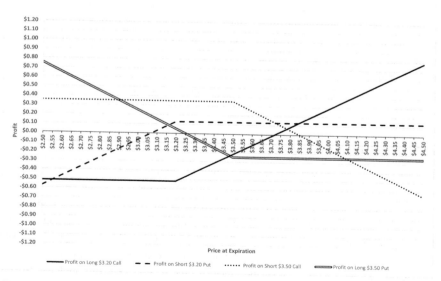

Figure 17.8 Box Spread Using Long $3.20 Call, $0.5175 Premium and Short $3.20 Put, $0.1275 Premium Plus Short $3.50 Call, $0.35 Premium and Long $3.50 Put, $0.25 Premium

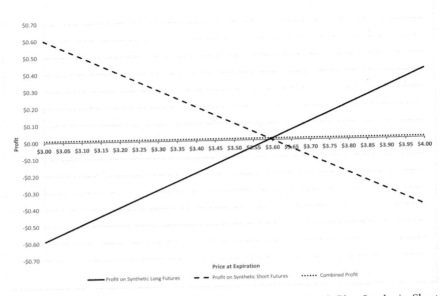

Figure 17.8A Box Spread Using Synthetic Long Futures at $3.59 Plus Synthetic Short Futures at $3.60

Notice that the combined profit line in Figure 17.8A is +$0.01 at all price levels. This is also equal to the difference between the $3.60 synthetic short futures position and the $3.59 synthetic long futures position. Selling a futures contract at $3.60 and buying the same futures contract at $3.59 results in a risk-free profit of $0.01, ignoring commissions and other transaction costs. This profit is due to small pricing discrepancies among the four components, and does not require the trader to have any opinion about market direction.

Bull Spreads and Bear Spreads

In contrast, bull spreads and bear spreads require an opinion about market direction (bull spreads and bear spreads were introduced in Chapter 11). As the names indicate, a bull spread will be profitable when the price of the underlying futures increases, while a bear spread will be profitable when the price of the underlying futures decreases. A call spread involves buying a call at one strike and selling a call at a different strike, while a put spread involves buying a put at one strike and selling a put at a different strike. For both call spreads and put spreads, the bull and bear designations describe the action taken with the lower-priced strike, so a bull spread – either a bull call spread or a bull put spread – involves buying the lower-priced strike. Conversely, a bear spread – either a bear call spread or a bear put spread – involves selling the lower-priced strike.

Bull Call Spread

In a bull call spread, the trader uses a long call at a lower-priced strike and a short call at a higher-priced strike, so the sale of the higher-strike call will partially offset the premium of the lower-strike call. As the underlying futures price moves higher, the lower-strike call will move in the money before the higher-strike call, and the lower-strike call will be in the money by a greater amount than the higher-strike call, up to a maximum amount equal to the difference between the two strikes.

For example, suppose that we have a bull call spread with a long $3.50 call at a premium of −$0.35 and a short $3.60 call at a premium of +$0.30. As shown in Table 17.4, at prices $3.50 and below, both call options are out of the money and the combined profit is −$0.05, which is the difference between the $0.35 paid for the long call and the $0.30 received for the short call. At prices between $3.50 and $3.60, the long $3.50 call moves in the money while the short $3.60 call remains out of the money, so the combined profit increases and eventually becomes positive. Finally, at prices $3.60 and above, the short $3.60 call moves in the money while the long $3.50 call moves deeper in the money. However, recall that the $3.60 call is short while the $3.50 call is long, so as both options move (deeper) in the money the short $3.60 call will generate losses while the long $3.50 call will generate gains. These losses and gains cancel, so the combined profit is +$0.05 at all prices $3.60 and above, as shown in Figure 17.9.

Table 17.4 Profit on Bull Call Spread Using Long $3.50 Call, $0.35 Premium and Short $3.60 Call, $0.30 Premium

Price	Profit on long $3.50 call	Profit on short $3.60 call	Combined profit
$3.00	−$0.35	$0.30	−$0.05
$3.05	−$0.35	$0.30	−$0.05
$3.10	−$0.35	$0.30	−$0.05
$3.15	−$0.35	$0.30	−$0.05
$3.20	−$0.35	$0.30	−$0.05
$3.25	−$0.35	$0.30	−$0.05
$3.30	−$0.35	$0.30	−$0.05
$3.35	−$0.35	$0.30	−$0.05
$3.40	−$0.35	$0.30	−$0.05
$3.45	−$0.35	$0.30	−$0.05
$3.50	−$0.35	$0.30	−$0.05
$3.55	−$0.30	$0.30	$0.00
$3.60	−$0.25	$0.30	$0.05
$3.65	−$0.20	$0.25	$0.05
$3.70	−$0.15	$0.20	$0.05
$3.75	−$0.10	$0.15	$0.05
$3.80	−$0.05	$0.10	$0.05
$3.85	$0.00	$0.05	$0.05
$3.90	$0.05	$0.00	$0.05
$3.95	$0.10	−$0.05	$0.05
$4.00	$0.15	−$0.10	$0.05

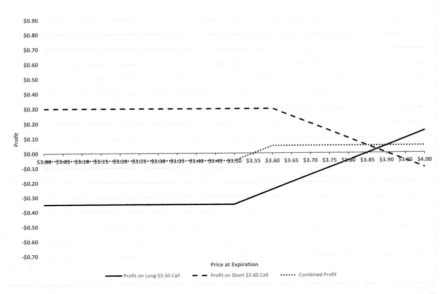

Figure 17.9 Bull Call Spread Using Long $3.50 Call, $0.35 Premium and Short $3.60 Call, $0.30 Premium

Notice that there are three distinct sets of outcomes in this profit diagram, and in the diagrams for all bull/bear call/put spreads: prices at and below the lower strike, prices between the two strikes, and prices at and above the higher strike. The maximum loss on a bull call spread is equal to the difference between the premium paid and the premium received (i.e., the net premium for the combined position), and occurs at prices at or below the lower strike. The maximum profit on a bull call spread is equal to the difference between the strikes for the two options, minus the difference between the premiums for the two options (i.e., the net premium for the combined position), and occurs at prices at or above the higher strike. A range of intermediate results occurs at prices between the two strikes.

Bear Call Spread

In contrast, a bear call spread uses a short call at a lower-priced strike and a long call at a higher-priced strike, so the sale of the lower-strike call will more than offset the premium of the higher-strike call. Like in the previous example, as the underlying futures price moves higher, the lower-strike call will move in the money before the higher-strike call, and the lower-strike call will be in the money by a greater amount than the higher-strike call, up to a maximum amount equal to the difference between the two strikes. Conversely, as the underlying futures price moves lower, the higher-strike call will move out of the money before the lower-strike call, and the higher-strike call will be out of the money by a greater amount than the lower-strike call, up to a maximum amount equal to the difference between the two strikes.

For example, suppose that we have a bear call spread with a short $3.50 call at a premium of +$0.35 and a long $3.60 call at a premium of −$0.30; notice that we can simply reverse the long and short positions and the respective profits used for the bull call spread in the previous example. As shown in Table 17.5, at prices $3.50 and below, both call options are out of the money and the combined profit is +$0.05, which is the difference between the $0.35 received for the short call and the $0.30 paid for the long call. At prices between $3.50 and $3.60, the short $3.50 call moves in the money while the long $3.60 call remains out of the money, so the combined profit decreases and eventually becomes negative. Finally, at prices $3.60 and above, the long $3.60 call moves in the money while the short $3.50 call moves deeper in the money. However, recall that the $3.60 call is long while the $3.50 call is short, so as both options move (deeper) in the money the long $3.60 call will generate gains while the short $3.50 call will generate losses. These gains and losses cancel, so the combined profit is −$0.05 at all prices $3.60 and above, as shown in Figure 17.10.

Notice that once again there are three distinct sets of outcomes in this profit diagram. The maximum loss on a bear call spread is equal to the difference between the premium paid and the premium received (i.e., the net premium for the combined position), and occurs at prices at or above the higher strike. The maximum profit on the spread is equal to the difference between the strikes for the two options, minus the difference between the premiums

Table 17.5 Profit on Bull Call Spread Using Long $3.50 Call, $0.35 Premium and Short $3.60 Call, $0.30 Premium

Price	Profit on short $3.50 call	Profit on long $3.60 call	Combined profit
$3.00	$0.35	−$0.30	$0.05
$3.05	$0.35	−$0.30	$0.05
$3.10	$0.35	−$0.30	$0.05
$3.15	$0.35	−$0.30	$0.05
$3.20	$0.35	−$0.30	$0.05
$3.25	$0.35	−$0.30	$0.05
$3.30	$0.35	−$0.30	$0.05
$3.35	$0.35	−$0.30	$0.05
$3.40	$0.35	−$0.30	$0.05
$3.45	$0.35	−$0.30	$0.05
$3.50	$0.35	−$0.30	$0.05
$3.55	$0.30	−$0.30	$0.00
$3.60	$0.25	−$0.30	−$0.05
$3.65	$0.20	−$0.25	−$0.05
$3.70	$0.15	−$0.20	−$0.05
$3.75	$0.10	−$0.15	−$0.05
$3.80	$0.05	−$0.10	−$0.05
$3.85	$0.00	−$0.05	−$0.05
$3.90	−$0.05	$0.00	−$0.05
$3.95	−$0.10	$0.05	−$0.05
$4.00	−$0.15	$0.10	−$0.05

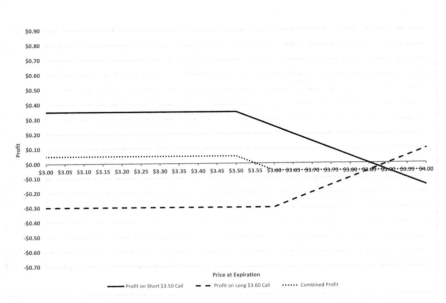

Figure 17.10 Bear Call Spread Using Short $3.50 Call, $0.35 Premium and Long $3.60 Call, $0.30 Premium

for the two options (i.e., the net premium for the combined position), and occurs at prices at or below the lower strike. A range of intermediate results occurs at prices between the two strikes.

Bull Put Spread

We can create similar examples of bull and bear spreads using puts. In a bull put spread, the trader uses a long put at a lower-priced strike and a short put at a higher-priced strike, so the sale of the higher-strike put will more than offset the premium of the lower-strike put. As the underlying futures price moves lower, the higher-strike put will move in the money before the lower-strike put, and the higher-strike put will be in the money by a greater amount than the lower-strike put, up to a maximum amount equal to the difference between the two strikes. Conversely, as the underlying futures price moves higher, the lower-strike put will move out of the money before the higher-strike put, and the higher-strike put will be in the money by a greater amount than the lower-strike put, up to a maximum amount equal to the difference between the two strikes

For example, suppose that we have a bull put spread with a long $3.40 put at a premium of −$0.20 and a short $3.50 put at a premium of +$0.25. As shown in Table 17.6, at prices $3.40 and below, both put options are in the money. The combined profit is −$0.05, which is the difference between the $0.25 paid for the long put and the $0.20 received for the short put. The $3.50 put is short while the $3.40 put is long, so as both options move (deeper) in the money the $3.40 put will generate losses while the $3.50 put will generate gains. However, these losses and gains cancel, so the combined profit is −$0.05 at all prices $3.40 and below. At prices between $3.40 and $3.50, the short $3.40 put is out of the money. However, as prices increase from $3.40 to $3.50, the long $3.50 put is in the money but by a decreasing amount, so the combined profit increases and eventually becomes positive. Finally, at prices $3.50 and above, both puts are out of the money, and the combined profit is +$0.05, as shown in Figure 17.11.

The maximum loss on a bull put spread is equal to the difference between the premium paid and the premium received (i.e., the net premium for the combined position). The maximum profit on a bull put spread is equal to the difference between the strikes for the two options, minus the difference between the premiums for the two options (i.e., the net premium for the combined position).

Bear Put Spread

Conversely, a bear put spread uses a short put at a lower-priced strike and a long put at a higher-priced strike, so the sale of the lower-strike put will partially offset the premium of the higher-strike put. As the underlying futures price moves higher, the lower-strike put will move out the money before the higher-strike put. Stated differently, as the underlying futures

Table 17.6 Profit on Bull Put Spread Using Long $3.40 Put, $0.20 Premium and Short $3.50 Put, $0.25 Premium

Price	Profit on long $3.40 put	Profit on short $3.50 put	Combined profit
$3.00	$0.20	−$0.25	−$0.05
$3.05	$0.15	−$0.20	−$0.05
$3.10	$0.10	−$0.15	−$0.05
$3.15	$0.05	−$0.10	−$0.05
$3.20	$0.00	−$0.05	−$0.05
$3.25	−$0.05	$0.00	−$0.05
$3.30	−$0.10	$0.05	−$0.05
$3.35	−$0.15	$0.10	−$0.05
$3.40	−$0.20	$0.15	−$0.05
$3.45	−$0.20	$0.20	$0.00
$3.50	−$0.20	$0.25	$0.05
$3.55	−$0.20	$0.25	$0.05
$3.60	−$0.20	$0.25	$0.05
$3.65	−$0.20	$0.25	$0.05
$3.70	−$0.20	$0.25	$0.05
$3.75	−$0.20	$0.25	$0.05
$3.80	−$0.20	$0.25	$0.05
$3.85	−$0.20	$0.25	$0.05
$3.90	−$0.20	$0.25	$0.05
$3.95	−$0.20	$0.25	$0.05
$4.00	−$0.20	$0.25	$0.05

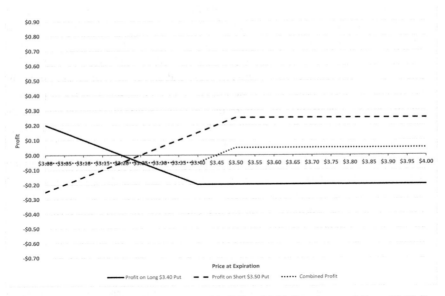

Figure 17.11 Bull Put Spread Using Long $3.40 Put, $0.20 Premium and Short $3.50 Put, $0.25 Premium

price moves lower, the higher-strike put will move in the money before the lower-strike put, and the higher-strike put will be in the money by a greater amount than the lower-strike call, up to a maximum amount equal to the difference between the two strikes.

For example, suppose that we have a bear put spread with a short $3.40 put at a premium of +$0.20 and a long $3.50 put at a premium of −$0.25; notice that we can simply reverse the long and short positions and the respective profits used for the bull put spread in the previous example. From Table 17.7, at prices $3.40 and below, both put options are in the money and the combined profit is +$0.05, which is the difference between the two strike prices, minus the net premium paid for the combined positions. At prices between $3.40 and $3.50, the short $3.40 put is out of the money. However, as prices increase from $3.40 to $3.50, the long $3.50 call is in the money but by a decreasing amount, so the combined profit decreases and eventually becomes negative. Finally, at prices $3.50 and above, both puts are out of the money, and the combined profit is −$0.05, which is the difference between the −$0.25 premium paid for the long $3.50 put and the +$0.20 premium received for the short $3.40 put, as shown in Figure 17.12.

The maximum loss on a bear put spread is equal to the difference between the premium paid and the premium received (i.e., the net premium for the combined position). The maximum profit on a bear put spread is equal to the difference between the strikes for the two options, minus the difference between the premiums for the two options (i.e., the net premium for the combined position).

Table 17.7 Profit on Bull Put Spread Using Long $3.40 Put, $0.20 Premium and Short $3.50 Put, $0.25 Premium

Price	Profit on short $3.40 put	Profit on long $3.50 put	Combined profit
$3.00	-$0.20	$0.25	$0.05
$3.05	-$0.15	$0.20	$0.05
$3.10	-$0.10	$0.15	$0.05
$3.15	-$0.05	$0.10	$0.05
$3.20	$0.00	$0.05	$0.05
$3.25	$0.05	$0.00	$0.05
$3.30	$0.10	-$0.05	$0.05
$3.35	$0.15	-$0.10	$0.05
$3.40	$0.20	-$0.15	$0.05
$3.45	$0.20	-$0.20	$0.00
$3.50	$0.20	-$0.25	-$0.05
$3.55	$0.20	-$0.25	-$0.05
$3.60	$0.20	-$0.25	-$0.05
$3.65	$0.20	-$0.25	-$0.05
$3.70	$0.20	-$0.25	-$0.05
$3.75	$0.20	-$0.25	-$0.05
$3.80	$0.20	-$0.25	-$0.05
$3.85	$0.20	-$0.25	-$0.05
$3.90	$0.20	-$0.25	-$0.05
$3.95	$0.20	-$0.25	-$0.05
$4.00	$0.20	-$0.25	-$0.05

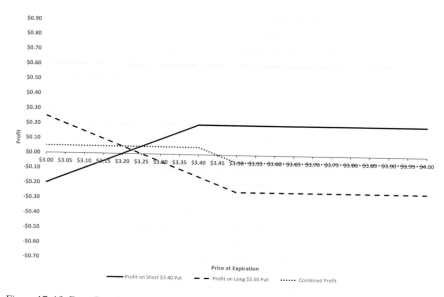

Figure 17.12 Bear Put Spread Using Short $3.40 Put, $0.20 Premium and Long $3.50 Put, $0.25 Premium

Identical Results from Bull and Bear Spreads

Notice that a bull call spread and a bull put spread with the same strikes will produce identical profits or losses; similarly, a bear call spread and a bear put spread with the same strikes will produce identical profits or losses. Recall from Chapter 15 that the profit diagram for a long call is the mirror image top-for-bottom of the profit diagram for a short call, and the profit diagram for a long put is the mirror image top-for-bottom of the profit diagram for a short put with the same strike. Also notice that the profit diagram for a long call is the mirror image left-to-right of the profit diagram for a long put with the same strike, and the profit diagram for a short call is the mirror image left-to-right of the profit diagram for a short put with the same strike. Finally, recall from numerous examples in this book that different combinations of instruments can produce identical profits – for example, synthetic futures positions and actual futures positions. Consequently, the ability to obtain identical results from a bull call spread and a bull put spread, or a bear call spread and a bear put spread, should not be surprising.

Box Spread Using Bull and Bear Spreads

In yet another example of this ability to obtain identical results from different combinations of derivatives, recall that our box spread example above used a long $3.20 call, a short $3.20 put, a short $3.50 call, and a long $3.50 put, which were then combined into a synthetic long futures contract (i.e., long $3.20 call plus short $3.20 put) and a synthetic short futures contract (i.e., short $3.50 call plus long $3.50 put). However, these four option positions also could be combined into a bull call spread (i.e., long $3.20 call plus short $3.50 call) and a bear put spread (i.e., short $3.20 put plus long $3.50 put). This brief example further illustrates the flexibility of options, and serves as a useful reminder to monitor the combined results of the portfolio and not become distracted by the performance of the individual positions.

18 Commodity Swaps

In Chapter 1, we described a swap as a type of off-exchange instrument that operates like a series of forward contracts. Now, in the final chapter of this book, we will take a brief look at how commodity swaps are constructed and how they are used.

Swaps and Forwards

Suppose we have two individuals, A and B. Person A sells a series of forward contracts for a certain commodity to Person B, with the forwards expiring in 1 year, 2 years, 3 years, and so forth. These forward contracts require Person B to pay a *floating price* or market price to Person A when each contract expires (i.e., 1 year, 2 years, 3 years, etc.), and simultaneously for Person A to provide the commodity to Person B.

At the same time, Person B sells a series of forward contracts for the same commodity to Person A, also with maturities in 1 year, 2 years, 3 years, and so forth. These forward contracts require Person A to pay a *fixed price* to Person B when each contract expires (i.e., 1 year, 2 years, 3 years, etc.), and simultaneously for Person B to provide the commodity to Person A.

Notice that Person A supplies the commodity to Person B, and Person B supplies the same commodity to Person A, so the exchanges of the commodity effectively cancel. However, the exchanges of payments (i.e., cash flows) likely will not cancel. For some expirations the fixed price will be higher than the floating price, and for other expirations the floating price will be higher than the fixed price. In practice, only the net amount, or difference between the fixed price and the floating price, would be exchanged instead of requiring both parties to make payments. It is this exchange of net cash flows that makes swaps a useful instrument for both hedgers and speculators.

Swap Features and Applications

Fixed and Floating, Long and Short

In our example above, Person A pays the fixed price and receives the floating price – commonly known as *pay fixed, receive floating* – and they will have a gain when the floating price is more than the fixed price. Notice that this is analogous to having a long position in a market where the price increases, so Person A effectively has a long position in the swap. Conversely, Person B pays the floating price and receives the fixed price – referred to as *pay floating, receive fixed* – so they will have a gain when the floating price is less than the fixed price. Notice that this is analogous to having a short position in a market where the price decreases, so Person B effectively has a short position in the swap. The fixed price is often referred to as the *reference price*, which underscores the fact that the outcome of a swap is determined by how the floating price changes relative to the fixed price.

In practice, a swap is used much like a futures contract, as either a hedging instrument or a speculative vehicle. When used in a hedge, a swap offsets both gains and losses, so it effectively locks in a net purchase or sale price for the commodity being hedged. Unlike a futures contract, which covers a single cash market transaction, a swap typically covers a series of cash purchases or sales over a period of months or years. A swap typically is used in conjunction with a large quantity or dollar value of the commodity, often corresponding to hundreds or thousands of futures contracts. Consequently, most swaps are transacted by large commercial firms and investment funds, rather than by the individual producers, consumers, and speculators who account for most futures trading activity. In addition, participation in the swap market is restricted to *eligible contract participants* or *ECPs*. Financial requirements to become an ECP include $10 million in assets for corporations and other entities, $10 million in investments for individuals, or $1 million in net worth for entities that are hedging commercial risks.

Commodity Swap Example

Adding some details to our simplified example above will illustrate how a swap can be used in a hedging application. Suppose that we have two parties, Trader A and Trader B, where Trader A is an overseas grain buyer and Trader B is a swap dealer. They enter into a swap for 1 million bushels of corn each month for the next 5 years, at a fixed price of $4.00 per bushel which reflects the export price at the Gulf of Mexico. The floating price is the midpoint of the Louisiana morning bid for US #2 yellow corn, as reported by the US Department of Agriculture in the daily "Louisiana and Texas Export Bids" (JO_GR112) report. Notice how specific the floating price must be, while the fixed price can simply be a number. In this example, Trader A is the fixed-price payer (and therefore the floating-price receiver), and Trader B is the floating-price payer (and therefore the fixed-price receiver). Stated differently, Trader A has a long position in the swap because they will gain from higher prices, and Trader B has a short position in the swap because they will gain from lower prices.

First Settlement Results

End of Month 1: The floating price is $4.10, so Trader A pays the $4.00 fixed price to Trader B and receives the $4.10 floating price from Trader B, both multiplied by 1 million.

Simultaneously, Trader B pays the $4.10 floating price to Trader A and receives the $4.00 fixed price from Trader A, both multiplied by 1 million. Consequently, the cash flows are $4 million (= $4.00 per bushel × 1 million bushels) from A to B, and $4.1 million (= $4.10 per bushel × 1 million bushels) from B to A. However, it is not necessary for the traders to exchange these gross amounts, and in practice only the net cash flow, or $100,000 (= $4.1 million − $4 million), is transferred from B to A.

Recall that Trader A is an overseas grain buyer and Trader B is a swap dealer. Trader A has budgeted to spend $4 million for each monthly cash purchase, based on the fixed price of $4.00 per bushel. At the end of Month 1, the cost of 1 million bushels is $4.1 million, so Trader A uses the $4 million they have budgeted plus the $100,000 received from Trader B and completes the cash purchase.

Notice that the swap is not a supply agreement, despite the fact that a swap is equivalent to two forward contracts, one short and one long. Unlike a forward contract, which links both the price and the cash transaction to a specific supplier, a swap allows Trader A to buy the cash commodity from any source. Also notice that the swap uses a specific cash price, rather than a futures price, so Trader A is protected from basis risk. This feature accounts for much of the popularity of swaps among end-users.

Trader B also will have hedged against a price change, typically by taking an offsetting position in futures, or by a *back-to-back* or *matched book* transaction using an offsetting position in swaps that it has structured for other customers. If the swap dealer hedges with futures, it also may engage in basis trading to manage the basis risk of the swap transaction. Notice that a swap dealer normally does not speculate on the price level, and earns its income from the *mark-up* or bid-ask spread plus various fees for the services it provides.

Second Settlement Results

End of Month 2: The floating price is now $3.80, so Trader A pays the $4.00 fixed price to Trader B and receives the $3.80 floating price from Trader B, both multiplied by 1 million. Simultaneously, Trader B pays the $3.80 floating price to Trader A and receives the $4.00 fixed price from Trader A, both multiplied by 1 million. The gross cash flows are $4 million (= $4.00 per bushel × 1 million bushels) from A to B, and $3.8 million (= $3.80 per bushel × 1 million bushels) from B to A. These amounts are reduced to a net cash flow of $200,000 (= $4 million − $3.8 million) from A to B. Trader A has budgeted to spend $4 million for each monthly cash purchase. At the end of Month 2, the cost of 1 million bushels is $3.8 million, so Trader A pays $200,000 to Trader B and uses the remaining $3.8 million for the cash purchase.

Subsequent Settlements

This process is repeated each settlement period for the duration of the swap. Notice how the swap provides the hedger (Trader A) with long-term price certainty, and provides the swap dealer (Trader B) with a steady stream of income.

Swap Contract Specifications

Swaps are used for speculative purposes much like futures contracts, only on a larger scale and for longer periods of time. An investor can participate by acting as a counterparty in a swap – for example, by replacing the swap dealer in our example but not hedging their short exposure to the corn market – or by having a swap dealer design a custom-tailored swap that meets the investor's specific needs. When the swap dealer is not directly involved as a counterparty, they still play an indirect role by overseeing settlements, facilitating payments between the counterparties, and performing various other administrative duties.

A swap is a legally binding contract, same as a futures contract or a forward contract. To simplify the contract-writing process, an organization known as ISDA, or the International Swaps and Derivatives Association, has standardized much of the necessary documentation for their members. The two most important parts of an *ISDA*, as these documents collectively are known, are the Master Agreement and the Credit Support Annex. Both use a multiple-choice, fill-in-the-blank format for the specific details of a particular swap. Despite having standardized definitions and other so-called boilerplate language as a starting point, it may take weeks or months for the two parties to negotiate the remaining details and finalize a swap agreement. The complete agreement for a straightforward swap may number several dozen pages, so the key details are usually summarized on a *term sheet* that is just a page or two.

Under current regulations, all swap transactions must be reported to a *swap data repository* or *SDR*, which compiles and reports this information to the general public and to the CFTC. The CFTC is responsible for regulating swaps and monitoring trading activity for potential manipulation. Some of the more common or plain vanilla swaps are traded on specialized exchanges known as *swap execution facilities* or *SEFs*, or regular exchanges known as designated contract markets or DCMs (discussed in Chapter 5). In addition, many swaps are cleared by a *derivatives clearing organization* or *DCO*, which serves as the central counterparty and guarantees the financial performance of the participants. The DCO also may require margins and issue margin calls, same as for a futures contract. Finally, there may be position limits for a particular swap, which can be coordinated with the position limits on a corresponding futures contract and related options to control the total number of derivatives for a particular commodity held by an individual or entity.

Flexibility vs. Liquidity

Swaps are not standardized, unlike futures contracts, so a swap can be constructed for any commodity, of any quality, in any *notional amount* (i.e., quantity), for any *tenor* (i.e., length of time) and series of expiration date(s). Each swap is constructed by a swap dealer, typically an investment bank or other financial institution, and is designed to meet the specific needs of the customer. This personalized, made-from-scratch nature is sometimes described as *bespoke*, a term traditionally used to describe a custom-tailored suit sewn to fit a specific person. Because most swaps are constructed for a particular application, there is usually little liquidity, similar to the forward contracts on which they are based. A customer who wants to *tear up* (i.e., cancel) or modify a swap prior to expiration must negotiate any changes with the *counterparty* (i.e., the other person involved in the swap).

In addition to specifying the value of the fixed price, the swap will list the official name and source of the floating price. Typically the floating price will be a market price or other published value that changes over time. The agreement may also list alternate data sources or describe steps that can be taken if the floating value is not available at settlement time.

The Market for Commodity Swaps

Swaps are widely used to hedge financial instruments, particularly those involving interest rates but also for exchange rates and a limited amount of equity (i.e., common stock) applications. In contrast, commodity swaps are much less common, accounting for less than 1% of all swaps outstanding based on notional value. The majority of commodity swaps are energy-related, with agricultural swaps accounting for a much smaller fraction.

One reason for the small size and slow growth of the commodity swap market is the difficulty of valuing them for accounting and trading purposes. Most financial instruments have actively-traded forward contract markets, with prices quoted month-by-month for years into the future – commonly known as the *forward curve* – that are available from commercial price quotation services. The value of a swap can be determined from the value of the corresponding forward contracts, but if these forward values are not readily available, then swap valuation becomes problematic.

The limited availability of forward prices for most commodities is tied to the fact that commodities can be difficult to transport and often derive much of their value from being in a place where they can be easily used. In contrast, the specific location of a financial instrument is normally not a factor in determining its value. Consequently, it is much easier to obtain, publish, and monitor a single set of forward prices for a financial instrument than dozens or hundreds of location-specific forward prices for a commodity.

The commodity swaps market may be relatively small, but it is nonetheless important because it allows hedgers to manage risks on commodities for which there are no exchange-traded futures contracts, or for which the quality specifications, quantity, and/or expiration schedule differ substantially from the standardized version. The ability to manage price risk and basis risk with a single instrument is highly attractive, and undoubtedly has been a factor behind the rapid adoption of swaps in the financial sector. We expect the same advantages will lead to the wider usage of swaps for a broader range of commodities.

INDEX

Locators in *italics* refer to figures and those in **bold** to tables, though these are not indexed separately when continuous with related text.

abandon option 5, 159, 161–3, 166, 196–7
actual basis 83, 128–9
actual cash price 83, 90, 121, 123, 128–9
aggregate limit 49
all-months-combined limit 49, 50
American-style options 161, 174–5
anticipatory hedge 97, 99
arbitrage 28, 43–4, 46, 176
assignment: futures 44, 166–7; options 165–7, 231
automatic exercise 166

back month 7
basis *see* hedging and the basis
basis trading: commercial 130–4; rolling a hedge 99, 135–46; swap dealer 253; *see also* spread-adjusted basis
bear call spread 242, 244–6, 250
bear put spread 242, 247–50
bear spread 143–4, 150, 242–4, 246, 250
bids: electronic trading 16–19, 21; pit trading 12
Black model 168, 170–7, 179, 181, 183, 221
Black-Scholes model 167–8, 170, 174
box spread 240–2, 250
branded products 1–2
broker 7, 9–13, 16, 19, 57
bull call spread 242–5, 250
bull put spread 242, 246–8, 250
bull spread 143–6, 150, 242–4, 250
butterfly: futures spread 150–1; options spread 234

buyer's remorse 3, 120
buying the spread 150

call option formula 170–2
carry spreads 150
carrying cost 28–31, 36
cash prices: actual 83, 90, 121, 123, 128–9; commodity swaps 253; correlation 67, 77, 78–9, 80–1; expected 83–95, 128; cash settlement 45, 48–9, 53, 67, 167
cash-futures arbitrage 43–4
cattle feeding margin 114–17
ceiling strategy 207, 219
central limit order book 16–17
certainty, derivatives 3–4, 253
change price 21
clearing firm 9, 13, 15, 38–42, 44, 54, 168
clearing house: delivery 44–5; futures trading 37–41, 40; options 165–8; regulation 54, 55; close price 20–1
collar strategy 207–15
commercial hedging 129–34, 146
Commitments of Traders report 51, 52, 152–7
commodities: inelastic supply and demand 2; meaning of 1–2; options on actuals 169; perfect competition model 2; undifferentiated vs branded products 1
commodity codes 13, 15, 22–3
Commodity Exchange Act 54–7

commodity funds 157

Commodity Futures Modernization Act (CFMA) 57

commodity futures, speculating 147–52, 157–8

Commodity Futures Trading Commission (CFTC) 54–7, 152, 168, 254

commodity pool operator (CPO) 157

commodity swaps: features and applications 251–5; market for 255; swaps and forwards 251

commodity trading advisor (CTA) 157

condor spread 234

contract expiration 23–4

contract month 7, 10, 13, 15, 18, 27–9, 43, 45, 48–50, 53–4, 99–102, 104, 135, 149, 150–2, 160, 165, 168–9, 205, 236

contract size 21–2, 47, 52

contrary instructions, options on futures 166

convergence 43

conversion strategy, speculating with options 236–40

correlation: corn futures 77–80; hedging and the basis 83; hedging with futures 67–8, 109–10

counter instructions, options on futures 166

counterparty: clearinghouse as central 38–44; swaps 255

covered call strategy 215–17

covered put strategy 215–17

credit controls 19

cross-hedging 105–10, 117–19

crude oil refining margin 114

customer protection features, electronic trading 18–19

daily price limits 52, 169, 229

daily settlement price 21, 41–2. 45, 168

daily settlement process 40–1, 167–8

default, futures contract 6, 39, 44, 49

deferred futures contract 143–6, 150

deliverable supply 49–50

delivery: final settlement 7, 36, 43–4; market regulation 48; options on futures 167

delivery date 48

delivery month 43

delivery notice 44–5

delta: hedging with options 217–21; option pricing 177–9; options on futures 169

demand, inelastic 2

demand for futures contracts 105

derivatives, meaning of 3–6

derivatives clearing organization (DCO) 254

designated contract market (DCM) 54, 254

directional trades 230–1

Disaggregated Commitments of Traders 152–4

discounts *see* premiums and discounts

Dodd-Frank Act 57–8

double hedging 99–100

dynamic hedging: example 218–20; using gamma 221

electronic trading 7, 15–9, 148

errors: electronic trading 19; pit trading 15

European-style options 161, 174–5

exchange functions 3–4

exchange traded fund (ETF) 157

exercise option 5, 159–63, 165–7, 174–5, 178–9

exercise price 159–61

expandable limits 52

expected basis 83, 90, 128–9

expected cash price 83–95, 128

expiration date 23–4, 43, 53, 101, 103, 159, 164, 167, 169, 221, 254

fair value 167–8, 172–3

fat finger errors 19

fat tails 174

final settlement via delivery 7, 36, 43–5; *see also* settlement

financial crisis (2007–2008) 57–8

financial engineering 229

Financial Industry Regulatory Authority (FINRA) 57

first-line regulator 53, 168

fixed prices, swaps 251–3, 255

flexibility, swaps 254–5

floating prices, swaps 251–3, 255

floor speculators 7–9, 15, 148

floor strategy 206–7

form, futures prices 33–6

forward contracts 3–6, 46, 56, 98–9; commodity swaps 154, 251; inverse hedging of 119–24

forward curve: basis trading 141–3; commodity swaps 255; futures prices 29–32, 150, *30, 31, 32*

front end, electronic trading 16–18

front month 7

fundamental analysis 149

futures commission merchant (FCM) 40, 54, 57, 157

futures contracts 4–6; electronic trading 15–19; pit trading 7–15; *see also* hedging with futures; market regulation

futures prices: interpreting different prices 28–36; quotes 20–4; *see also* hedging and the basis

futures trading: final settlement 7, 36–8, 43–5, 48; margins 37–42; *see also* hedging with futures

futures-equivalent 169, 178, 220

gamma, option pricing 177, 179, 221

going long 24

going short 24

Grain Futures Act 54

Greeks: hedging with options 217–21; option pricing 176–83; *see also* delta; gamma; rho; theta; vega

gross profit margin 111

hand signals 12, *13*

hedge ratio 106–10, 117, 178

hedgers, position limits 50

hedging: anticipatory 99; basis behavior 83–96; commercial 129–34; inventory 97–9; inverse 119–24; long hedge 84–90; profit margin 111–19; short hedge 90–6

hedging and the basis 82–3; basis behavior 83–96; long hedge 84–90; redefining the basis and the cash price 125–9; short hedge 90–6

hedging enhancements: cross-hedging 105–10; rolling a hedge 99–104

hedging with futures: corn futures example 77–80; correlation 67–8; long hedge 68–70, 72; options 222–9; prices 68–77; returns 80–1; short hedge 72–7

hedging with options: delta-neutral 217–21; strategies 206–17; synthetic futures 222–9

high price 20

historical volatility 173–4

holder, options on futures 160–1

in the money 161–8, 171, 173, 177–84, 191, 193, 195–6, 199, 203, 206, 211–12, 215–16, 218–20, 243–8

industry self-regulation 57–8; *see also* market regulation

inelastic supply and demand 2, 32

initial margins 37–8, 41–2

input-output, futures prices 33–6, 109, 151

insurance, and options 163, 207, 215

inter-market spread 151–2

intra-market spread 150–1

intrinsic value: hedging with options 218; options 162–7, 170–2, 191–6; speculating with options 230–1

inventory hedge 97–9

inverse collar strategy 213–15

inverse hedging 119–24

investment, vs speculation 147–8

last price 20

last trading date 45, 53

legislation *see* market regulation

limit-down 52–3

limit-up 52

linear profits 184–5

liquidity, swaps 254–5

locals 7–9, 15, 148, 221

location for delivery 4, 6, 32–3, 36, 44, 48

lock in 67–9, 71–2, 74–5, 98, 114, 129, 135, 139

locked limit 52

long calls 189–91, 193, 196, 200–3, 207, 213, 215, 219–20, 222–6, 231–2, 243–5, 250

long futures 43, 49, 69–70, 72, 80, 82, 98, 119, 120–2, 127–8, 145, 160, 165, 167–9, 178, 184–5, 187, 191, 196, 200–3, 205, 216–17, 219, 222–3, 225–7, 236–8, 240–2, 250

long hedge: hedging and the basis 84–90; hedging enhancements 98–9, 100–2, 102–4;

hedging with futures 68–70; inverse hedging 120–2; rolling 135–9, 143; *see also* short the basis

long position 24–5, 41, 44, 49, 73–4, 80, 90, 127, 135, 149, 151, 155–6, 161, 165, 167, 187, 215, 221–2, 225, 252

long puts 43, 193–8, 206–8, 211, 223–6, 231–3, 246–7, 250

long the basis 126–8, 131, 143

maintenance margins 37–8, 41–2

managed money 52, 155–7

margins: futures trading 37–42; options on futures 166–8, 185, 231

market makers 148, 221

market regulation: by exchanges 53–4; by Federal Government 54–7; by futures contract specifications 46–53; by industry 57–8; options on futures 168–9; other sectors and countries 58

matching engine 16–7

merchants, reportable traders 52, 154–6

minimum price increment 21, 52, 148, 169, 175

month codes 22–3, **23**

National Association of Securities Dealers (NASD) 57

National Futures Association (NFA) 57–8, 168

net purchase price 72

net sale price 73

nonlinear profits 189–205

nonreportable positions 156–7

non-spot limits 49–50

nonstorable commodities 31–2, 50

notional amounts, swaps 254–5

offers (asks): pit trading 12–3; electronic trading 16–7, 19–20

old crop-new crop spread 150

oldest long 44, 166–7

open interest 24–8, 50, 52, 54, 152–7, 166

open outcry trading 12; *see also* pit trading

open price 20

option buyers 4–5, 160–6, 164–9, 191, 193, 195–8, 206, 216, 231

option pricing: Black model 170–5, 183; Greeks 176–83; put-call parity 175–6; sensitivity analysis 176–7

option sellers 5, 160–3, 164–9, 191, 193, 195–6, 198, 206, 216, 231

option trading 163, 167–8, 183

options on actuals 5, 169

options on futures 1, 5, 56, 161–68, 170, 174, 189–205, 229; *see also* hedging with options; speculating with options

order execution 10–12

order ticket 10–13, 15–6

order types 10–12, 18

order-fillers 7

other reportables 52, 155–7

out of the money 161–6, 173, 177, 179, 183–4, 191, 193, 195, 212, 218, 220, 233, 236, 243–8; par quality 47

payoff diagrams *see* profit diagrams

pays and collects 40–1, 168

percent volatility 174

perfect competition model: commodities 2; futures contracts 46; market regulation 55

pit trading 7–15, 167

position limits 48–50, 58, 169, 178

position traders 149, 151, 156–7

premiums and discounts, contract specifications 47–8; price determination 6

price discovery 5–6

price quotes, futures 20–1; see also change price, close price, high price, last price, low price, open price, settle price

price reporting 13–15

price stability, derivatives 3

price-later contracts 3–4

pricing vs. exchange of goods 3–4

processing margin 111–19, 151

processing spread 151–2

processors, reportable traders 52, 154–6

producers, reportable traders 52, 154–6

profit diagrams: linear profits 184–9; nonlinear profits 189–91, 193–200, 202–5; synthetic long futures 226–7; synthetic short futures 227–9; see also hedging with futures, hedging with options

profit margin hedging 111–19
profit tables 184–5
put option formula 172–3
put–call parity 175–6, 183, 240

quality differentials, futures prices 33–6, 47
quotes, futures prices 20–1

real estate option 159–60
realized volatility 173–4
regression equations 107–10
regulation *see* market regulation
reportable levels 50–2
reportable traders 52, 152, 154–6
returns: to speculation 157–8; use in hedging
    with futures 80–1, 83, 90, 109; use in options
    164, 173–4; reversal strategy, speculating with
    options 236–40
reverse hedging *see* inverse hedging
rho, option pricing 177, 181, 183
risk management: *see* hedging with futures;
    hedging with options
rolling a hedge 99–104, 135–46
runaway trading 19

scalpers *see* locals
seasonality 31
self-regulatory organization (SRO) 53
seller's remorse 3–4, 120
selling the spread 149–50
sensitivity analysis 176–7
settle price 21
settlement: commodity swaps 252–5; futures
    daily 21, 41–2, 52, 58; futures final via cash
    settlement 45, 48–9, 53, 67; futures final via
    delivery 4, 7, 36–7, 43–5, 48, 67; options on
    futures 167–8, 174
short calls 178, 191–3, 196, 198–200, 222–5, 211,
    215–6, 223–4, 226, 234, 236, 243–4, 250
short futures 43, 49, 72–3, 75–7, 80, 90, 99,
    122–4, 126, 128, 160, 165, 169, 178, 185–9,
    193, 195, 197–200, 203, 216–17, 222, 224,
    226–7, 229, 236–8, 240–2, 250
short hedge: hedging and the basis 90–6; hedging
    enhancements 98–9; hedging with futures

72–7; inverse hedging 122–4; rolling 139–43;
    see also long the basis
short position 24–5, 41–2, 49, 52, 68, 70, 80,
    82–3, 127, 140, 144, 149–52, 154–6, 161, 165,
    178, 187, 193, 196, 211, 216, 222, 225–6, 245,
    248, 252
short puts 43, 160, 178, 195–8, 203–5, 215–16,
    223–6, 234, 236, 246–7, 250
short squeeze 49
short the basis 126–8, 133, 143
single month limit 49
soybean crush margin 34, 111–14, 151
space, futures prices 32–3, 36, 125
SPAN (Standard Portfolio ANalysis of Risk)
    37–8
speculating with futures: market impact 152;
    styles 148–52; vehicles 157; vs investment
    147–8; *see also* commitments of traders; returns
    to speculation
speculating with options: intrinsic value strategies
    230–1; spread strategies 236–50; time value
    strategies 231; volatility strategies 231–6
speculators, position limits *see* position limits
spot limits 49
spot month 49–50
spot prices *see* cash prices
spread *see* bear call spread; bear put spread;
    bear spread; box spread; bull call spread; bull
    put spread; bull spread; implicit bear spread;
    implicit bull spread; speculating with futures;
    speculating with options; spread-adjusted basis;
    spread-adjusted futures price
spread-adjusted basis 138–9, 141–2, 144–5
spread-adjusted futures price 137–8, 141, 144–5
spread impact 143–6
spread orders 99
spreaders 149–52
stability, derivatives 3, 75
storage spread *see* carry spreads
straddle strategy 231–5
strangle strategy 233–6
strike price 159, 162
supply, inelastic 2, 32
supply of futures contracts 105
swap contracts 5, 251–5

swap data repository 254

swap dealers 52, 154–7, 252–4

synthetic futures 178, 222–9, 236, 240, 250

synthetic options 222–6

tear up, swaps 255

technical analysis 149

technology, electronic trading 15–19, 167

telescoping price limits 52

tenor, swaps 254–5

term sheets 254

textbook hedging 129–30

theta, option pricing 177, 179–81, 183

tick size 21–2, 52, 176

ticker symbols 22–3

time, futures prices 28–32, 36, 125; time and sales reports 20

time value, options 163–5, 167, 170, 173, 231; *see also* theta

Tokyo Stock Exchange 19

total reportable positions 155, **156**

trading activity measures 24–8

trading card 12, *14*

trading limits 19

undifferentiated products 1

users, reportable traders 52, 154–6

vega, option pricing 177, 181–3

volatility, option pricing 164–5, 167, 170–4, 177–80, 231–4; *see also* vega

volatility smile 174

volume, trading activity 4, 6, 15, 19, 21, 24–8, 152

writer, options on futures 160–1

zero-cost collar strategy 211–13

zero-sum game 41, 152, 168